THE ILLUSTRATED GUIDE TO
TANKS
OF THE WORLD

THE ILLUSTRATED GUIDE TO
TANKS

GEORGE FORTY

HERMES
HOUSE

Contents

This book is dedicated to my son
Jonathan who helped immeasurably
with its preparation.

This edition is published by Hermes House

Hermes House is an imprint of
Anness Publishing Ltd
Hermes House
88–89 Blackfriars Road
London SE1 8HA
tel. 020 7401 2077
fax 020 7633 9499
info@anness.com

© Anness Publishing Ltd 2005, 2006

A CIP catalogue record for this book
is available from the British Library.

Publisher: Joanna Lorenz
Editorial Director: Judith Simons
Project Editor: Felicity Forster
Copy Editor and Indexer: Tim Ellerby
Jacket Design: Michael Reynolds
Designer: Design Principals
Editorial Reader: Jay Thundercliffe
Production Controller: Steve Lang

10 9 8 7 6 5 4 3 2 1

PAGE 1: **Mark III Valentine Infantry Tank.**
PAGE 2: **M1A1/2 Abrams Main Battle Tanks.**
PAGE 3: **Uparmoured Swedish Army
Strv 102 (Centurion).**

Introduction

What is a tank? Expressed in its simplest terms, a tank can be defined as a means of transporting firepower about on the battlefield, with its weapon system and crew protected from direct enemy fire. This revolutionary weapon has been in existence for under a hundred years, and in that time it has become one of the most important and indispensable components of the battle-winning All Arms Team. The tank is just one of the many types of Armoured Fighting Vehicle (AFV) found on the modern battlefield. What makes it special is the careful blend of its three basic characteristics – firepower, protection and mobility – into a lethal mix that can bring instantaneous, accurate, direct fire to bear, whenever and wherever it is needed, day and night, whether on the move or stationary. These three characteristics can be blended together in differing amounts to produce very different results, as can be seen in the directory sections of this book.

Firepower is undoubtedly the most important characteristic because it is a tank's reason for being. The type and size of weapon system can vary enormously, and as this becomes larger and more sophisticated, the carrying vehicle invariably increases in both size and weight as there is more to protect.

If a tank is to achieve its mission, then an effective means of protection is vital. Although this can be achieved in a variety of ways, the basis is usually some form of armour plate composed of steel, aluminium, plastic-sandwich, ceramic, reactive or other materials, which inevitably increases the

TOP: **Firepower. Challenger MBTs of A Squadron, 1st Royal Tank Regiment, night-firing on Castlemartin Ranges, Pembrokeshire, Wales, 2001.**
ABOVE: **Protection. The massively thick, advanced Chobham type armour on the hull and turret of this Abrams M1A1 MBT gives protection against ATGWs (Anti-Tank Guided Weapons) and other battlefield weapons.**

tank's size and weight. Main Battle Tanks (MBTs) of today weigh around 60–70 tons, including much weighty armour. There are also other ways of providing protection, such as limiting size, lowering silhouette, camouflaging the tell-tale shape and using aids such as local smoke to help it "disappear". Inevitably as the tank's protection has become more and more sophisticated, so too have the anti-tank weapons ranged against it. Therefore its protection must be able to deal with all manner of attacks,

LEFT: **River Crossing. Royal Engineers have constructed this Class 80 ferry, to practise ferrying a Challenger 2 during training at Bovington, Dorset, England.** BELOW: **Mobility. A Challenger 2, belonging to the Armour Centre at Bovington, Dorset, England, powers its way effortlessly through thick mud on the training area.** BOTTOM: **Sea Movement. Challenger tanks being loaded at Zebrugge, Belgium, bound for the Middle East during the first Gulf War.**

from ground level – such as mines – through a vast range of hand-held/vehicle-borne guns and guided missiles that can attack at any level, to specific top-attack weapons. As far as possible, it must also now protect against nuclear, biological and chemical weapons. To all of this must be added a tank's deadliest foe – another tank, with its weapon system firing more and more sophisticated ammunition specifically designed to penetrate armour.

Mobility is the third vital characteristic, and again as the tank has become larger and heavier, increasingly more powerful powerplant, transmission and suspension are needed to move it over all types of terrain. Cross-country, the track clearly wins over the wheel, and good mobility is essential if the tank is to achieve its varying missions. Weight affects its portability, especially by air or over water. MBTs have probably now reached their ultimate size and weight, and so there is now a trend towards lighter, smaller, more portable tanks. This in turn puts the smaller tank at a distinct disadvantage in any tank versus tank engagements, when faced with a larger, better protected and better armed enemy, so tank development can be a vicious circle.

This book contains a wide selection of tanks through the ages. We have deliberately confined our coverage to the more important and interesting models worldwide, so while it is definitely not an exhaustive encyclopedia, it will give the reader a good indication of what the tank is all about.

The tank ended World War II in a pre-eminent position in the land battlefield and has lost none of its usefulness during the turbulent days that have followed. The last two conflicts in Iraq

have again shown that it is still a potent force, not yet superseded as "Queen of the Battlefield" by any other weapon system. In the hands of well-trained, highly professional soldiers, the awesome power of the tank still lives on and will continue to do so into the foreseeable future. FEAR NAUGHT!

The History of Tanks

The history of the tank has very largely been the history of 20th-century ground warfare, this revolutionary new weapon being conceived to help break the early battlefield stalemate of World War I. Later it had mixed fortunes in the years of peace following 1918, but came back into its own during World War II and has maintained its pre-eminent position ever since. Tanks have been produced in all shapes and sizes throughout their history. Nevertheless, without exception, they have all had the basic characteristics of firepower, protection and mobility. It is how these are balanced together that makes a critical difference to their effectiveness. During the tank's history some of its original roles have been taken over by other types of Armoured Fighting Vehicle (AFV). Nevertheless, the ability of the tank to carry firepower about on the battlefield with a protected crew and weapons has remained essential. We are now seeing a requirement for lighter AFVs to replace current Main Battle Tanks (MBTs), which poses the question: "Will the tank as we currently know it still be with us by the end of the 21st century?"

LEFT: **The Type 61 MBT was the first tank produced by Japan after World War II. After almost a decade in development, it ended a long period when Japan had no armaments industry.**

Evolution of the tank

Since earliest times humankind has searched for bigger and better weapons with which to defend themselves and destroy their enemies. Without doubt each one must have initially appeared to be invincible on the battlefield, more fearsome than its predecessor. None has been more effective than the tank, a revolutionary weapon system, tracing its ancestry back partly to the war chariot, partly to the armoured war elephant and partly to a mechanical war machine in the fertile mind of Leonardo da Vinci. Not until the 20th century was it possible to propel a suitably armoured vehicle containing a crew and its weapons across all types of terrain. The invention of the internal combustion engine, modern methods of fabricating armour plate and the caterpillar track all combined to make this possible.

The stimulus for this new weapon came about in 1914, following the stalemate on the Western Front after the First Battle of Ypres. Neither side could advance because the defences of the other were too strong. The artillery shell, machine-gun, barbed wire and never-ending trenches stretching from the Belgian coast to Switzerland, had effectively brought war to a grinding halt. Until some way could be found of providing mobile, protected fire support for the attacker, this impasse could not be broken.

Before World War I there had been a number of designs proposed for bizarre-looking mechanical devices in both Britain and France, but all had been summarily discounted or pigeon-holed. These included a tracked armoured vehicle using Diplock caterpillar tracks and another, the "Big Wheel", which was propelled along by three enormous wheels. Ad hoc armoured vehicles were also produced by bolting sheet armour plate on to early motor cars and were used to rescue downed British pilots from behind enemy lines and for light "cavalry" raids by the Belgian Army. Foremost of these

ABOVE: **Wooden model of the "War Machine" as taken from Leonardo da Vinci's notebook. The model was something of a guess as Leonardo never actually built it. Motive power was to be provided by a man inside turning a handle that can be seen connected to the axles, so its engine power was "one manpower"! This model was on show at the Israeli Tank Museum at Latrun, but has now been dismantled.** BELOW: **The "Big Wheel" project must have seemed like something out of H.G. Wells'** *War of the Worlds***. It was designed to move an armoured vehicle forward on huge 12.2m/40ft diameter wheels, but was never completed. The man in the bowler hat is William Tritton, managing director of William Foster's who would build the first tanks.**

inventors was a British Royal Engineer officer, Ernest Swinton, whose proposal was for an armoured vehicle using American Holt farm-tractor caterpillar tracks for cross-country propulsion. Fortunately Swinton had the backing of Winston Churchill, then First Lord of the Admiralty, otherwise his "landship" might never have seen the light of day. Instead, a Landships

"And the Lord was with Judah, and he drove out the inhabitants of the mountain, but he could not drive out the inhabitants of the valley, because they had chariots of iron."
Judges, Chapter 1, Verses 19 and 20

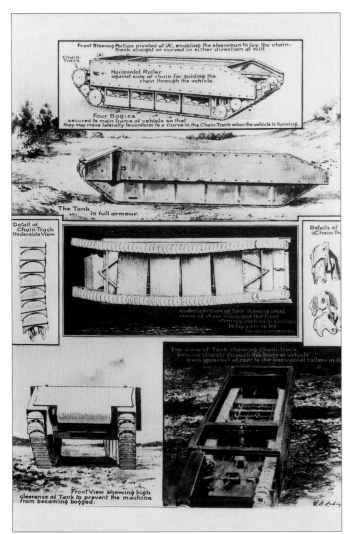

ABOVE: **An early tank? An artist's impression of Lancelot de Mole's designs for an armoured fighting vehicle which he submitted to the War Office in about 1912, only to be completely ignored.** ABOVE RIGHT: **William Tritton, managing director of William Foster's, admires the "Tritton Trench Crosser" which he designed. As can be seen, it carried its own bridge with which to cross trenches.** RIGHT: **"Mother", also known as "Big Willie" or "HMLS Centipede", at the Burton Park trials in 1916. Having been designed in August 1915, it moved under its own power on January 13, 1916 – an astonishing achievement.**

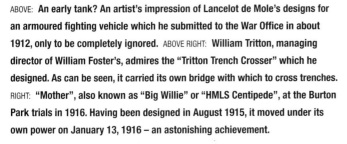

"The structure of the machine in its early stages being boxlike, some term conveying the idea of a box or container seemed appropriate. We rejected in turn – container – reservoir – cistern. The monosyllable TANK appealed to us as being likely to catch on and be remembered."
The Landships Committee

Committee was formed, chaired by Tennyson d'Eyncourt, Director of Naval Construction, and included remarkable men such as William Tritton, managing director of William Foster and Co. Ltd of Lincoln (the firm that would build the first tanks), Royal Naval Lieutenants Walter Gordon Wilson and Albert Stern, and of course Ernest Swinton.

Designed by Tritton and Wilson, the No. 1 Lincoln Machine (also called the "Tritton Machine"), and later, after a complete track redesign, given its more familiar name of "Little Willie", came into existence on September 18, 1915. Weighing 18 tons, it was to have had a centrally mounted turret although this was never fitted. This was almost immediately superseded by "Big Willie" also known as "HMLS Centipede" or more affectionately as "Mother", despite being a "Male" tank armed with two long-barrelled 6pdr guns ("Females" had only machine-guns). She was completed in January 1916, and

secretly moved to a trials area near Hatfield Park. Here, on February 2, 1916, "Mother" performed magnificently before a VIP audience and again six days later to His Majesty The King, who was also most impressed. One hundred Mark Is were ordered and given the nickname "Tank" because this was thought to be most likely to catch on and to be memorable.

Other nations were also coming to terms with the need for such a weapon system – first and foremost the French, once Colonel Estienne put forward plans to develop a land battleship, the *Cuirasse terrestre*, after witnessing British trials of the Holt tractor towing artillery guns. This led not only to the production of both the Schneider and St Chamond heavy tanks, but also the remarkably effective FT-17 light tank series. The Americans, Italians, Russians and surprisingly even the Germans would drag their heels somewhat, but eventually all the major nations would produce their own versions of the tank.

The tank crew

Like every other crew-served weapon system, a tank is only as good as its crew, which is at all times an integral and indispensable component. The first tanks had of necessity either large crews in heavy tanks – the German A7V topped the bill at eighteen, while the British Mark I and the French Saint Chamond had eight and nine respectively – or small crews of only two or three such as those in the tiny French FT-17 and British Whippet. The average-sized tank during World War II and after would have a crew of four men – a driver, a gunner, a loader/radio operator and a commander. They each had their allotted space in the driving or fighting compartment and were allocated personal hearing and vision devices.

The driver was seated at the front surrounded by his controls and instruments. Sometimes he operated a bow machine-gun, or there was a co-driver seated alongside to do so. The other three crewmen were in the turret/fighting compartment, normally with two on one side of the main armament (gunner in front of commander) and one (loader/ operator) on the other. All were located close to their controls and had dedicated seats, vision and intercommunication devices and access/escape hatches.

Today's tank crew live, eat, sleep and fight in their tank throughout the 24-hour battlefield day, but can and do dismount when necessary. Modern tanks are equipped so that the crew can live on board – eating, sleeping and defecating within a filtered atmosphere so that they do not need to wear NBC

ABOVE: **Members of the crew of a British Mark V heavy tank inspect a captured German 13mm/0.512in anti-tank rifle. Up to and including the Mark IV, the crew was eight men, four of whom were the commander and driving team (including two secondary gearsmen); the other four were gunners/loaders.**
BELOW: **A Challenger 1 tank commander of 7th Armoured Brigade (note his Desert Rat flash) in his turret during Operation "Desert Sabre".**

(nuclear, biological and chemical) clothing or respirators once inside and pressured up. In the early days, British tank crews wore chain-mail visors to protect against cuts from spawl (flakes of metal chipped off from bullet strikes outside), while heat, fumes and poisonous gas were other hazards they faced. Modern tanks are now designed to be fought closed down, very different to World War II when commanders normally had to have their heads out. The radio system in a tank provides both inter-communications between crewmen as well as long- and short-distance external communications.

Although an individual tank can operate alone, it should never do so, and usually functions as part of a troop or platoon of three or four tanks, or in a larger subunit or unit. Furthermore, tank formations should not operate in isolation, needing infantry, engineer and other all-arms support, especially when holding ground by night, or when operating in urban areas.

Traditionally, tank crews have been all-male, although there were a few cases of women crew members serving in the Red Army during World War II, and there is now an increasing trend towards integration. In some cases, robotic accessories can also take the place of crew members – the most obvious being an automatic loader for the weapon system. While this usually works well, it does inevitably mean that there is one less person to carry out the many and varied other crew tasks such as replenishing ammunition, fuel and rations, gun cleaning, basic maintenance and even the simple yet essential tasks of mounting guard and radio watch, cooking and making the cups of tea or coffee, without which no tank crewman can survive!

"Tank aces" occur in any conflict; however, it is always difficult to single out an individual for special praise because a tank crew lives and fights as a team, and it is this teamwork that wins battles. However, there can be little doubt that the tank commander has the most difficult job, especially if he is commanding other tanks as well as his own, maybe at troop, squadron or regimental level. This requires him to listen constantly on the radio via his headphones (which are now built into his helmet), read a map, guide the driver, locate targets, give fire orders to the gunner, specify what type of ammunition to load, and a hundred and one other things – all at once!

ABOVE LEFT: **Map-reading is one of the many skills a tank commander has always required. Nowadays, an on-board Global Positioning System (GPS) helps.**
ABOVE: **Commander (in rear) and gunner use their vision devices to acquire targets in the turret of this closed-down Chieftain. The complexity and compactness of their controls is well evident.** BELOW: **Time for a brew! The crew of a Chieftain use their cooking stove to brew up a "cuppa" during training. The canned rations, known as Composite Packs ("Compo" for short) are ideal for tank crews and can be carried in the external bins.**

As warfare becomes more sophisticated, so inevitably do modern tanks, and consequently more skills are needed by all members of tank crews to enable them to survive and to fight effectively. The success of the American and British tank crews in the recent war in Iraq is testament to this continuing ability.

World War I

On August 13, 1916, the first detachment of British tanks left for France, the crews departing from Southampton but, because there was no crane there capable of loading them, the tanks left from Avonmouth. They then moved forward by train to the Somme where the great Allied offensive had opened on July 1, with horrendous casualties (British losses were 60,000 on the first day). The Commander-in-Chief of the British Expeditionary Force, General Sir Douglas Haig, was desperate to find a solution to the mounting casualties and seized on the handful of tanks as a panacea, despite the tanks being initially met with amused tolerance or contemptuous scepticism. Haig's plan was to deploy the available tanks (49 in total) over the entire front in twos and threes.

First tank action

On the morning of September 15, 1916, Zero Hour was at 06:20 hours, the tanks being on the move much earlier to reach the start line in time. Some broke down or were ditched moving forward, so where they did get into action, they were available only in ones or twos. Despite this, the effect upon the battle was out of all proportion to their number. Typical were the exploits of D 17 (Dinnaken) of 3 Section, D Company, which was reported in the British Press as "walking up the High Street of Flers with the British Army cheering behind!". German war correspondents were more dramatic: "One stared and stared as if one had lost the power of one's limbs," wrote one, "the monsters approached slowly, hobbling, rolling and rocking, but they approached. Nothing impeded them;

ABOVE: **Moving up for the Battle of Cambrai. British Mark IV heavy tanks, belonging to 4 Battalion, at the Plateau Railhead. Note that they have brushwood fascines (to help in trench crossing) on their fronts and unditching beams on their rears.** BELOW: **Into battle. A British Mark I heavy tank advances, with infantry on foot behind its tail-wheels. This was a device to help with steering but was soon discarded because the wheels fell into shell-holes or trenches, thus proving more a hindrance rather than a help.**

a supernatural force seemed to impel them on. Someone in the trenches said, 'The devil is coming,' and the word passed along the line like wildfire."

Cambrai

Unfortunately their very success worked against them and they continued to be deployed in small numbers for over a year, normally on appalling mud, the thick morass being so bad that tank officers took to carrying long ash sticks to test the depth

in front of their tanks. Eventually Haig allowed Brigadier Hugh Elles, who had taken over command of the Tank Corps from Swinton, to plan a battle on ground of his own choosing. The result was that on November 20, 1917, the entire Tank Corps of 476 tanks took part in the Battle of Cambrai, with Elles in the lead tank, flying the Tank Corps colours from his ash plant.

Zero Hour was 06:00 hours, and after ten hours the battle was won as far as the Tank Corps was concerned; the most rapid advance of the entire war had been achieved at minimal cost – only some 6,000 casualties instead of the anticipated 250,000 or more. Had the British been able to take advantage of this remarkable breakthrough, then a great victory might have been achieved – a remarkable feat by just 690 officers and 3,500 men of the Tank Corps. The Tank Corps had proved itself beyond all expectations, Haig writing in his dispatches that "the great value of the tanks had been conclusively proved".

Five months earlier, however, at Berry au Bac, Estienne's fledgling French tank arm had fought its first battle with 132 Schneiders taking part, but unfortunately involving a long approach march in full view of the enemy. The French tanks quickly encountered heavy artillery fire and many obstacles, 76 tanks being lost without much success. The Germans concluded that tanks were not very effective weapons – a conclusion they would live to regret! One of the main reasons for such heavy losses was the Schneider's vulnerability to the new German "K" anti-tank bullet, but this failure was to make the French concentrate their efforts on the highly successful light FT-17 two-man tanks.

Despite continuing British success, the Germans were slow in appreciating the potential of the new weapon system. However the Americans, who entered the war in April 1917, formed a special board to look into their employment, concluding that the tank was destined to become an important element in the war. They formed a separate tank corps, equipped with a mixture of British heavy and French light tanks. First to make his name in the new corps was a young cavalry captain, George S. Patton, Jnr, destined to become a famous tank commander in World War II.

TOP: **A battlefield scene showing American "doughboys" advancing across enemy trenches, with tank support from the ubiquitous FT-17s.** ABOVE: **A good rear view of a column of Medium Mark A Whippet tanks pausing on its way forward. No doubt the infantry who were passing would have liked a ride!** BELOW: **Two crew members of a British Mark V heavy tank talking to an infantryman. This is of course a modern-day re-enactment at the Tank Museum Bovington, Dorset, England, but the crew members are wearing authentic khaki overalls and the composite/leather crew helmets (affectionately known as "Dead Tortoises"), while their chain-mail face masks (to prevent cuts from spawl) are hanging around their necks.**

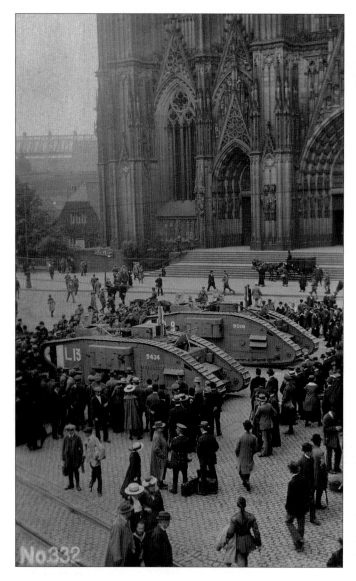

ABOVE: **"Goodbye to boots and saddles!" An M2A4 light tank passes a column of horse-mounted cavalry during exercises in the USA during 1940.** LEFT: **British Army of Occupation in Germany. Taken in 1919, these two Mark V tanks of 12th Battalion Tank Corps are seen outside Cologne Cathedral, on their way to the station to welcome General Petain who was visiting that day.** BELOW: **"Thank God for the French Army!" French AMR 33 light tanks on parade in Paris on Bastille Day, June 14, 1935, when President Lebrun took the salute. France had more tanks than Germany at the start of World War II, but they were still deployed using the old fashioned infantry tactics and spread out in "penny packets", unable to stand up to the new German Blitzkrieg.**

Between the wars

Between September 1916 and November 1918, British tanks took part in 3,060 separate engagements, French in 4,356 and American in 250, so it is not surprising that one German historian commented that they had been defeated "not by the genius of Marshal Foch, but by 'General Tank'". Despite their successes, the tanks were in for some lean years following World War I, principally due to cost, but also as a result of prejudice against all things mechanical. The British Tank Corps was reduced from 25 battalions when the Armistice was signed to five just a year later. Not until 1922 was a firm decision made to retain a permanent British Tank Corps, while the Americans abolished theirs completely and subjugated their tanks under infantry control. They fared a little better in France, where their tank arm was retained, but seen only as support for the all-powerful infantry, while the cavalry re-emerged, despite their proven battlefield vulnerability.

Apart from the tank element of the British Army of Occupation in Germany, the only exciting episode was the "Russian Stunt", when British tanks were sent to southern

> 'The Germans were beaten ... not by the genius of Marshal Foch but by 'General Tank'."
> German historian Gen der Infanterie AWH von Zwehl

Russia to help fight against the Bolsheviks, the tank once again showing its prowess – a single tank capturing an entire city. Remarkably the city was Tsaritsin, renamed Stalingrad after the Revolution, which an entire German Army could not capture during World War II.

The 1920s was a great time for armoured theorists, especially in the UK, where Fuller and Liddell Hart produced a stream of books on the theory and practice of armoured warfare. Most remained ignored at home but were avidly read abroad, especially by the Germans. While British, American and French tank soldiers had to fight against the anti-armour prejudice pervading their respective armies, the Germans, despite the crippling restraints of the Versailles Treaty, secretly planned for the future, designing tanks and forming tank units to man them. In Britain prejudice was eventually overcome and mechanization began slowly in 1926, still to be incomplete at

the outbreak of World War II. There was no shortage of able tank designers with men such as Martel in the UK designing cheap, small tanks ideal for training, and J. Walter Christie in the United States creating a revolutionary suspension which allowed high-speed cross-country movement.

The newly emerging Soviet Union did not take an interest in tank development until the start of their first "Five Year Plan" in 1929, thereafter building large numbers of poorly designed tanks. Stalin hindered their armoured development when he carried out his savage purges, removing many of those who had been advocating the theories of Fuller and Liddell Hart. Covertly the Soviets also helped the Germans by allowing them to send prototypes of their new tanks to the secret tank testing ground at Kazan.

When Hitler came to power he quickly realized the potential of the tank and by 1934, having thrown aside all pretence of obeying the Versailles Treaty, began tank-building on a large scale. He created the *Panzerwaffe* (Tank Arm), the first three panzer divisions being formed on October 15, 1935. Their organization bore a close resemblance to the British experimental armoured force of 1927. Officers and men of these divisions would gain useful combat experience as

ABOVE: **Hitler reviews his panzer troops. This scene is in pre-war Berlin, where any excuse for a military parade – such as Hitler's birthday, heroes' memorial days and foreign visitors – was snapped up. Here, Hitler is inspecting his big six-wheeled armoured cars and troop carriers, but on the other side of the Platz are the panzers and crews in their distinctive black uniforms.**

"volunteers" in the German Condor Legion, fighting for General Franco during the Spanish Civil War. It was during this time that the new tactics of *Blitzkrieg* (Lightning War) were perfected, which soon came to revolutionize the battlefield, employing innovative elements such as air–ground support, with dive-bombers and tank formations working closely together. Much of their tactics and training was based on the teachings of General Heinz Guderian, the armoured guru, who had been the first to realize that the panzer division would be the weapon of decision in the new German Army. He visualized armoured forces which did not only contain tanks, but a mix of all fighting arms and services, thus differing from the "all-tank" theories of Fuller and from the policy of tying tanks to infantry as adopted by the French and Americans. His new panzer arm would be the primary striking force in the coming war, and not just a supporting player.

Blitzkrieg!

On September 1, 1939, two German Army Groups swept across the Polish frontier, spearheaded by two Panzer Corps, their aim being to encircle and destroy the Polish Army in a gigantic pincer movement. Germany knew the Poles would fight stubbornly, buoyed up by promises of British and French support. However, unbeknown to Poland and her allies, there was a Nazi–Soviet Pact in which Poland was to be divided in two, the Russians attacking from the rear.

The Germans unleashed a new tactical system on the Poles, perfected by Guderian, which pierced the enemy's front and then encircled and destroyed all or part of their forces. Its key elements were surprise, speed of manoeuvre, shock action from both ground and air, and the retention of battlefield initiative. It required that all commanders used their initiative to the full. Reconnaissance elements led, accompanied by Artillery Forward Observers and Luftwaffe Forward Air Controllers, who could quickly call for fire support. Having located the enemy main positions, the reconnaissance would bypass these strong-points and quickly press on to maintain momentum. They were in constant radio communication with the force commander who controlled the speed of advance, deciding whether the whole force should bypass enemy positions or engage them. The *Schwerpunkt* ("centre of gravity") of the assault was where the commander, being well forward, decided was the best point to attack. Overwhelming force was then concentrated against this point, as Guderian put it, "*Klotzen nicht Kleckern!*" ("Thump them hard, don't pat them!"). The aim of this initial attack was to punch a hole through their lines, to be immediately followed by another element of the force that would pass through and press on,

ABOVE: **At the Channel Coast. The date is May 20, 1940, the place Dunkirk, the tank a PzKpfw 38(t) built by the Czechs and "appropriated" by the Germans.**
BELOW: **Blitzkrieg in action! In the suburbs of Warsaw, a column of German tanks, led by a PzKpfw II Ausf F, passes a 7.5cm/2.95in infantry gun as they batter their way into the city, September 1939.**

avoiding main enemy positions, creating havoc in their rear. Following this up would be motorized infantry, who would "mop up" any remaining resistance, ensuring that the gap was permanent. Such operations demanded teamwork, good communications, command and control, and where possible, surprise. There were no more massive build-ups, long artillery barrages or set-piece attacks which gave the enemy time to prepare. Instead, the overwhelmingly powerful attacking force would hit without warning, smashing through on a narrow front. No wonder Guderian's nickname was *Schnelle Heinz* ("Hurrying Heinz")!

Blitzkrieg was repeated on May 10, 1940, when the Germans invaded the Low Countries and then crossed the Meuse into France. The disorganized and demoralized French

FAR LEFT: **On into Russia! A column of PzKpfw III Ausf Es leaving a ruined Russian village as they head for the steppes.**
LEFT: **The prime architect of the German Blitzkrieg tactics was General Heinz Guderian, seen here during pre-war training.**
BELOW: **The All Arms team was one of the vital components of the German Blitzkrieg. The infantry had to work closely with tanks, as shown here, where they use a tank to get them nearer to the enemy. However, they will have to dismount once the action begins, so that the tank can traverse its turret and engage targets.**

had their armour spread out in "penny packets" and were no match for the German assault, while the British Expeditionary Force (BEF) soon struggled to escape over the Channel. However, a few important challenges to the German offensive occurred, most notably at Arras where a counter-attack by the 4th and 7th Royal Tank Regiments held up the panzers long enough to prevent the BEF from being cut off from their escape ports. By June 18, Paris had capitulated, followed by the complete surrender of France on June 24. The *Panzerwaffe* was in the ascendancy.

Operation "Barbarossa"

Just under a year later, on June 22, 1941, the Germans unleashed three massive army groups against their erstwhile Soviet ally. Similar to the campaigns in Poland and France, panzers spearheaded the German forces, with a front line extending 3,219km/2,000 miles from the Baltic to the Black Sea. The Red Army retreated everywhere, losing more than 3,000 tanks. By autumn the Germans had advanced 885km/

550 miles and occupied 1.3 million sq km/500,000sq miles of Soviet territory, inflicting 2.5 million casualties on the Red Army and capturing over a million prisoners.

On the other side of the world, the USA had begun to awaken, and its massive armaments and tank-building industry swung into action, anticipating its entry into the war. This would change the US Army into the most mechanized force in the world. The British were grateful to receive American tanks to boost their armoured divisions because they were still bedevilled with tank design problems, having too many models that were under-armoured, under-gunned and restricted by turret rings too small to take larger calibre weapons.

Elsewhere, other countries, such as Axis partners Italy and Japan, began increasing their tank-building programmes, but were never very successful. Commonwealth tank development also played its part, although the Allies were to rely on the industrial output of the USA to build the tanks they needed for their armoured forces. On every battlefield, the tank had begun to play a more pivotal role than ever before.

Tanks in other theatres

Of all the unlikely places for tanks to prove their abilities, the barren Western Desert of North Africa was probably the strangest. Yet despite problems caused by the extremes of heat and cold, combined with the effect of sand and grit on their engines and running gear (let alone on their crews), tanks once again proved themselves the dominant arm, this time in desert warfare. Initially it was British tanks against Italian that would capture the headlines, the Matilda II swiftly earning the title "Queen of the Desert". The Italian invasion of Egypt and their subsequent trouncing by a much smaller British and Commonwealth force culminated in the surrender of the entire 10th Italian Army at Beda Fomm, Libya, in February 1941. Here the British 7th Armoured Division (the "Desert Rats") took 20,000 prisoners, together with immense quantities of vehicles, arms and ammunition, for the loss of just nine killed, fifteen wounded and four tanks knocked out.

However, the British would not have it all their own way for long, once General Erwin Rommel and his *Deutsches Afrika Korps* (DAK) arrived. The "Desert Fox", as he was called by both sides, soon proved that he was in his element in the desert, leading from the front and dominating battles by his sheer personality. Hard-fought campaigns then took place

> **"We have already reached our first objective which we weren't supposed to get to until the end of May ... You will understand that I can't sleep for happiness."**
> **Rommel in a letter home to his wife**

TOP: **"Queen of the Desert". The British Matilda Mark II was far superior to any of the Italian tanks in the Western Desert because its protection was far better.** ABOVE: **Across the steppes. Blasting their way through Russian defences, the panzers initially made good progress on the wide open steppes until winter set in.**

from one end of the Western Desert to the other between March 1941 and October 1942. The turning point came with the Battle of El Alamein, Egypt, which gave victory to General Montgomery and his British 8th Army. The DAK then fought a stubborn withdrawal action all the way back to Tunisia, where they were finally forced to surrender on May 12, 1943.

The Japanese bombed Pearl Harbor on December 7, 1941, and in so doing brought the USA into the war, switching their enormous armaments industry to full-scale production. Over 88,400 tanks were built during the war years, nearly four times the production of Germany or Britain. The American armed forces soon numbered over 12 million and a goodly proportion of these fought the Japanese in the Pacific "island-hopping" campaigns that saw tanks being used in a wide variety of new roles. In other parts of the Far East, British and Commonwealth armour fought in unlikely jungle settings, winning victories where tanks were not expected to be able to survive, let alone operate.

From mid-1943, the tide had turned against the Axis powers in nearly every theatre of the war, nowhere more so than on the Russian steppes where the Red Army was able to employ its excellent new tanks – the T-34 and KV-1 – built in ever larger numbers at factories that had been moved safely eastwards. Soon they turned the tables on the overstretched Nazis and were pushing them inexorably back to the Fatherland, in the process winning some enormous tank battles such as the one at Kursk in July–August 1943.

In the Mediterranean theatre, tanks also played a major part in the conquest of Sicily and Italy. In north-west Europe, with the opening of the Second Front on D-Day, June 6, 1944, specialized armour in the form of the Funnies was used to great effect in these landings. Once a breakout from the beaches had been achieved, tanks led the way on all fronts with armoured commanders such as General Patton racing to go further and faster than his fellow generals, giving the Germans no opportunity to regroup.

Nevertheless, the Germans still had a surprise up their sleeve with their heavy armour playing a major role in a totally unexpected counter-attack through the Ardennes region in a conflict which became known as the "Battle of the Bulge".

TOP: **"*Panzer Rollen in Afrika Vor!*" A PzKpfw IV belonging to the *Deutsches Afrika Korps* negotiates a sand dune in the North African desert.**
ABOVE LEFT: **The Red Army resists. Russian medium tanks pressing the Germans back towards Rostov during the autumn of 1942.** ABOVE: **A US Marine Corps Sherman M4A2 medium tank operating deep in the jungle of Cape Gloucester. Tanks proved their worth in jungles all over the Pacific theatre, being used to great effect by both the US Army and USMC.**

This nearly succeeded in breaking through the Allied forces, but proved to be a last gasp, and Allied tanks were soon hammering on the gates of Berlin from all sides. Following Hitler's suicide, Germany sued for peace, surrendering unconditionally on May 7, 1945. Fighting in the Pacific would take a further three months to force Japan into a similar surrender on August 14, bringing World War II to a close.

Would the atom bomb, which had so dramatically heralded in the nuclear age, lead to the demise of the tank?

Wartime development

As World War II progressed, most major tank-building nations produced larger, more powerful, better armed and better armoured tanks. The UK, once the world leader, had been left woefully far behind by the others with tanks that were under-equipped and ill-prepared for the Blitzkrieg tactics of modern war. Their machine-gun armed light tanks were suitable only for peacetime training or possibly reconnaissance tasks, a role soon to be taken over by armoured cars. Likewise, the cruiser and infantry tanks mounted either a tiny 2pdr high velocity anti-tank gun or a 75mm/2.95in close support howitzer. The former was adequate in the anti-armour role but of little use firing High-Explosive (HE) in support of infantry. Unfortunately, the diameter of their turret rings was mainly too small to allow the mounting of larger-calibre weapons. German tanks did not suffer from this design fault. The PzKpfw IIIs and PzKpfw IVs, designed in the early 1930s and forming the backbone of the *Panzerwaffe*, were still in quantity production in the early 1940s, well able to be up-armoured and up-gunned.

The Americans had recognized the need for a dual-purpose main tank armament and the advantages of stabilizing the gun platform so as to hit targets on the move – in most tank versus tank battles the one who hit first usually won. The introduction of American Medium M3 Lee/Grants into British service in the North African desert was the first time they had had a tank gun of this size with dual capability since the naval 6pdr of the Heavy Mark V in World War I. Despite this advantage, the 75mm/2.95in gun remained in service far too long, not being replaced by the much improved 76mm/2.99in gun until later in the war. The British did not produce a real match-winner until the A34 Comet, with its excellent 77mm/3.03in gun, which entered service in March 1945.

ABOVE: **The backbone of the panzer divisions for many years was the PzKpfw IIIs and IVs. This interesting line-up shows (from left to right) Pz IV Ausf F, Pz III Ausf L/M, Pz III Ausf H and Pz IV Ausf F, taken in March 1944.**
BELOW LEFT: **The deeper the Germans penetrated into the Soviet Union, the farther east the Soviets had to move their tank-building factories, like this one that was producing their new heavy tank, the KV-1.**

Although the Germans mostly led the field in tank design – with obvious exceptions such as the Soviet T-34, probably the best all-round tank of the war – they could not match the Americans or the Russians in mass production output. Curiously, they squandered much of their precious production capacity on building ever larger tanks. They created behemoths such as the 68-ton King Tiger, 70-ton Jagdtiger and the last of which was too late to see combat, the 180-ton Maus. These tanks were very difficult to manoeuvre, slow, needed specially reinforced bridging and guzzled fuel, although they could see off every other tank they met with ease. Had they concentrated on producing the PzKpfw V Panther, things might have been different.

Protection became more of a problem as anti-tank weapons improved and the means of penetrating armour became more varied. In addition to conventional Kinetic Energy penetration by solid shot, a new method, High-Explosive Anti-Tank (HEAT) was introduced, which relied on the chemical energy generated

by a high-velocity, high-temperature jet of HE. This was fired at low velocity and was thus most accurate at shorter ranges in hand-held weapons such as the bazooka. This led to the fitting of "stand-off" armour to protect suspensions and turrets, while front glacis and turret frontal arcs became ever thicker. Other methods of protection included painting with anti-magnetic mine paste (*Zimmerit*) and fitting local smoke dischargers, which fired a pattern of local smoke allowing a tank to escape to cover. Internal protection was improved by not storing ammunition above the turret ring (apart from ready rounds) and by fitting ammunition bins with water jackets.

Engine and track performance also improved, but in many cases petrol engines still had to be used instead of the more robust (and less inflammable) diesels because the majority of diesel fuel was needed for the navies. "Duckbills" (track extensions) were fitted in some cases to improve traction in muddy conditions, while the ingenious Culin Hedgerow Cutter, a device that could cut its way through the thick *bocage* hedgerows of Normandy, won a medal for the American NCO who invented it.

Undoubtedly the biggest continual threat to tanks came from the air in the form of specialized "tank busters" or *Jabos* (*Jagdbombers*), constantly searching out and destroying tank columns, a particular problem for the Germans thanks to the Allies' almost complete air superiority.

TOP: **As well as tank crews, technicians had to learn about new tanks as they came into service – like these REME (Royal Electrical and Mechanical Engineers) craftsmen removing the 75mm/2.95in gun and mantlet from this US M24 Chaffee, the last of the American light tank line of World War II.** ABOVE: **Stand-off armour. As can be seen on this German PzKpfw III, side plates to protect the suspension and turret sides give the tank improved protection against HEAT (High-Explosive Anti-Tank) projectiles.** BELOW: **Light tanks had to be able to be carried in gliders to support airborne operations. Here a 7-ton British Light Tank Mark VII Tetrarch exits from the nose of a glider.**

The Funnies

Crucial to the success of the Allied armies landing on the Normandy beaches was the support they had from all manner of specialized armour. The driving force behind these strange devices – the product of many inventive minds – was one man, arguably the greatest trainer of British armoured soldiers: Major-General Percy Hobart. He had already proved his prowess before World War II on Salisbury Plain and then in Egypt where he turned the Cairo Mobile Division into the world-famous 7th Armoured Division – the original "Desert Rats" – and following this by forming and training the formidable 11th Armoured Division. However, the 79th Armoured Division, "Hobo's Funnies" (although he detested the nickname), was his crowning achievement.

Strange-looking tanks, fitted with deep-water wading screens, mine-clearing flails, portable bridges, flamethrowers or tank-borne searchlights, joined the more conventional armoured bulldozers and armoured engineers assault vehicles to provide the fire support and assist more conventional tanks over and through the natural and man-made beach obstacles. The Division went on playing an important role right up to and over the Rhine Crossing, when it had a strength of 21,000 all ranks and 1,566 tracked vehicles (compared with 14,000 men and 350 AFVs in a normal armoured division), but always operating in "penny packets" spread across the front line. "Hobo's eagle-eye" appeared to be everywhere, and his contribution to the Allied success was enormous.

As the photographs here and in the directory section show, the majority of Funnies were based upon either the highly adaptable American Sherman M4 Medium Tank or the equally versatile British A22 Churchill Infantry Tank Mark IV. Before the

TOP: **The Churchill "Crocodile" Flamethrower was a fearsome weapon that was still in service in the 1950s. In fact, a squadron's worth went to Korea with the Commonwealth Division as part of the United Nations force, but were only ever used as gun tanks.** ABOVE: **A Sherman DD enters the water during training before D-Day. Note the propellers on the rear (run off the engine and yet to be lowered) and the raised canvas screen which gives the tank the necessary buoyancy.**

LEFT: **The 79th Armoured Division, "Hobo's Funnies", took a bull's head as its insignia.**

formation and equipping of 79th Armoured Division, there had been some limited specialized armour, mainly used in the Middle East, such as Matilda and Valentine-based mine-sweeping tanks, the Matilda nightfighting searchlight (known as the Canal Defence Light) and the Valentine amphibious tank (using a collapsible screen and fitted with Duplex Drive propellers to enable it to swim). These clearly led on to the Sherman/Churchill derivatives that were much improved versions of the originals. Here are some of the most widely used Funnies.

Sherman DD (Duplex Drive)

First ashore with the leading troops was a Sherman gun tank fitted, like the Valentine, with DD propellers and a collapsible screen. Unfortunately, those on the American beaches were launched too far out and many sank before they could reach shore. However, on the British and Canadian beaches they landed successfully and proved invaluable.

LEFT: **A Churchill gun tank uses a Churchill Great Eastern Ramp to surmount an extra high wall.** BELOW LEFT: **One of the very few Sherman DDs left in existence is this one on show at the Tank Museum, Bovington, as part of the D-Day exhibits.** BELOW: **A Churchill AVRE (Armoured Vehicle Royal Engineers) fitted with a fascine carrier and brushwood fascine ready to be dropped into any ditch or crater that blocked its way.** BOTTOM: **One of the most successful mine-clearing devices was the Sherman Flail (British designation: the Sherman Crab) that used flails attached to a front-mounted spinning drum to literally blast the mines out of the ground or set them off.**

Sherman Crab

This was again a Sherman gun tank fitted with a flail mine-sweeping device which could sweep a safe lane through a minefield, wide enough to allow tanks and other vehicles to negotiate it in safety.

Churchill AVRE (Armoured Vehicle Royal Engineers)

These were Churchill Mark III or IV tanks, modified to mount a 290mm/11.42in spigot mortar, together with other devices such as various bridges, Bobbin "carpet-layers", fascines and mine exploders. The spigot mortar was used to destroy pill-boxes and was known as a "Flying Dustbin".

Churchill ARKs

A turret-less Churchill tank, modified to carry ramps for use in obstacle crossing. The Germans were completely surprised by these strange-looking vehicles which had no counterpart in the German Army. The Funnies accomplished many tasks on D-Day, including crossing sea walls and anti-tank ditches; breaching sea walls and other obstacles; knocking out gun emplacements and defended buildings; filling ditches and craters with fascines or crossing them with tank bridges.

After D-Day other Funnies were brought into action, such as Churchill "Crocodile" Flamethrowers, "Kangaroo" armoured personnel carriers (based on Ram tanks) and other types of bridges, bulldozers, etc. No wonder they were called the "tactical key to victory".

On to victory!

Once the Rhine was crossed, with armour leading on all fronts, the Allied armies moved deeper and deeper into Germany. Now the lighter, faster American mediums and British cruisers really came into their own, their speed, reliability and overwhelming numbers counting for more in the end than the superior enemy firepower and protection. I remember being told of one German tank commander who, having boasted that one Tiger was better than ten Shermans, then smiled ruefully and said, "but you alvays haff eleven!" Nevertheless it was no easy ride, especially with the added danger from a proliferation of hand-held anti-tank weapons, such as the *Panzerfaust* and *Panzerschreck*. The once proud panzer divisions were by now a shadow of their former selves, yet single Tigers and Panthers still performed miracles until they were taken out by superior numbers or by the dreaded *Jabos*.

The Allies were also fielding better tanks, the American M26 General Pershing heavy tank, with its highly effective 90mm/3.54in M3 gun, had reached Europe in January 1945 and even saw action in the Pacific theatre before the war ended. The highly effective British Comet entered service at about the same time as the Pershing, but unfortunately its successor, the world-beating A41 Centurion, was not in prototype stage until January 1945 with the first six vehicles

ABOVE: **Brilliant British commander Field Marshal Bernard Montgomery always wore a Royal Tank Regiment black beret and badge on to which was sewn his General's badge. "Monty" had his own M3 Grant medium tank in the Western Desert, now in the Imperial War Museum, London.**

ABOVE: **One of the greatest German armoured commanders was Field Marshal Erwin Rommel, who commanded the *Deutsches Afrika Korps* in North Africa, then Army Group B on the Atlantic Wall and Channel Coast. Implicated in the bomb plot against Hitler, he was forced to commit suicide.**

being rushed to Germany for testing in combat conditions in May 1945. This gives a measure of how far behind the British were in the tank development race.

On the Eastern Front the Red Army "Steamroller" moved closer to Berlin, headed by the ubiquitous T-34 and the new JS-1, JS-2 and JS-3, with their 122mm/4.8in gun and thick armour. Particularly deadly was the JS-3 with its new ballistically shaped cast hull and smoothly curved turret, but all were more than a match for their aging opponents.

Tank destroyers

Before closing on World War II it is perhaps relevant to deal here with tank destroyers. All the major tank-building nations employed them because they were an ideal way of getting a

> "Armor, as the ground arm of mobility, emerged from World War II with a lion's share of the credit for the Allied victory. Indeed armor enthusiasts at that time regarded the tank as being the main weapon of the land army."
> US Army Lineage series *Armor-Cavalry*

more powerful anti-armour weapon into battle on a smaller, lighter or almost obsolescent tank chassis, thus prolonging its effective battlefield life. The Americans, however, viewed things slightly differently. Early in the war they had been heavily influenced by the way German tanks had sliced through the opposition in Poland, France and Russia, and this had a bad effect on American morale. They came to the conclusion that the answer was to have masses of fast-moving, high-velocity anti-tank guns whose primary task was to knock out enemy tanks. This led to the creation of Tank Destroyer Command (with their motto "Seek, Strike and Destroy!"), which at its peak in early 1943 contained 106 active tank destroyer battalions – only 13 less than the total number of US tank battalions. From then on, numbers started to decline, principally because the expected massed German tank formations were not used against the Americans, being needed more on the Eastern Front. Nevertheless, the M10 Wolverine, the M18 Hellcat and the M36 tank destroyers all gave useful service in the US Army, while both the British and the Germans made full use of their tank destroyers for many tasks, often in lieu of normal gun tanks. The British up-gunned some of their M10s by installing their 17pdr Mk V gun, the resulting highly effective tank destroyer being known as the "Achilles". Undoubtedly the German *Jagdpanther* was one of the best tank destroyers ever built, while *Jagdtiger* was the heaviest German AFV to go into active service. Smaller tank destroyers, like the Hetzer, which utilized well-proven

TOP LEFT: **One of the smallest number of tanks in any theatre were those of the composite squadron of Light Mark VI and Matilda Mark II on Malta. Note the strange camouflage to blend in with the hundreds of dry stone walls on the island.** TOP RIGHT: **America's most famous armoured general was General George S. Patton, Jr, whose flamboyant style made him instantly recognizable everywhere. This evocative statue of Patton stands at Ettelbruck, Luxembourg.** ABOVE: **Berlin at last! A column of Red Army JS-2 heavy tanks drives through the Brandenburg Gate, sealing the fate of the Third Reich.**

components of the Czech-built PzKpfw 38(t), continued to be used by the Swiss Army long after the end of the war.

"Armor, as the ground arm of mobility, emerged from World War II with a lion's share of the credit for the Allied victory. Indeed armor enthusiasts at that time regarded the tank as being the main weapon of the land army." That is how the US Army Lineage series *Armor-Cavalry* put it, and it would be hard to disagree. "General Tank" had done it again!

The Cold War

While there is no doubt that World War II had proved once again that tanks could win major battles, just as after World War I, the American and British armoured forces were reduced significantly to peacetime levels – 20 cavalry regiments and eight from the Royal Tank Regiment (RTR) respectively – the rest disbanded, despite worldwide commitments such as the dismantling of the British Empire. In addition, the spectre of nuclear war between the Super Powers hung over Europe, with NATO and the Warsaw Pact countries facing each other across the Iron Curtain. Bolstering up the Soviet threat to the West was a mass of armoured units that appeared ready to strike at any moment and whose purpose was to follow-up a pre-emptive nuclear strike. To guard against such an eventuality the US, UK and other NATO nations stationed many of their tank units in north-west Europe, or had complicated "Reforger" programmes in which the tanks were

ABOVE RIGHT: **On the other side of the Iron Curtain, American M60s, belonging to their armoured regiments stationed in West Germany, got on with their training for battle. These three are firing on the open range.** BELOW: **The Cold War was certainly cold on the eastern side of the Iron Curtain. Here Red Army soldiers on manoeuvres in the early 1950s use a platoon of T-34/76s to help them move through thick snow.**

kept in specially weatherproofed shelters in Europe while the crews were at home – ready to be flown out to man them at a moment's notice. Either way it was an expensive and time-consuming business, but the threat was real enough, both sides fearing that the other would strike first.

The "shield and sword" principle of NATO undoubtedly did much to prevent a third world war during the remainder of the 20th century. Had war occurred, tank battles would have been a major feature. Cracks in the Warsaw Pact were apparent from time to time, such as with the Hungarian uprising in October 1956, but these were savagely repressed,

LEFT: **Guns rear, a column of M60s return to their barracks after manoeuvres in southern Germany. They are passing another armoured column led by an M113 APC.** BELOW LEFT: **Driving home in the morning mist. A German Leopard 1 returning to barracks at the end of an exercise through mist-shrouded pine forests.** BELOW: **NBC (Nuclear, Biological, Chemical) warfare was yet another feature of the Cold War, which required tank soldiers to wear special uniforms, including respirators, and to decontaminate their tanks. Here a German crew practise decontamination drills, with suitable detergent sprays.**

slowly starting up their own tank-building industry once again, but this time with very different objectives. It was soon clear that German tank-building expertise was as good as ever, clearly demonstrated by the Leopard 1 and later Leopard 2 tanks. For anyone stationed in Germany during the 1940s to the 1970s, this was a time of considerable change, encompassing initially an era of massive free-wheeling exercises that saw tanks running on their tracks over much of the countryside, and then of tactical training becoming more and more restricted as costs increased and land became more precious.

The training expedients that had to evolve are dealt with later in this book, but it is worth noting that as the lethality of tank gun ammunition increased, so too did the size of army firing-range danger areas in order to safeguard the public; alternatively, other methods of training tank gunners would have to evolve. Nevertheless, the threat of armoured conflict was always present, making this type of training essential at all levels.

There was also an important shift in some countries, such as Great Britain, for their armies to change from conscripts to regular soldiers, causing considerable changes to the training cycle of tank crews. In general terms, after some teething problems, this was to produce a far more professional and well motivated tank crewman, whose expertise has been evidenced in the last two Gulf Wars. Tanks were also becoming ever more sophisticated, requiring that the training of tank crewmen also had to develop and improve continually.

using in this case over 1,000 tanks to crush it. At the same time the whole world was becoming "awash" with tanks – the highly successful Soviet T series, for example, being widely available and mirroring the similar worldwide availability of such small arms as the AK-47 Kalashnikov assault rifle. NATO countries favoured the American M47, M48, M60 series or the British Centurion, all of which were produced in large numbers both at home for export and under licence abroad. Additionally, other "sleeping giants" like China had also begun to develop their own tank-building industry.

The Armies of Occupation in Germany gradually became less "occupying forces" and more equal partners as the erstwhile enemies were welcomed back into the fold, even

Korea and Vietnam

On June 25, 1950, Blitzkrieg struck again, this time in the Far East where a two-pronged assault, spearheaded by tanks, raced south across the 38th Parallel dividing North Korea from South Korea. Their success was stunning, although the North Korean Peoples Army (NKPA) based their armoured tactics more on those of the Red Army than of the *Panzerwaffe*. The South Koreans and the Americans, who were there as an army of occupation, could muster just a handful of M24 Chaffee light tanks, which the NKPA T-34s dealt with easily. Somehow, the Americans managed to hold on and regroup, bring in some Pershings and Shermans from Japan, and then one battalion of more modern M46 Pattons. By the third week in August, there were over 500 US tanks in the Pusan perimeter, and by early September, US tanks outnumbered the NKPA by at least five to one.

The United Nations forces (the defending force was now approved by the UN) soon went on to the offensive, driving the North Koreans back over the 38th Parallel and into North Korea. By now there were small numbers of both British and French tanks in the UN command, the British Centurion proving conclusively to be the best tank of the campaign. The war looked like drawing to a victorious close, but on November 25, 1950,

TOP: **Invasion! On the morning of June 25, 1950, some 10,000 North Korean infantry supported by more than 50 tanks (Soviet-built T-34/85s) swept across the 38th Parallel, spearheading the invasion of South Korea. They were followed by more troops and more tanks, and swiftly over-ran most of the country.** ABOVE: **Shermans of 2nd US Infantry Division blast enemy positions during an assault on the Chinese Communist Forces on the East Central Front in Korea, September 1951.**

the Chinese launched a massive offensive, the front not being stabilized until early April, back along the 38th Parallel. Thereafter, although tanks had shown themselves well able to operate in the rugged terrain, the use of armour both in attack and defence was sidelined and the war lapsed into an uneasy truce.

Since those days, the NKVA has built up a massive army containing over 6,500 tanks, half of which are main battle tanks of Russian or Chinese manufacture. South Korea has some 4,650 tanks, of which some 2,330 are also main battle tanks. The latter is tasked to absorb and then defeat any Blitzkrieg-type assault with prompt support from the US Army.

LEFT: Sweeping for mines. An M48 tank with an automatic mine-sweeper checks the road from Cam Lo to Mai Loc, Vietnam, in the northern I Corps area near the Demilitarized Zone (DMZ), September 16, 1970.
BELOW: An M155 Sheridan tank belonging to Troop "A" of the 1st Battalion, 1st Cavalry Regiment, American Division, pauses beneath some trees about 30.6km/19 miles north of Tam Ky, Vietnam, March 18, 1970.

Indo-China and Vietnam

The French fought a guerrilla war here from 1951–54 against the Viet Minh, in the end suffering a humiliating defeat at Dien Bien Phu, Vietnam. They used American World War II armour, including less than 500 tanks and tank destroyers spread over an area of some 72,520sq km/28,000sq miles. By comparison, when it came to be the Americans' turn to fight there, they employed some 600 tanks and over 2,000 other AFVs in an area less than one-third that size. A terrain study carried out in Vietnam by a team of US tankers in 1967 showed that nearly half the country could be traversed by AFVs all year round. Nevertheless, in the difficult areas like the Mekong Delta and the Central Highlands the lightly equipped, fast-moving Vietcong were far more capable of carrying out full-scale mobile war.

While the main American AFV used was the M113 (almost in the role of a light tank), M41s and later M48s were introduced as the war escalated. From 1967–68 the Australians sent a

squadron of medium tanks (British-built Centurions), and they fought a number of successful actions before being withdrawn from 1971–72. New equipment arriving in the late 1960s included the Sheridan Light Tank, with its wholly inappropriate 152mm/5.98in anti-tank missile that was never used in anger. Tank versus tank combat took place only twice: once at Ben Het in March 1969 between two tanks of US 69th Armour and a number of North Vietnam Army (NVA) PT-76s, two of which were knocked out; and in Laos in March 1971, where South Vietnamese M41s clashed with NVA tanks.

In their spring offensive in 1972, Viet Cong Russian-built T-54s and their Chinese equivalent Type 59s fought it out with American M48A3s of the South Vietnamese 20th Tank Regiment. Unfortunately the South Vietnamese not only let the initiative pass to the enemy, but also used their armour in a static role, inviting piecemeal destruction. Thus, as in Indo-China, a seemingly unsophisticated "peasant" army had shown itself better able to handle armour than its far more armour-conscious opponent.

LEFT: USMC flamethrowing M67s (developed from the M48), burning fields in Vietnam, near the 1st Battalion, 3rd Regiment command post, 3rd Marine Division, January 1966.

The uneasy peace

In addition to the Korean and Vietnam Wars, the 20th century saw many other conflicts taking place all over the world, for example on the Indian subcontinent, in the ever-turbulent Middle East, and even on the "roof of the world" in Afghanistan. Tanks have been employed in all of these wars, as the following four examples demonstrate.

India–Pakistan

Following World War II, the British Army found itself responsible not only for occupation duties in Europe but also for "Imperial Policing" in the British Empire as trouble flared in Palestine, then Malaya, Cyprus, Aden, Borneo and elsewhere, as erstwhile colonies sought their independence. Those units involved in such activities were mostly armoured cars and scout cars, but on some occasions tanks were deployed. Indeed, it was the norm for British armoured regiments to serve tours in the armoured reconnaissance role, the lighter AFVs being more suitable for aid to the civil power and counter-insurgency operations.

Such disturbances also occurred on the Indian subcontinent, as both Hindus and Muslims sought self-government. Then on August 14, 1947, India and Pakistan became separate countries. This momentous event was sadly accompanied by widespread communal violence, which inevitably led to war between the two new nations – first of all over Kashmir in November 1947, then over the Rann of Kutch in January 1957.

The United Nations mediated and a ceasefire was effected, but not before a number of major tank battles had taken place, in which the Indian-manned, British-built Centurions took on and beat the more sophisticated American-built Pakistani M48 Pattons. In 1965 during the 22-day war, the largest tank battle ever fought in Asia took place, with over 1,500 tanks involved and many being knocked out. On January 10, 1966, the two countries signed an uneasy truce, but in 1971, the Awami League declared East Pakistan to be the independent republic of Bangladesh. This led to Pakistan attacking India from West Pakistan in the "Lightning War". India retaliated by sending some eight divisions, including over 700 tanks (more than 400 Soviet-built T-55s and 300 home-produced Vickers Vijayanta, plus a number of Centurions, French-built AMX-13s and

BELOW: **An Indian Commanding Officer issues orders to his squadron commanders on the eve of battle, April 13, 1948. The Stuart Light Tank behind them is now on a plinth at the Indian War Museum.**

Russian amphibious PT-76s), forcing the Pakistanis into a humiliating surrender. Since then no major conflicts have occurred and both countries now have their own main battle tanks under construction (with outside assistance).

Iran–Iraq

The Iran–Iraq conflict is often forgotten despite being one of the longest-running wars of the 20th century. On September 22, 1980, Saddam Hussein attacked Iran, anticipating a short three-week Blitzkrieg-type campaign, leading to victory using more than 3,000 mainly Soviet-built tanks. Instead the war lasted for eight years and resulted in over a million casualties. Western arms dealers were only too happy to supply both sides with weapons, especially Iran, whose tanks were in a parlous state after years of neglect following the deposing of the Shah, who had taken a great interest in all things military.

Russo-Afghan War

In December 1979, the USSR attempted to take over Afghanistan, invading it with more than 100,000 troops supported by large numbers of tanks, helicopters and jet fighters. For the next ten years they fought a bitter, bloody war against the Mujahedin, who were clandestinely aided by Western finance. Eventually the Soviets realized that they could not win and signed a peace agreement in April 1988, withdrawing troops in 1989. Fighting has continued there ever since, but with different protagonists.

The Balkans

Closer to Europe, the Balkans has been a potential and actual battleground throughout the 20th century. During his lifetime, Marshal Tito managed to hold the various ethnic components of Yugoslavia together – an explosive mixture of Serbs, Croats and Slovenes – and fought successfully against the Germans in World War II. However, following his death the situation deteriorated, with widespread ethnic violence, leading to UN intervention in which British and American main battle tanks were employed in peace-keeping operations.

Sadly, this handful of examples is only the tip of the iceberg, as shown only too often by the twisted hulks of burnt-out tanks found all over the world.

ABOVE LEFT: **Indo-Pakistan conflict. This Pakistani M48 Medium Tank was knocked out by Indian Centurions during the war in 1965.** ABOVE: **Some Indian tank commanders pose with one of their victorious Centurions.**
BELOW: **Soviet tanks on the streets of Bratislava in 1968. A stone-throwing youth uses the leading Soviet T-62 to provide cover from the other Russian tanks in this failed uprising, August 1968.** BOTTOM: **War in the Falklands. A small number of British tanks were used in the Falklands War in 1982. Here a Scimitar CVR(t) gains extra protection by being dug in.**

The Arab-Israeli wars

It is ironic that after World War II the dashing image of the *Panzerwaffe* should have been taken over by Jewish tank commanders – the people the Nazis most reviled. The Israeli Armoured Corps was born in battle from small beginnings, yet rapidly became one of the most formidable armoured forces the world has known. Their commanders learned the hard way – on the battlefield – at all levels, putting lessons into practice immediately, instituting a rigorous system of discipline, yet without stifling individual initiative. The resulting potent mixture enabled them time and again to overcome the far larger, better-equipped forces of their Arab neighbours.

During the initial War of Independence in 1948, they had to organize effective armoured units while at the same time obtaining tanks from all over the world. Their first (and only) armoured brigade contained just one tank battalion comprising one company of smuggled in French Hotchkiss Light Tanks, manned by Russian immigrants who spoke little Yiddish, and one company of two Cromwells and one Sherman (stolen from the British), manned by British and South African volunteers. Nevertheless, they performed miracles.

1956 saw another upsurge in violence following the nationalization of the Suez Canal and the decision by Britain and France to send in troops to maintain free, open transit

TOP: **Patton tanks of Israel Defence Force (IDF) 7th Armoured Brigade breaking into Khan Younis on the morning of June 5, 1967, when the Six Day War began.** ABOVE: **Yom Kippur. Israeli Patton tanks advancing across the desert in central Sinai, making for the Suez Canal.**

through the canal. British Centurion tanks landed and took Port Said, but the major armoured effort came from two Israeli armoured brigades – part of their invasion force from Sinai. The Israeli 7th Armoured Brigade, for example, reached the Suez Canal in less than 100 hours, having travelled 241km/150 miles and having fought several fierce battles on the way.

A period of hasty reorganization followed, in which a number of new armoured brigades were formed, and in 1960 the Israelis took delivery of British Centurions, which soon proved their worth against Syrian tanks in border skirmishes. They were followed by more modern tanks, such as American M48A2 Pattons, fortunately in time for the Six Day War of 1967,

> "The outcome of the war will depend on our performance ...
> If we fail the outcome will be disastrous for the whole campaign ...
> There will be heavy fire and the Egyptians will fight well,
> so keep moving ... fire from as far as possible, knocking
> out enemy tanks and anti-tank guns at long range."
> General Israel Tal, then Director of the Israeli Armoured Corps
> to his tank commanders

ABOVE: **Part of a company of Merkava MBT in a Palestinian camp. The Israelis are probably the most experienced army in the world as far as street fighting is concerned.**

LEFT: **Paratroopers with armoured support (Sherman M4A1 Horizontal Volute Spring Suspension with 76mm/2.99in gun and wet stowage) break through to the American colony, north-west of the Old City wall of Jerusalem.**
BELOW: **An excellent photograph of two Israeli Centurions churning through the sands of Sinai during the lightning campaign that lasted just six days.**

in which the Israeli armour did particularly well, the individual tank gunnery skills of their tank crews completely dominating their Egyptian and Syrian opponents.

Then followed the War of Yom Kippur in October 1973, when the Egyptians took the initiative, launching a surprise attack across the Suez Canal. The Bar Lev Line was heavily attacked by 280,000 troops and 2,000 tanks, and many defending Israeli tanks were knocked out by man-portable, Soviet-made "Sagger" guided missiles. By the morning of October 8, the Egyptian Army had achieved a tremendous success and had put five divisions across the Canal. Nevertheless, despite being taken by surprise, the Israeli

reservists were soon rushing to join their units, two armoured divisions reaching Sinai during the night of October 7–8. Instead of the expected Egyptian breakout, there followed a period when they merely held their positions and knocked out many of the counter-attacking Israeli tanks. Clearly the Israelis needed to regain the initiative, and so they decided to re-cross the Canal and infiltrate their armour behind the Egyptian lines. After some delay, this was achieved at dawn on October 15, and by October 19 they had the best part of three tank divisions across. They were soon threatening Port Tewfik and the Gulf of Suez, encircling the Egyptians and forcing them into a ceasefire by October 24. Success on the Golan against the Syrians soon followed.

Since then there has been much activity but no all-out war, although Israeli armour, in particular their remarkable Merkava tank (one of many home-grown armoured successes) has been in constant action along their disputed frontiers with the Palestinians. The Israelis have certainly become experts in the difficult art of urban warfare, using heavy armour effectively against short-range urban targets. This requires specialized ammunition for the main armament and the use of the tank's excellent target-acquisition capability coupled with on-board machine-guns to deal with snipers and other threats. Another highly successful weapon on the latest Merkava Mk IV is the remotely activated, internally mounted Soltam 60mm/2.36in mortar which is used most effectively against tank-hunting parties.

Improvements in basic characteristics

Following World War II, while the speed and quantity of tank-building worldwide has slowed down, there are still plenty of new tanks being built, with some new countries indulging in first-time manufacture or in the improvement of less modern tanks so that they are capable of holding their own in future battles. All three of the basic characteristics have seen improvements, as have many other, less vital features.

Regarding firepower, Main Battle Tanks (MBTs) now mount main guns of 120–122mm/4.72–4.80in calibre. However, the fitting of conventional rifled guns has been overtaken by smooth-bore weapons of similar calibre, the only exception among the latest MBTs being the British CR2. Both have a similar range of anti-armour projectiles, which now include fin-stabilized, long rod, DU (Depleted Uranium) penetrators. These are necessary to defeat new forms of armour like the British Chobham – the latest type being called "Dorchester",

which gives a significant increase in protection against both KE (Kinetic Energy) and CE (Chemical Energy) attack. In 1988 the USA announced a new version on the M1A1 with steel-encased depleted uranium armour, two and a half times the density of steel.

Gun performance has also been significantly improved by a wide variety of new vision and gun-laying devices designed to improve the chances of a first-round hit by day or night. For example, some of the fire-control equipment found in the US Army Abrams M1A1 MBT includes a laser rangefinder, a full solution solid-state digital computer and a stabilized day/thermal night sight. The stabilizer allows for accurate firing on the move, the gunner merely placing the reticule in his sight on to the target and using his laser rangefinder to measure the range. The computer then works out and applies the weapon sight offset angles necessary to hit the target, and the gunner

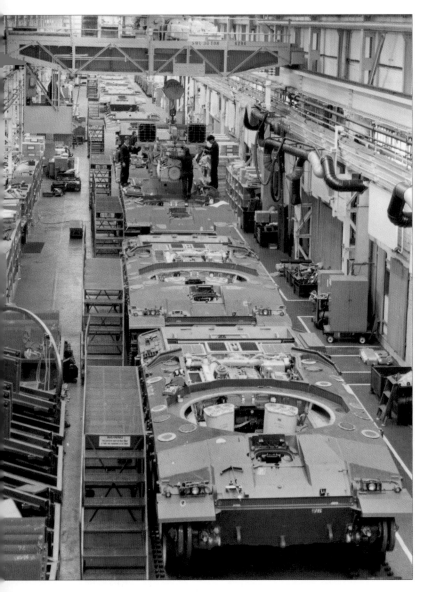

LEFT AND ABOVE: **In these two photographs taken inside the Challenger building plants at what was the Royal Ordnance Factory, Leeds (now closed), tank turrets are being fitted with Chobham armour for increased protection. Compare them with the normal Chieftain turrets alongside.**

opens fire. The gun has a muzzle reference system to measure any bend in the gun tube, while other sensors check wind speed, barrel temperature, ammunition temperature, etc, and automatically feed the results into the computer.

Added protection is afforded to many MBTs by the external fitting of reactive armour in the form of explosive-filled tiles. These detonate and explode outwards when struck by a shaped-charge projectile, thus disrupting the armour-piercing jet and negating its penetrative effect. Internally, sliding armoured doors and armour-protected boxes isolate crew members from on-board ammunition explosions, while automatic fire extinguishing systems will react to a fire and extinguish it.

Engines are now invariably run on diesel or are kerosene-based and despite being smaller in size are more powerful, having to deal with an MBT normally weighing between 60–70 tons. They are also generally simpler to maintain, the Abrams power pack (a Lycoming Textron AGT 1500 gas turbine), for example, being capable of removal and replacement in less than one hour (compared with four hours for the M60 series). Equally, modern-day suspensions give a smoother ride, not only benefiting the crew, but also making the weapon stabilization system more effective.

In addition to all these major new items, there are land-navigation and battlefield information systems, and better day/night viewing devices together with longer-range yet more compact radios. The inevitable result of all these improvements, however, has been a considerable increase in manufacturing costs. Thus, there has been a significant consolidation and specialization within the armaments industry, for example in the UK, first the acquisition of Vickers Defence Systems by Alvis plc in late 2002, and then the take-over of Alvis Vickers by BAe Systems. Building MBTs is clearly an expensive business.

ABOVE LEFT: **Even "bombing-up" a tank on the ranges and not under battlefield conditions is still a time-consuming job. Here crewmen load practice ammunition (note the colour is different from service rounds). In the photograph there are APDS (Armour-Piercing Discarding Sabot) and HESH (High-Explosive Squash-Head) practice rounds, plus bag charges, vent tubes (in the small can he is holding) and belts of machine-gun ammunition for the coaxial machine-gun.**

ABOVE: **Modern tank ammunition includes Armour-Piercing Fin-Stabilized Discarding Sabot rounds such as these for a British 120mm/4.72in tank gun. The part that does the damage is the Long Rod Penetrator (two versions are on show here) to defeat Depleted Uranium armour.** BELOW: **Amphibious light tanks are still extremely useful for reconnaissance purposes. Here a number of Soviet PT-76s swim ashore during a training exercise.**

Training expedients

Immediately post-World War II, armoured training on both sides of the Iron Curtain was intensified at all levels, with major exercises being held by NATO and Warsaw Pact forces at varying levels of realism. However, it soon became clear that other cheaper and more sustainable methods of training had to be found if vast training damage bills were to be avoided – not to mention the wear and tear on AFVs. Nevertheless, tank crews still had to be kept at the right level of readiness so that they could go to war at a moment's notice.

Considerable work was therefore done on improving indoor static-training devices such as Classroom Simulators, especially for both tank driver/commander and tank gunner/loader/commander skills. While this could not entirely replace actual hands-on training in the AFV, it certainly could and did give all crew members good, basic training and made it easier to sustain follow-on training in regiments, so that tank crews could be kept at a suitable level of operational readiness. In military schools such as the Armor School at Fort Knox, USA, and the RAC (Royal Armoured Corps) Centre (now called the Armour Centre) in the UK and in training regiments, suites of

ABOVE: **Gunnery training simulators were essential to save both expensive training areas and equally expensive track mileage. This Classroom Armament Instructional Mounting for a Chieftain was used by the REME (Royal Electrical and Mechanical Engineers) to instruct gun-fitters.**

such training devices have been installed and are used extensively. In addition, it was realized that training a tank driver did not require an AFV with a vastly expensive fighting compartment (i.e. a turret), so now MBTs such as CR2 have a specially built turret-less Driver Trainer Tank (DTT).

Regular gunnery training periods on open ranges are still essential if crews are to become accustomed to live firing. However, the increased range and lethality of tank gun ammunition has made it necessary to invent new training rounds which have similar characteristics to service ammunition, but without the same range or lethality.

Another perennial problem for training at lower levels has been finding a suitable method of registering hits on two-sided exercises. Initially this could only be done by means of on-the-spot umpires, but this not only required manpower, but was in many cases ineffective. There are now training devices that can be fitted to tanks, anti-tank guns/missile launchers, and even to individual personal weapons, which give a realistic impression

FAR LEFT: The "business end" of an early driver-training simulator. This shows the TV camera on a Link Miles Driving Simulator which was moved on a gantry across a terrain model.
LEFT: Instructor's console for the Link Miles Driving Simulator. Note the replica driving controls below the TV screen and the map of the terrain model above them.

ABOVE: Bale out! With a coloured smoke pyrotechnic belching smoke (for 30 seconds) denoting a "kill", the crew of this Chieftain bale out of their "knocked-out" tank. BELOW: Fording water obstacles is another part of tank training. Note the tall "conning tower" fixed to the commander's hatch of this Chieftain and the rubber sealing covers to prevent water from getting inside the tank.

both to the firer and at the target end. When an accurate hit by a suitable type of armour-piercing round is registered on the target vehicle, coloured smoke may be emitted, a siren sounded, or the vehicle engine or gun control computer may be shut down by means of suitably located detectors on board. However, this must be carefully controlled so that the "knocked-out" tank and its crew are not put at risk. The firer also gets a suitable reaction, even as far as reducing the amount of his on-board ammunition, so that in due course he must replenish if he is to continue to take part in the battle.

Restrictions on space in Europe have led to the British seeking training areas further afield. None has been more successful than the British Army Training Unit, Suffield (BATUS), in Alberta, Canada. Armoured units stationed in the UK and Germany now regularly train at BATUS against "live" enemy. In addition, the lowering of the Iron Curtain and the dismantling of the Berlin Wall has led to NATO and erstwhile Warsaw Pact armies exchanging training grounds and working together to deal with common problems.

Additionally, the mere fact that much of the equipment on a modern tank is computer-controlled means that built-in training devices are commonplace, allowing crews to practise their drills without even having to leave the tank hangar.

Wars in Iraq

In early August 1990, tiny oil-rich Kuwait was invaded by its neighbour Iraq, which boasted the fourth largest and supposedly most powerful army in the world. The Iraqis used thousands of Russian-built T-series tanks (such as T-62 and T-72 MBT) to spearhead their invasion in typical Blitzkrieg style. Fortunately, apart from a few "prophets of doom", Saddam Hussein found few allies, while the United Nations, with America leading the way, imposed an immediate naval blockade. This was swiftly followed by an impressive build-up of sea, land and air forces in Saudi Arabia, to back up the UN resolution ordering Iraq to withdraw. Operation "Desert Shield", as it was called, was followed by Operation "Desert Storm" in which first Coalition air forces and then ground troops were employed. The ground offensive, Operation "Desert Sabre", was launched on February 23, 1991. Meticulously planned and executed with élan, its speed and direction came as a complete surprise to the Iraqis. With armour to the fore – in particular the main battle tank playing a major role – it was yet another example of a highly successful all-arms team action. It was also fought on a 24-hour battlefield day, in which the vastly superior night-fighting capability of the British Challenger and the American Abrams tanks was in evidence from the outset.

The battle went so quickly that many observers could not believe what they saw on their television screens all over the world. Thousands of the enemy were killed, wounded or captured – out of all proportion to the small numbers of Coalition casualties. The much-vaunted Soviet tanks were a disaster, and in many cases dug in so deeply that they could not traverse their turrets, while their AFV batteries had been removed and used to light underground shelters rather than work their vehicle electrical systems! The fourth largest army in the world turned out to be a paper tiger thanks to the sheer professionalism of the Allied tank crews. Pentagon officials estimated that some 4,000 Iraqi tanks were destroyed in the 100-hour battle, which ended on February 28 when the Coalition forces cut the highway from Kuwait to Basra, thus preventing the bulk of the battered and defeated Iraqi Army from escaping.

ABOVE LEFT: **Operation "Desert Storm". Crews of British Challenger 1s carry out last-minute adjustments before going into battle.** ABOVE: **The detritus of war. In the foreground are the knocked-out blackened hulks of two Iraqi tanks during the aftermath of Operation "Desert Storm", barely recognizable as once combat-ready MBTs. A convoy of Coalition force vehicles can be seen in the background.** BELOW: **A British Challenger 1 advances to meet the enemy.**

The second Gulf War

World opinion prevented the Coalition forces from "finishing the job" and calling Saddam Hussein to account. Instead, for the next 14 years they vacillated, while Iraq threatened its neighbours with supposed "Weapons of Mass Destruction" and the Iraqi leader continued to oppress his own people. Eventually the Allies once again decided to act, although this time world opinion was not as solidly behind

BELOW: **Operation "Telic".** Striking picture of the "business end" of a 2nd Royal Tank Regiment Challenger 2. Note the 7th Armoured Brigade "Desert Rat". BOTTOM: **Gunner action!** A CR2 belonging to the 2 RTR Battlegroup traverses on to a target.

the USA and UK as it had been on the first occasion. Nevertheless, on March 20, 2003, the Allied armies invaded Iraq from Kuwait, the British elements targeting the southern city of Basra, while the Americans drove all-out for Baghdad. The success of the armour-led Allied columns was even more spectacular than in 1991, the war-fighting being over in a matter of just a few days. Once again the American and British main battle tanks had shown their complete

superiority – a testament to how effective tanks still are on the modern battlefield, provided they are manned by thoroughly professional, properly motivated, well-disciplined and well-trained tank crews. Operation "Iraqi Freedom", as it was known by the Americans, and Operation "Telic", as it was called by the British, showed once again that it is the all-arms team that wins battles and that the human element in the shape of the tank crew is still the most important ingredient.

The future

As must be evident from what has been covered already, the tank undoubtedly played a major part in securing victory in both World Wars and has gone on to prove itself time and time again ever since, being employed in most of the high-intensity conflicts that have occurred worldwide. There was also a large armoured presence on both sides of the Iron Curtain ready to take part in World War III if the unthinkable had ever happened and the world had descended into nuclear war. This led to increasingly large numbers of sophisticated Main Battle Tanks (MBTs) being built by both sides before the thaw in the Cold War started.

There is now, however, no doubt that things are changing, principally because the end of the Cold War has seen a downsizing of most European armies, leading to considerable over-capacity in tank-building and associated armaments industries, despite the continuing lucrative trade in the upgrading and modernization of older MBTs. However, this has not been the case worldwide where countries in the Far East, such as China, Japan and the Republic of Korea, now have their own tank-building industries, some even exporting to neighbours and further afield. In the West there has thus been a declining MBT market, especially as a number of countries, including the USA and UK, have started to favour a more balanced force composition. Therefore, as well as needing a "heavy" element based upon MBTs, infantry fighting vehicles and Self-Propelled (SP) artillery, they have now stated a requirement for a "light" element that can be air-transportable

TOP: **One of the obvious employments for British armour will be in peacekeeping operations on behalf of NATO and the UN, as in Kosovo. The photograph shows three elements of IFOR, including a Challenger 2 MBT and a CVR Scimitar Light Tank.** ABOVE: **Fitting old tanks with more powerful guns, power packs, etc, is now big business all over the world. Here an American-built M48 has been fitted with a more powerful diesel engine – the AVDS 1790 2C tank engine – by means of installing a TCM/GPD simplified dieselization kit.**

in medium-range transport aircraft, such as the C-130 Hercules. This challenges the armaments industry to produce a class of tank weighing about 16 tons – a very demanding requirement for any would-be manufacturer who must produce a new tank with firepower, protection and mobility on a par with the current 70-ton MBT, but weighing some 75 per cent less. This calls for considerable innovation, and consideration is now being given to lighter, smaller, wheeled AFVs as well as tracked vehicles. Miniaturization of components and the use of machinery to perform crew tasks (such as automatic loaders) so as to cut down on the space requirements also becomes a major issue.

In addition, the use of non-conventional, lighter, composite armour is also being studied. An example of such lighter systems is the much-debated American "Future Combat System". It is early days yet and, at least for the time being, MBTs will continue to rule.

Various MBTs and other AFVs are now being offered with a variety of alternative subsystems – such as varying power packs, fire-control systems and night/day vision devices – to suit all customers' needs. As mentioned before, the British CR2 is now the only top-grade MBT with a rifled gun. This could possibly change as consideration is currently being given to replacing it by one of a number of similar calibre smoothbore guns. New types of ammunition specifically for urban warfare have been developed, such as the American Multi-Purpose Anti-Tank round (MPAT) to create breaches in buildings for assault team access and the Israeli Anti-Personnel Anti-Material tank round (APAM) containing six sub-munitions with thousands of tungsten cubes for controlled fragmentation.

Suffice it to say that for the time being anyway, there is little chance of the MBT going out of fashion or being replaced by some other weapon system such as the armed helicopter. Although the balance of the "Firepower, Protection and Mobility" equation may alter and thus produce a more varied selection of the weapon system that we call the "Tank", their future place on the battlefield as an indispensable member of the battle-winning all-arms team still appears secure.

LEFT: **Added protection against HEAT (High-Explosive Anti-Tank) projectiles is achieved by the fitting of tiles of Explosive Reactive Armour (ERA), as on this Russian T-72 tank.** BELOW: **Testing new materials for the future. An early test model, developed in 2000 by the Defence Evaluation and Research Agency (DERA) in partnership with Vickers Defence Systems, to examine the trend towards smaller, lighter MBTs. It has a plastic/glass fibre composite hull rather than one made of conventional steel. It was known as the Advanced Composite Armoured Vehicle Platform (ACAVP), but christened by some the "Tupperware Tank"! Its basic purpose was for stress and strain analysis under field conditions.**

ABOVE: **On guard at the edge of Podujevo during Operation "Agricola". A close-up of the CR2 belonging to the Commanding Officer of 2 RTR, 7th Armoured Brigade (note the "Desert Rat" emblem).** LEFT: **After many years without an armaments industry, Japan, like other Far Eastern countries, now makes its own tanks. These are Type 61 MBTs, the first home-produced tank since World War II.**

A–Z of World War Tanks

1916–45

The size and shape of the first tanks of 1916 depended more upon the need to cross trenches and deal with machine-gun nests than any other factor. Improvements were then rapidly made, the "International" Mark VIII of 1918 being way ahead of the original Mark I, while the tiny French FT-17, which was the first tank with a fully traversing turret, was sought worldwide. From 1918 onwards, financial restrictions put paid to progress among the victors, leaving it to Germany to develop armoured warfare. Tanks like the Panzer III and IV stayed in production for most of World War II, while the Allies floundered, building a plethora of generally inferior models. In the end it was the remarkable transformation of American industry that saved the day, producing vast numbers of reliable, adaptable tanks like the Sherman. Towards the end of World War II, the Soviets also produced some excellent medium and heavy tanks, including perhaps the best Allied tank of all, the T-34. Nevertheless, ask anyone to name the outstanding tank of the war and they will invariably say the German Tiger I, whose dreaded 8.8cm/3.46in gun and thick armour made it feared everywhere.

LEFT: **This British Heavy Mark V of 1918 is still in full running order at the Tank Museum, Bovington, Dorset, despite having seen action on the battlefields of France during World War I.**

A7V Sturmpanzerwagen

At the start of World War I the Germans lacked anyone at ministerial level prepared to put their weight behind any tank projects; consequently no attempt was made to build one until after British tanks had already appeared. Ultimately only one German tank type took part in the war, the A7V, with 100 being ordered but less than a quarter of that number being built.

Weighing 30,480kg/30 tons, this leviathan consisted of a basic massive steel box superstructure built over a tractor chassis. It had a suitably enormous crew of 18, 12 of whom were machine-gunners, divided into pairs, with one team stationed at the rear and the rest along the sides. The main armament was a 5.7cm/2.24in gun mounted in the nose. The A7V's cross-country performance was poor, although it had a top road speed of 14kph/9mph. Despite this and its frightening appearance, it was remarkably ineffective, being both cumbersome and mechanically unreliable.

The first tank versus tank battle took place at Villers Bretonneux, France, on April 24, 1918, when three British tanks (two Female and one Male) met three A7Vs. Two of the enemy were too far away to be engaged, but the British Male, a Mark IV, opened up on the leading A7V. The British tank crews had been badly gassed the previous day, two of the Mark IV Male's crew being evacuated and the remainder still suffering from the effects of the mustard gas. This made it very difficult for the British tank gunners to see properly to engage their enemy.

TOP: **The only surviving A7V is in the Australian War Museum. However, the German Panzer Museum at Munster now has a full-scale replica which is seen here in a panorama setting in their museum.** LEFT: **A captured A7V arriving at Erin near Bermicourt, France, the location of the Tank Corps Central Workshops.**

ABOVE: **Two A7Vs in a village near Villers Bretonneux, France. The vehicles were "Hagen" and "Wotan".** RIGHT: **According to the chalk marking, this A7V was captured by the New Zealanders.** BELOW: **Thirteen of the eighteen-man crew are seen here riding on the outside of the tank – probably to escape from the heat, fumes and noise inside.**

A7V Sturmpanzerwagen

Entered service: 1917
Crew: 18
Weight: 30,480kg/30 tons
Dimensions: Length – 8m/26ft 3in
   Height (over turret hatch) – 3.4m/11ft 2in
   Width – 3.2m/10ft 6in
Armament: Main – 5.7cm/2.24in gun
   Secondary – 6 x 7.92mm/0.31in Maxim-Spandau
   08/15 machine-guns
Armour: Maximum – 30mm/1.18in
Powerplant: 2 x Daimler-Benz 4-cylinder petrol,
   74.5kW/100hp
Performance: Speed – 15kph/9mph
   Range – 60–70km/37–44 miles

Their first rounds missed, and the A7V quickly replied with armour-piercing machine-gun fire, causing "splash" and sparks inside the British tanks. The German tank engaged the two Female tanks, damaging both and forcing them to withdraw. The British commander of the Male, Second Lieutenant Frank Mitchell then halted his tank to give the gunner a steady shot. They were both delighted to see the A7V keel over, but it had simply run down a steep bank and overturned. This was nevertheless counted as the first tank kill.

A1E1 Independent

In December 1922, the War Office asked Vickers to design a new heavy tank to replace the World War I Mark V. The chosen design was for a tank with a main gun in an all-round traversing turret and machine-guns in four small separate turrets with limited traverse only. The "land warship" idea, pioneered by the British with this tank, would enjoy a brief European-wide popularity before its shortcomings became apparent and the practical problems of command, crew control, weight and size made it redundant.

However, as an experimental model it anticipated and influenced future tank design with various new developments, including: a self-cleaning drive sprocket; an aero-marine inertia starter; a prototype intercom system using the laryngaphone and mechanical indicators; as well as better battle stations for increased crew comfort and safety.

The controls of the A1E1 were hydraulically operated by the driver at the front, with the engine at the rear and the tracks slung low with the hull between them. Main armament was a 3pdr in the main turret, with four Vickers machine-guns in the subsidiary turrets. Its 296.7kW/398bhp Armstrong-Siddeley V12 engine theoretically gave the A1E1 a road speed of 40kph/25mph, but in practice it was lower (32kph/20mph) because it consumed oil heavily. The engine was also notoriously difficult to start – hence the fitting of the aero-marine inertia starter.

With the weight at 32,514kg/32 tons, the engine, final drive, suspension, rubber tyres of the road wheels and the brakes all gave constant trouble because the tank was too heavy, out of proportion and too long for its width. This in turn made it difficult to steer, and caused serious problems at the rear where the track frames started to peel away from the hull. Eventually after an expensive but useful seven-year development cycle, the project was shelved after costing over £150,000 – a high price at that time.

TOP: **Built in 1926, this multi-turreted, heavily armed British tank was designed, as the name implies, for independent action. Its design was very advanced for the time, and it set a trend for similar tanks in France, Germany and Russia. The only A1E1 built still survives at the Tank Museum, in Dorset. During World War II it was taken out of the Museum and used to guard the approaches to Bovington.**

LEFT: **Internal photograph of the main armament of the Independent.**

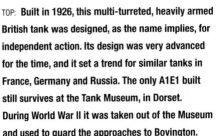

A1E1 Independent	

Entered service: This tank never entered service
Crew: 8
Weight: 32,514kg/32 tons
Dimensions: Length – 7.6m/24ft 11in
    Height (over turret hatch) – 2.72m/8ft 11 in
    Width – 2.67m/8ft 9in
Armament: Main – 3pdr QF (quick-firing) gun
    Secondary – 4 x Vickers machine-guns in subsidiary turrets
Armour: Maximum – 30mm/1.18in
Powerplant: Armstrong-Siddeley air-cooled V12, 296.7kW/398bhp
Performance: Speed – 32kph/20mph
    Range – 150km/93 miles

LEFT: **Two A9s are prepared by their crews for action in the Western Desert. Early on in the Desert War they could hold their own against the Italian tanks, but they were outclassed once the panzers arrived.**

A9 Cruiser Tank Mark I

A9 Cruiser Tank Mk I

Entered service: 1938
Crew: 6
Weight: 12,190 kg/12 tons
Dimensions: Length – 5.79m/19ft
  Height (over turret hatch) – 2.54m/8ft 4in
  Width – 2.54m/8ft 4in
Armament: Main – 2pdr gun
  Secondary – 3 x Vickers 7.7mm/0.303in machine-guns (one coaxial, two in separate turrets)
Armour: Maximum – 10–14mm/0.39–0.55in
Powerplant: AEC Type A179 6-cylinder petrol, 111.9kW/150bhp
Performance: Speed – 40kph/25mph
  Range – 241km/150 miles

Medium tanks lacked speed, while light tanks lacked both firepower and protection. This led to the design of a series of "Cruiser" tanks, the A9 being the first. Sir John Carden completed the design in 1934, trials started in 1936, and production in 1937. One hundred and twenty-five tanks were built in total, and saw service from 1938–41.

The weight of the A9 being relatively low allowed it to be powered by a commercially available 9.64 litre AEC bus engine, which gave it a top speed of 40kph/25mph. It also had a distinctive "slow-motion" suspension system with the triple-wheel bogies on springs mounted with Newton hydraulic shock absorbers.

It was armed with a 2pdr main gun and three machine-guns, one coaxial in the main turret and the other two in separate auxiliary turrets, and it was the first British tank with an hydraulic-powered turret traverse.

Combat experience in France in 1940 proved that the design had two critical drawbacks: the armour was too thin and the speed too slow for the cruiser role. It also fought in the Western Desert in North Africa, where, although adequate against the Italian armour, it was just too slow and thinly armoured when confronted by contemporary German tanks.

A10 Cruiser Tank Mark IIA

The A10 shared various features with the A9, including the same designer, Sir John Carden. It had the same basic turret and hull shape but with the two secondary turrets removed and additional armour installed by simply bolting extra plates on to the outside of the hull and turret, making it the first British tank built in this composite fashion. One hundred and seventy-five vehicles were ordered and completed by September 1940. A10s were issued to units of the 1st Armoured Division, and were used in France in 1940 and in the Western Desert until late 1941. However, like its predecessor, it was too slow and lightly armoured when confronted by contemporary German tanks.

A10 Cruiser Tank Mk IIA

Entered service: 1940
Crew: 5
Weight: 13,970kg/13.75 tons
Dimensions: Length – 5.51m/18ft 1in
  Height (over turret hatch) – 2.59m/8ft 6in
  Width – 2.54m/8ft 4in
Armament: Main – 2pdr QFSA (quick-firing semi-automatic) L/52 gun
  Secondary – 2 x 7.92mm/0.31in Besa (one coaxial and one hull)
Armour: Maximum – 22–30mm/0.87–1.18in
Powerplant: AEC Type A179 6-cylinder petrol, 111.9kW/150bhp
Performance: Speed – 26kph/16.16mph
  Range – 161km/100 miles

LEFT: **Sir John Carden designed the A10 Cruiser Tank Mark II. It was more heavily armoured than its A9 predecessor, and replaced the two separate machine-gun turrets with a single Besa machine-gun. This model has been painted in the original British wartime desert camouflage pattern rather than that used in temperate climates.**

A11 Infantry Tank Mark I Matilda I

The first pilot model of the A11 was designed by Sir John Carden and produced by Vickers in 1936. It had a maximum speed of only 13kph/8mph because at the time it was considered that Infantry tanks were only required to keep up with the infantry as they advanced at a walking pace. It was armed with either a 7.7mm/0.303in or 12.7mm/0.5in machine-gun.

To keep costs to a minimum, the construction was kept very simple. A commercial Ford V8 engine and transmission were installed with the steering, brakes, clutches and suspension adapted from those used

in the Vickers Light Tanks and Dragon gun tractors. The body was of an all-riveted construction, with the exception of the turret which was cast.

The first production order for 60 vehicles was placed in April 1937, and later increased to 140, all of which were completed by August 1940. Although they were cheap and reliable, they were soon obsolete – being outgunned from the start. Nevertheless, they did see action in the early days of World War II and thereafter were used for training purposes only.

There are a number of stories as to how the tank got its nickname Matilda,

one being that when General Sir Hugh Elles saw the tank's comic, duck-like appearance and gait, he named it after a cartoon series of the day. In fact, the codeword "Matilda" appears on the original proposal for the A11 in John Carden's handwriting.

A11 Infantry Tank Mk I Matilda I

Entered service: 1938
Crew: 2
Weight: 11,160kg/11 tons
Dimensions: Length – 4.85m/15ft 11in
  Height (over turret hatch) –1.85m/6ft 1in
  Width – 2.29m/7ft 6in
Armament: 1 x 12.7mm/0.5in or 7.7mm/0.303in
  Vickers machine-gun
Armour: Maximum – 60mm/2.36in
Powerplant: Ford V8 petrol, 52.22kW/70bhp
Performance: Speed – 13kph/8mph
  Range – 129km/80 miles

TOP: **The small but heavily armoured A11 Infantry Tank Mark I Matilda I. It was invulnerable to anything but the largest enemy anti-tank guns because of its thick armour. However, it was only armed with a single machine-gun, and was very slow.**

LEFT: **A somewhat battle-scarred Matilda I – this model is the A11E1 prototype.**

A12 Infantry Tank Mark II Matilda II

In 1936, design began on the successor to the Matilda I, which was to mount a 2pdr main gun and have an increased road speed of around 16–24kph/10–15mph. It was hoped to modify the A11, but it soon became apparent that this would not be practical. Instead, the new design, designated the A12 Infantry Tank Mark II, would be based on the A7 Medium Tank, and built by the Vulcan Foundry of Warrington. Twin ganged AEC diesel engines and a Wilson epicyclic gear box were installed, and the tank was armed with a coaxially mounted 2pdr and 7.92mm/0.312in Besa machine-gun.

The powered turret could be traversed in 14 seconds using a system adapted from that fitted to the Vickers A9. The hull armour was cast and the tracks were protected by one-piece armour side skirts with five mud chutes.

The Matilda played its most important role in the early Western Desert campaigns. In Libya in 1940, its heavy armour was soon found to be almost immune to Italian anti-tank and tank fire. Until the appearance of the German 8.8cm/3.46in Flak gun in 1941, used in an anti-tank role, it was the most effective of the British tanks.

ABOVE: **The Bovington Tank Museum's A12 Infantry Tank Mark II Matilda. It is painted in the original Western Desert camouflage and named "Golden Miller" in honour of Major General Bob Foote's tank which he commanded when, as Commanding Officer of 7 RTR, he was awarded the Victoria Cross for outstanding courage and leadership over the period from May 27 to June 15, 1942.**

Unfortunately, as the Matilda turret could not fit the 6pdr due to the small size of its turret ring, its importance began to diminish. There were, however, many special purpose variants produced, including:
• Matilda CDL (Canal Defence Light): a powerful searchlight used to illuminate battlefields at night.
• Baron I, II, III and IIIA: flail mine-clearers.
• Matilda Scorpion: flail mine-clearer.
• Matilda with AMRA (Anti-Mine Roller Attachment): mine-clearer using rollers.
• Matilda with Carrot (Carrot demolition charge): 272kg/600lb HE (High-Explosive).
• Matilda Frog: flamethrower developed in Australia.
• Matilda Murray: flamethrower also developed in Australia.

ABOVE RIGHT: **Sandstorm approaching! A Matilda Mark II – the Commanding Officers's tank of 4 RTR – in the desert, alongside his heavy-utility staff car, as a _Khamseen_ (dust storm) blows up behind them.**
LEFT: **A Matilda II in the shadow of St Paul's Cathedral, London.**

A12 Infantry Tank Mk II Matilda II

Entered service: 1939
Crew: 4
Weight: 26,924kg /26.5 tons
Dimensions: Length – 5.61m/18ft 5in
    Height (over turret hatch) – 2.52m/8ft 3in
    Width – 2.59m/8ft 6in
Armament: Main – 2pdr OQF (ordnance quick-firing) gun
    Secondary – 1 x coaxial 7.92mm/0.312in Besa machine-gun
Armour: Maximum – 78mm/3.07in
Powerplant: 2 x AEC 6-cylinder diesels, 64.8kW/87bhp
Performance: Speed – 13kph/8mph
    Range – 258km/160 miles

LEFT: Developed from the high-speed Christie-type BT tanks then in service with the Red Army, the A13 was based on a Christie model imported from the USA. It saw operational service both in France and the Western Desert.

A13 Cruiser Tank Mk III

Entered service: 1938
Crew: 4
Weight: 14,225kg/14 tons
Dimensions: Length – 6.02m/19ft 9in
   Height (over turret hatch) – 2.59m/8ft 6in
   Width – 2.54m/8ft 4in
Armament: Main – 2pdr QFSA (quick-firing semi-automatic) gun
   Secondary – 1 x coaxial Vickers 7.7mm/0.303in machine-gun
Armour: Maximum – 14mm/0.55in
Powerplant: Nuffield Liberty V12 petrol, 253.64kW/340bhp
Performance: Speed – 48kph/30mph
   Range – 145km/90 miles

A13 Cruiser Tank Mark III

The A13 originated in late 1936 after British War Office observers had witnessed the high speed of the Russian Christie-type BT tanks in service with the Red Army. The Nuffield Company was asked to design a similar tank based on the Christie design as a high-speed replacement for the A9 and A10. The A13 was based on an actual Christie vehicle imported from the USA, developed in under two years and in service by 1938. It had the Christie suspension system, a high power-to-weight ratio, and a very high top speed of over 48kph/30mph. The engine could be started electrically or by using compressed air. The simple flat-sided turret gave the tank a distinctive appearance. It was used by the 1st Armoured Division in France 1940 and in small numbers with the 7th Armoured Division in the Western Desert in 1940–41, but was too lightly armoured and under-gunned when compared to its German contemporaries.

A13 Mark II Cruiser Tank Mark IV

The A13 Mark II was the up-armoured version of the A13 with extra armoured steel plates giving added protection and eliminating shot traps. Hollow "V"-sided plates were added to the original A13 type turret – some A13s were also upgraded to similar standards – and this gave the turret a very distinctive appearance with its faceted sides. Due to the high power-to-weight ratio of the Nuffield Liberty V12 petrol engine, the extra armour did not adversely affect the vehicle's performance. The A13 Mark II was in production in 1938, and used in France in 1940 and in the Western Desert in 1940–41. Features included Christie suspension and varied patterns of mantlet. Some 655 were built in total. Once more it was under-gunned, its 2pdr being a satisfactory anti-tank weapon but far too small when used with HE (High-Explosive) munitions.

LEFT: The A13 Mark II Cruiser Tank Mark IV was essentially an up-armoured version of the Cruiser Tank Mark III. The excellent power-to-weight ratio meant that the increase in armour had little effect upon its top speed.

A13 Mk II Cruiser Tank Mk IV

Entered service: 1940
Crew: 4
Weight: 15,040kg/14.8 tons
Dimensions: Length – 6m/19ft 9in
   Height (over turret hatch) – 2.59m/8ft 6in
   Width – 2.59m/8ft 6in
Armament: Main – 2pdr OQF (ordnance quick-firing) L/52 gun
   Mk IVCS close-support) 94mm/3.7in howitzer
   Secondary – 1 x coaxial 7.7mm/0.303in or 7.92mm/0.312in Besa or 7.7mm/0.303in Vickers machine-gun
Armour: Maximum – 30mm/1.18in
Powerplant: Nuffield Liberty V12 petrol, 253.64kW/340bhp
Performance: Speed – 48kph/30mph
   Range – 145km/90 miles

A13 Mark III Cruiser Tank Mark V Covenanter

Built by the London, Midland and Scottish Railway Company, the Covenanter was based on the A13 Mark II and used many of its parts in order to keep costs down. It had a powerful purpose-built Meadows Flat-12 engine and a low-set Christie suspension. However, a design flaw of this vehicle was the positioning of the engine at the rear while the cooling radiator was placed at the front alongside the driver. As a result, the vehicle was plagued by overheating, causing continual mechanical problems.

It saw service from 1940–43, later versions having a better engine-cooling system, a different mantlet, and a number of other improvements.

However, the Covenanter's problems were never satisfactorily solved. As a result, the vehicle never saw action, but was used in a training role and in the development of variants, including:
• Covenanter CS: close-support version, armed with a 76.2mm/3in howitzer in place of the normal 2pdr.
• Covenanter with AMRA (Anti-Mine Roller Attachment): mine-clearing device pushed in front of the tank in order to set off mines by pressure.

TOP: **An excellent view of an A13 Mark III Cruiser Tank Mark V Covenanter taken during "Battle Day" at Bovington, Dorset. The ill-fated Covenanter was a failure due to engine overheating problems, and it never saw action.** ABOVE: **Despite its stylish appearance, the unhappy Covenanter was never a success and was plagued with mechanical problems. (The Tank Museum's model was dug up some years ago and restored to cosmetic order before going on show.)**

• Covenanter OP (Observation Post), Command: with extra radio equipment and a dummy gun.
• Covenanter Bridgelayer: bridgelayer with 10.36m/34ft bridge.

A13 Mk III Cruiser Tank Mk V Covenanter

Entered service: 1940
Crew: 4
Weight: 18,289kg/18 tons
Dimensions: Length – 5.8m/19ft
   Height (over turret hatch) – 2.24m/7ft 4in
   Width – 2.62m/8ft 7in
Armament: Main – 2pdr OQF (ordnance quick-firing) gun
   Secondary – 1 x coaxial 7.92mm/0.312in Besa machine-gun
Armour: Maximum – 40mm/1.57in
Powerplant: Meadows DAV1 12-cylinder petrol, 223.8kW/300bhp
Performance: Speed – 50kph/31mph
   Range – 161km/100 miles

A15 Cruiser Tank Mark VI Crusader

The Crusader was built by Nuffields utilizing a large number of components from the A13 series, including both the Christie suspension and Liberty engine of the original design, as always to keep down costs, production time and vehicle weight. It too had a riveted hull, welded turret and an extra outer layer of armour bolted on.

Ready by March 1940, production was then increased and a consortium produced 5,300 Crusaders by 1943 as it became the principal British tank from spring 1941 until the arrival of the American Sherman.

However, the Crusader always suffered from poor reliability, which reflected the urgency with which it had been rushed into production. It first saw action near Fort Capuzzo, Libya, in June 1941 and did well against Italian armour, but although the Germans respected its speed, it was no match for the PzKpfw III

or indeed the 5.5cm/2.17in, 7.5cm/2.95in and 8.8cm/3.46in anti-tank guns.

After withdrawal from front-line use in May 1943, it was mainly used for training, but also converted for special purposes, including:
• Crusader OP (Observation Post) and Crusader Command: vehicles modified with dummy gun and extra radio and communications equipment.
• Crusader III, AA (Anti-Aircraft) Marks I/II/III: Mark I – the turret was removed and replaced by single Bofors 40mm/ 1.57in Anti-Aircraft mount; Mark II – a new enclosed turret with twin 20mm/ 0.79in Oerlikon AA cannon; Mark III – similar to the AA Mark II but with radio equipment removed from turret and installed in hull.
• Crusader II, Gun Tractor Mk 1: open-topped box superstructure converted as a fast tractor for 17pdr anti-tank gun and its crew.

ABOVE LEFT: **This is the Tank Museum's Crusader III, the final production model, armed with a 6pdr instead of the original 2pdr gun.** ABOVE: **Tank crewmen hard at work. The crew of a Crusader III, belonging to the 16th/5th Royal Lancers cleaning their 6pdr gun in Tunisia, April 1943.**

• Crusader ARV (Armoured Recovery Vehicle): removal of turret and addition of recovery equipment.
• Crusader Dozer: turret removed, winch and jib fitted for working dozer blade.
• Crusader with AMRA (Anti-Mine Roller Attachment): mine-clearer.

LEFT: **Tanks in line! This mixed 8th Army tank column, photographed in the Western Desert, is being led by two Crusaders, the front one being a Crusader IICS (mounting the close-support 76.2mm/ 3in howitzer instead of a 2pdr). The Crusader was the best of the early cruisers.**

A15 Cruiser Tank Mk VI Crusader

Entered service: 1940
Crew: Mk VI – 5; Mk III – 3
Weight: Mk I/II – 19,255kg/18.95 tons
  Mk III – 20, 067kg/19.75 tons
Dimensions: Length – Mk I/II – 5.99m/19ft 8in
  Mk III – 6.3m/20ft 8in
  Height (over turret hatch) – 2.24m/7ft 4in
  Width – 2.64m/8ft 8in
  Mk III – 2.79m/9ft 2in
Armament: Main – Mk I/II – 2pdr OQF (ordnance quick-firing) L/52 gun
  Mk III – 6pdr OQF gun
  Secondary – 1 or 2 x 7.92mm/0.312in Besa machine-guns
Armour: Maximum – 51mm/2.01in
Powerplant: Nuffield Liberty Mk III/IV V12 petrol, 253.64kW/340bhp
Performance: Speed – 44kph/27mph
  Range – 161km/100 miles

A17 Light Tank Mark VII Tetrarch

Following on from the light Mark VI family, Vickers built the Tetrarch (originally called Purdah) in 1937. It was accepted by the British Army in 1938, but production was delayed until 1940, by which time it was obsolescent, light tanks having been almost entirely replaced by armoured cars in the reconnaissance role. Eventually, however, about 180 were built, some being sent to the USSR (Lend-Lease),

while a squadron's worth saw action in Madagascar in May 1942. They proved unsuitable for the desert (due to inadequate cooling), but were given a new lease of life in 1943 when adopted for use as an air-portable tank to support airborne forces (the Hamilcar glider being specially designed to carry it). Some saw action on D-Day and others at the Rhine Crossing. A few were converted to perform a close-support role mounting

a 76.3mm/3in howitzer instead of the usual 2pdr. The Tetrarch's unique feature was its new suspension with large road wheels which could be partially skid-steered to improve turning.

A17 Light Tank Mk VII Tetrarch

Entered service: 1942
Crew: 3
Weight: 7,620kg/7.5 tons
Dimensions: Length – 4.11m/13ft 6in
  Height (over turret hatch) – 2.12m/6ft 11.5in
  Width – 2.31m/7ft 7in
Armament: Main – 2pdr QFSA (quick-firing semi-automatic) gun
  Secondary – 1 x coaxial 7.92mm/0.312in Besa machine-gun
Armour: Maximum – 14mm/0.55in
Powerplant: Meadows MAT 12-cylinder petrol, 123kW/165bhp
Performance: Speed – 64kph/40mph
  Range – 225km/140 miles

LEFT: **Designed in 1937 as a private venture, the A17 Light Tank Mark VII Tetrarch came into its own with the development of airborne forces. An airborne reconnaissance regiment was specially formed as a part of 6th Airborne Division for the Normandy invasion. Tetrarchs remained in service until 1949 when the Hamilar glider, which had been designed to carry them, was withdrawn from service.**

A25 Light Tank Mark VIII Harry Hopkins

Last of the Vickers Light series and originally known as Tank, Light Mark VII, revised, this model underwent two more changes in name – officially being called the Mark VIII but more colloquially Harry Hopkins after the American President Roosevelt's confidential advisor. Although there were improvements, including a revised faceted hull and

turret, thicker armour and hydraulically assisted steering, the Harry Hopkins was still small, unreliable and vulnerable when compared to the opposition. It was perhaps just as well that it was destined never to see action.

Instead, some were used as the basis for the Alecto dozer and other self-propelled gun projects mounting:

a 95mm/3.74in howitzer (Alecto I); a 6pdr (Alecto II); a 25pdr howitzer (Alecto III); and a 32pdr (Alecto IV) – although only the first two were actually built, and none entered service.

A25 Light Tank Mk VIII Harry Hopkins

Entered service: 1944
Crew: 3
Weight: 8,636kg/8.5 tons
Dimensions: Length – 4.27m/14ft
  Height (over turret hatch) – 2.11m/6ft 11in
  Width – 2.71m/8ft 10.5in
Armament: Main – 2pdr OQF (ordnance quick-firing) gun
  Secondary – 1 x 7.92mm/0.312in Besa machine-gun
Armour: Maximum – 38mm/1.5in
Powerplant: Meadows 12-cylinder petrol, 110.3kW/148bhp
Performance: Speed – 48kph/30mph
  Range – 201km/125 miles

LEFT: **The A25 Light Tank Mark VIII Harry Hopkins was designed as a successor to the Tetrarch. Although some 100 were built in 1944, they were never used in action. The Alecto Dozer had a hydraulically operated dozer blade in place of the gun mount, so it was turretless.**

A22 Infantry Tank Mark IV Churchill

The Churchill was the first British tank to be completely designed during World War II, and was in production throughout the conflict. The earliest model was built in 1941, armed with a 2pdr gun in the turret and a 76.2mm/3in close-support howitzer in its nose. With thick armour and a good cross-country performance (albeit slow), it was undoubtedly one of the best and most well-liked British tanks of the war. It was also the first British tank to mount the US 75mm/2.95in gun – the guns and mantlets being salvaged from knocked-out Shermans in Tunisia.

With less than 100 tanks in the UK after Dunkirk, the A22 was built hurriedly by a consortium of companies, and this rushed development programme led to frequent breakdowns and problems with the early Marks. Its size was limited by the British railway loading gauge restrictions, and it suffered from the same disadvantages of other contemporary British designs, namely that it was too narrow to take a larger turret needed for the 17pdr gun. Thus, by 1944–45 it was under-gunned by German standards, although this was offset by heavy armoured protection.

The other factor which made the Churchill one of the most important British tanks of 1939–45 was its adaptability to specialized armour roles (the Funnies) needed for the invasion of Europe in 1944, for example:

• Churchill Oke/Crocodile: flamethrowers.
• Churchill AVRE (Armoured Vehicle, Royal Engineers) Mark I and II: to carry and support assault engineers charged with breaching heavy defences. Fitted with demountable jibs, front and rear, earth spade at rear, and two-speed winch. Also a 290mm/11.42in spigot mortar for demolition tasks.
• Churchill Ark Mark I/II/III: bridge-carrying vehicles able to lay ramps across sea walls or span defence ditches and craters.
• Churchill AMRA (Anti-Mine Roller Attachment)/AMRCR (Anti-Mine Reconnaissance Castor Roller)/CIRD (Canadian Indestructible Roller Device)/Plough/Snake/Conger: mine-clearers using various systems, usually front-mounted to detonate mines.
• Churchill with Bobbin/Twin Bobbins: mat layers for use during beach landings.
• Churchill with mine plough (A–D, Bullshorn/Jeffries and Farmer Ploughs).

ABOVE: **An A22 Infantry Tank Mark IV Churchill. The Churchill Mark I mounted a 2pdr gun and had a 76.2mm/3in howitzer in the hull. From Churchill Mark III onwards its main armament was a 6pdr, and from Mark VIII a 75mm/2.95in gun.**

A22 Infantry Tank Mk IV Churchill (family)

Entered service: 1941
Crew: 5
Weight: Mks III–VI – 39,626kg/39 tons
Mks VII–VIII – 40,642kg/40 tons
Dimensions: Length – 7.44m/24ft 5in
   Height (over turret hatch) – 3.25m/10ft 8in
   Mks VII–VIII – 3.45m/11ft 4in
   Width – 2.74m/9ft
   Mks I–II – 2.49m/8ft 2in
Armament: Main – Mk I – 76.2mm/3in nose-mounted gun and 2pdr turret-mounted gun
   Mks III, IV – 6pdr OQF (ordnance quick-firing) Mk III or V gun
   Mks V, VIII – 95mm/3.74in gun
   Mks VI, VII – 75mm/2.95in L/40 gun
   Secondary – 1 or 2 x 7.92mm/0.312in Besa machine-guns, coaxial or hull-mounted
Armour: Maximum – 102mm/4.02in
   Mks VI–VIII: 152mm/5.98in
Powerplant: Beford 12-cylinder petrol, 261.1kW/350bhp
Performance: Speed – 25kph/15.5mph
   Range – 193km/120 miles

A43 Infantry Tank Black Prince

In December 1943, Allied tanks were still out-gunned and out-armoured by the Germans. Neither the Challenger A30 nor the Sherman Firefly, both of which mounted 17pdr guns, had adequate armoured protection to engage the German Panther and Tiger tanks on equal terms. It was therefore planned to put the 17pdr gun into the more heavily armoured Churchill. The design of the turret was to be governed by the size of the gun – although consideration had still to be given to the possibility of a later even larger calibre gun such as the 94mm/3.7in Mark VI, which had a penetration performance of 25 per cent better than that of the 17pdr.

Owing to the larger turret ring diameter required for the 17pdr gun, the standard Churchill hull was too narrow. An enlarged version was therefore designed, using as many Churchill A22 components as possible, and with the same thickness of armour.

Vauxhall built six pilot models designated A43 and known as Black Prince, with full production scheduled to start by the spring of 1945. Unfortunately, the combination of two other factors caused the project to be shelved. First, the standard 261kW/350hp Bedford engine was found not to be powerful enough for the A43 which weighed 50,802kg/ 50 tons (some 10 tons heavier than the Churchill). Secondly, by the time plans had been made to replace it with the 447.4kW/600hp Rolls-Royce Meteor engine, a decision had been taken to concentrate the future tank programme on one class of tank only, namely the world-beating Centurion, which was on the point of being built.

A43 Infantry Tank Black Prince

Entered service: 1945
Crew: 5
Weight: 50,802kg/50 tons
Dimensions: Length – 8.81m/28ft 11in
  Height (over turret hatch) – 2.74m/9ft
  Width – 3.43m/11ft 3in
Armament: Main – 17pdr gun
  Secondary – 2 x 7.92mm/0.312in Besa machine-guns
Armour: Maximum – 152mm/5.98in
Powerplant: Bedford 12-cylinder petrol, 261kW/350hp
Performance: Speed – 18kph/11mph
  Range – 161km/100 miles

BELOW: **The A43 Infantry Tank Black Prince or Super Churchill. It mounted a 17pdr gun, which required the redesign and widening of the hull. Six prototypes were built. However, the A41 Centurion proved to be a far superior tank, and Black Prince was scrapped.**

A24 Cruiser Tank Mark VII Cavalier

LEFT: **The A24 Cruiser Tank Mark VII Cavalier was requested in late 1940 to overcome all the problems inherent in the earlier cruisers. Fitted with a Mark III or Mark V 6pdr gun, the latter was distinguishable from the prominent counterweight on the muzzle.**

A24 Cruiser Tank Mk VII Cavalier

Entered service: 1941
Crew: 5
Weight: 26,925kg/26.5 tons
Dimensions: Length – 6.35m/20ft 10in
    Height (over turret hatch) – 2.44m/8ft
    Width –2.9m/9ft 6in
Armament: Main – 6pdr OQF (ordnance
    quick-firing) gun
    Secondary – 1 or 2 x 7.92mm/0.312in Besa
    machine-guns
Armour: Maximum – 76mm/2.99in
Powerplant: Nuffield Liberty V12 petrol,
    253.64kW/340bhp
Performance: Speed –39kph/24mph
    Range – 266km/165 miles

Experience with Crusader and its predecessors in World War II led to the production of the first new wartime Cruiser, the Cavalier, which had thicker armour, a bigger gun (the 6pdr) and wider tracks. All this increased its weight by over an extra 5,080kg/5 tons more than the Crusader and consequently reduced its top speed because it used the same engine and power train despite improvements in its suspension.

Externally it was almost identical in appearance to both the Cromwell and Centaur. The Cavalier was only built in small numbers and was never used operationally as a gun tank. Some had the 6pdr gun replaced with a dummy barrel and were used for artillery OP (Observation Post), while others were converted to an ARV (Armoured Recovery Vehicle) role with the turret removed and a winch and a demountable A-frame jib fitted.

A27L Cruiser Tank Mark VIII Centaur

LEFT: **The A27L Cruiser Tank Mark VIII Centaur. Like the Cavalier, it too was initially called Cromwell, but changed to Centaur. Nearly 1,000 were built, with 80 mounting the 95mm/3.74in close-support howitzer instead of the 6pdr gun.**

A27L Cruiser Tank Mk VIII Centaur

Entered service: 1942
Crew: 5
Weight: 28,849kg/28.4 tons
Dimensions: Length – 6.35m/20ft 10in
    Height (over turret hatch) – 2.49m/8ft 2in
    Width – 2.9m/9ft 6in
Armament: Main – Mk I – 6pdr OQF (ordnance
    quick-firing) gun
    Mk IV – 95mm/3.74in howitzer
    Secondary – 1 or 2 x 7.92mm/0.312in Besa
    machine-guns
Armour: Maximum – 76mm/2.99in
Powerplant: Nuffield Liberty V12 petrol
Performance: Speed – 43.5kph/27mph
    Range – 266km/165 miles

Next in the Cruiser line was the A27L Centaur, which was unfortunately compromised from the start by production shortages. The intention was to fit this tank with a new powerful Rolls-Royce Meteor engine. However, supplies were not available because all production was required for aircraft. Consequently the old Liberty V12 engine was fitted instead. Some Centaurs were later upgraded to Cromwells (the Mark X) with a Meteor engine retro-fit, while

others had their existing engines up-rated, and were armed with a 95mm/3.74in howitzer to be used by the Royal Marines to give supporting fire from LCTs (Landing Craft Tanks) during the D-Day landings. A few were also converted for special-purpose roles, including AA (Anti-Aircraft) tanks, ARVs (Armoured Recovery Vehicles), OP (Observation Post) vehicles, and Dozers, all being used in the 1944–45 north-west Europe campaign.

A27M Cruiser Tank Mark VIII Cromwell

Early Cromwells closely resembled the Cavalier and Centaur, except, of course, for the fitting of the Meteor engine – hence the letter "M" in their title. The Meteor engine was a 447.4kW/600hp V12, and made Cromwell the fastest Cruiser tank so far, with increased reliability. It went on to become the most used British cruiser tank of World War II, and formed the main equipment of British armoured divisions from 1944–45, together with the US-built Sherman M4.

Cromwell's hull and turret were of simple box shape and its construction composite – an inner skin with an outer layer of armour bolted on. An important difference between early and later models was the introduction of all-welded construction process in place of riveting, which further simplified the mass production of the vehicle.

ABOVE: **An excellent photograph of an A27M Cruiser Tank Mark VIII Cromwell. Light, fast and armed with a 75mm/2.95in gun, initially it did not do well in Normandy but came into its own when the battle became more fluid.** BELOW: **A cutaway drawing of the Cromwell showing its main components, with the engine and transmission at the rear.**

Undoubtedly there were misgivings among many tank crews when they were converted from Sherman to Cromwell (the 7th Armoured Division was re-equipped with Cromwells when they returned to the UK from Italy to prepare for D-Day) because of its lack of firepower – it was armed with either a 75mm/2.95in or a 6pdr gun, neither of which was a real match for the German Tiger and Panther tanks. The narrowness of the Cromwell's hull prevented it from being further up-gunned until an

extensive redesign had been implemented, and it was not until after the end of World War II that this took place. Here is how one experienced 7th Armoured Division tank crewman summed up the Cromwell: "I think it was a useless tank – fast enough – but without adequate armour and under-gunned." To be fair, however, once the Normandy "bocage" country was left behind and speed became more important than tank versus tank battles, then the Cromwell did far better, although its basic faults remained.

The design was also flexible enough to be fitted with wider tracks and employed in specialist roles. These included:
• Cromwell ARV (Armoured Recovery Vehicle): vehicle with turret removed and winch and demountable A-frame jib fitted.
• Cromwell Command/OP (Observation Post): fitted with dummy gun and extra radio equipment.
• Cromwell CIRD (Canadian Indestructible Roller Device): vehicle fitted with CIRD mine-exploder.
• Cromwell Prong: standard vehicle fitted with Culin Hedgerow Cutting Device fitted to cut through "bocage" hedgerows.

A27M Cruiser Tank Mk VIII Cromwell

Entered service: 1943
Crew: 5
Weight: 27,941kg/27.5 tons
Dimensions: Length – 6.35m/20ft 10in
    Height (over turret hatch) – 2.49m/8ft 2in
    Width – 2.9m/9ft 6in
Armament: Main – Mk I–III – 6pdr gun
    Mks IV, V, VII 75mm/2.95in OQF (ordnance quick-firing) gun
    Mks VI, VII – 95mm/3.74in howitzer
    Secondary – 1 or 2 x 7.92mm/0.312in Besa machine-guns (one coaxial, one hull-mounted)
Armour: Maximum – 76mm/2.99in (101mm/3.98in with appliqué)
Powerplant: Rolls-Royce Meteor V12 petrol
Performance: Speed – Mk I–III – 64.4kph/40mph
    Mk IVs on – 52kph/32mph
    Range – 278km/173 miles

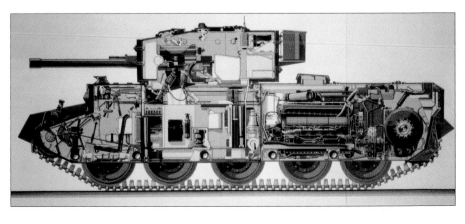

A30 Cruiser Tank Challenger

The main drawback to Cromwell was its lack of firepower, thus it was logical to produce a tank packing a bigger punch, and so the Challenger was specifically designed to mount the British 17pdr gun which had been developed in 1941. This required a larger turret and led to the need to increase both the length and width of the Cromwell hull. A sixth road wheel was then also added to accommodate this change, and the all-up weight increased to 33,022kg/ 32.5 tons. Production of Challenger was much slower than the Sherman Firefly (also mounting the British 17pdr), and by September 1944 there were only enough to provide three armoured regiments with twelve apiece.

LEFT: **The A30 Cruiser Tank Challenger. This was an attempt to mount a more powerful gun into a cruiser tank, the gun being the British 17pdr which had already been mounted successfully in the Sherman Firefly.**

A30 Cruiser Tank Challenger

Entered service: 1943
Crew: 5
Weight: 33,022kg/32.5 tons
Dimensions: Length – 8.15m/26ft 8.75in
  Height (over turret hatch) – 2.77m/9ft 1.25in
  Width – 2.91m/9ft 6.5in
Armament: Main – 17pdr OQF (ordnance quick-firing) gun
  Secondary – 1 x 7.62mm/0.3in coaxial Browning machine-gun
Armour: Maximum – 101mm/3.98in
Powerplant: Rolls-Royce Meteor V12 petrol, 447.4kW/600bhp
Performance: Speed – 52kph/32mph
  Range – 193km/120 miles

A30 Tank Destroyer Avenger

An alternative version of the A30 was also developed from 1943–44, namely an SP (Self-Propelled) anti-tank gun called the Avenger. This was a British attempt to produce a tank destroyer armed with a 17pdr gun and with an open-topped turret in order to reduce weight. The Avenger was a stopgap weapon while the Valentine Archer SP was being put into production and before the British began to receive supplies of the US M10. Unfortunately it was not ready for use operationally, and by the time the pilot model was completed it had been decided to switch production effort to the Comet instead.

LEFT: **The A30 Tank Destroyer Avenger self-propelled gun was similar to the A30 Challenger, but its open-topped turret was nearly 0.6m/2ft lower and the overall battle weight about 1,524kg/1.5 tons lighter. The turret had a mild steel canopy to give the crew some protection. The Avenger was not designed to fire on the move, hence the absence of vision devices.**

A30 Tank Destroyer Avenger

Entered service: 1943–44
Crew: 4–5 (optional second loader)
Weight: 31,498kg/31 tons
Dimensions: Length – 8.71m/28ft 7in
  Height (over turret hatch) –2.21m/7ft 3in
  Width – 3.05m/10ft
Armament: Main – 17-pdr OQF (ordnance quick-firing) gun
  Secondary – 1 x 7.7mm/0.303in Bren machine-gun on an AA (anti-aircraft) mount
Armour: Maximum – 101mm/3.98in
Powerplant: Rolls-Royce Meteor V12 petrol, 447.4kW/600bhp
Performance: Speed – 52kph/32mph
  Range – 169km/105 miles

A33 Heavy Assault Tank Excelsior

LEFT: **Only two pilot models of the A33 Heavy Assault Tank Excelsior were ever built. The requirement disappeared following the success of the Churchill in Tunisia and Italy, so there was no production order. The pilot model mounted a 6pdr gun, although a 75mm/2.95in had been originally proposed.**

A33 Heavy Assault Tank Excelsior

Entered service: 1943 (prototypes only)
Crew: 5
Weight: 45,722kg/45 tons
Dimensions: Length – 6.91m/22ft 8in
  Height (over turret hatch) – 2.41m/7ft 11in
  Width – 3.39m/11ft 1.5in
Armament: Main – 75mm/2.95in OQF (ordnance quick-firing) gun
  Secondary – 2 x 7.92mm/0.312in Besa machine-guns
Armour: Maximum – 114mm/4.49in
Powerplant: Rolls-Royce Meteor V12 petrol, 447.4kW/600bhp
Performance: Speed – 39kph/24mph
  Range – 209km/130 miles

Following the debacle of the raid on Dieppe, France, in August 1942, the poor performance of the early production Churchills forced the British to question its continuation and consider an alternative tank which combined the "cruiser" and "infantry" roles – the Excelsior. Based on the A27 hull and mounting a 75mm/2.95in dual-purpose gun – capable of firing both HE (High-Explosive) and AP (Armour-Piercing) ammunition – and with additional armour and wider tracks, it was an attempt to mount as large a gun as possible on an existing hull. It had an up-rated Meteor engine of 447.4kW/600bhp, giving it a top speed of 39kph/24mph – considerably faster than the Churchill. A second pilot model was built with widened, Cromwell-type tracks, known as the R/L Heavy Type.

In the end the Excelsior never went beyond the prototype stage. The Churchill's performance in North Africa redeemed its reputation, and the Excelsior project was quietly shelved with production effort being switched to the new all-purpose medium tank, the Comet.

A38 Infantry Tank Valiant

A38 Infantry Tank Valiant

Entered service: 1943–45 (prototypes only)
Crew: 4
Weight: 27,433kg/27 tons
Dimensions: Length – 5.36m/17ft 7in
  Height (over turret hatch) – 2.13m/7ft
  Width – 2.82m/9ft 3in
Armament: Main – 6pdr or 75mm/2.95in OQF (ordnance quick-firing) gun
  Secondary – 2 x 7.92mm/0.31in Besa machine-guns
Armour: Maximum – 114mm/4.49in
Powerplant: GMC diesel, 156.5kW/210bhp
Performance: Speed – 19kph/12mph
  Range – 129km/80 miles

LEFT: **The A38 Infantry Tank Valiant was an improved version of the Valentine with an up-rated diesel engine and other mechanical parts of its predecessor.**

Conceived as a successor to the Valentine, this small 27-ton tank was some 10,160kg/10 tons heavier than its predecessor. Design began in 1943, two pilot models being built, one with a GMC 156.5kW/210bhp engine and AEC gearbox, the other with a Rolls-Royce Meteor 261kW/350hp engine and gearbox. With a wider, longer turret than the Valentine, it could mount either a 6pdr or a 75mm/2.95in gun, as well as having space for three men – thus freeing the commander from having to load the gun. However the war ended, and in preference to other more successful types the project was shelved.

A34 Cruiser Tank Comet

The next logical development of the Centaur/Cromwell design was to produce a tank that really had the firepower, protection and mobility to match its German counterparts. This was to be the Comet, which, like the last Marks of Cromwell, was of an all-welded construction and at 35,560kg/ 35 tons was nearly 5,080kg/5 tons heavier than the last up-armoured version of the Cromwell series. It was to all intents and purposes an up-gunned, up-armoured Cromwell, retaining many similar features and components, as well as the same general layout. The initial Comet prototype was the last British cruiser to have the Christie suspension (the same as the Cromwell but with the top rollers) and it had a good cross-country performance and a top speed of 47kph/29mph.

Where it departed from its predecessor was in mounting a completely redesigned main gun, a 76.2mm/3in, known as the 77mm, which had just about the same performance as the 17pdr, but was smaller and lighter.

TOP: **Undoubtedly the best British tank of the war was the A34 Cruiser Tank Comet. Bearing the Black Bull divisional sign of 11th Armoured Division, this one was photographed at Bovington, Dorset. Comet was not available in sufficient numbers until after the Rhine Crossing in March 1945.** ABOVE: **Comets of the 1st Royal Tank Regiment on parade in Berlin, September 20, 1945, when they were inspected by Field Marshal Montgomery.**

Fast and reliable, the Comet was the best all-round British tank produced during World War II, but was introduced far too late to have much effect on tank versus tank combat. Production deliveries started late in 1944, but regiments did not receive issues until after the Rhine Crossing in March 1945. Fast and reliable, it was the first British tank to begin to match the German PzKpfw V Panther in all-round performance,

especially firepower. It would remain in service for the next 15 years, the last Comets not being withdrawn from British service until 1960. Its successor was the A41 Centurion.

Visually, Comet is quickly distinguishable from Cromwell by virtue of the four return rollers above the road wheels. Note also the prominent commander's all-round vision cupola, the forward-sloping turret roof and the large counterweight on the turret rear.

Comet was thus the last British tank to be developed during World War II and the last in the cruiser line, as its successor the A41 Centurion was classed as the first "universal" tank. Initially there was some criticism of Comet concerning the retention of the hull gunner and the thinness of the belly armour, as mines became more and more of a threat during the later stages of the campaigns of north-west Europe. However, these faults were deliberately ignored in order to get it into operational service.

A34 Cruiser Tank Comet

Entered service: 1945
Crew: 5
Weight: 35,560kg/35 tons
Dimensions: Length – 7.66m/25ft 1.5in
　Height (over turret hatch) – 2.68m/8ft 9.5in
　Width – 3.05m/10ft
Armament: Main – 77mm (76.2mm/3in) OQF (ordnance quick-firing) gun
　Secondary – 2 x 7.92mm/0.312in Besa machine-guns (one coaxial and one hull-mounted)
Armour: Maximum – 101mm/3.98in
Powerplant: Rolls-Royce Meteor V12 petrol, 447.4kW/600bhp
Performance: Speed – 47kph/29mph
　Range – 198km/123 miles

TOP: **Ready for battle! A Comet tank "bombed up" and ready for action.**

ABOVE LEFT AND ABOVE: **Views of the Comet during the war. Comet remained in British Army service for many years after the end of World War II. It was also in service with the Irish Army from 1950–70. It was the "end of the line" for British cruiser tanks, which had begun with the A9 and A10 in the early 1930s.**

LEFT: The massive A39 Heavy Assault Tank Tortoise. Six pilot models were built from August 1945 onwards but were not trialled until 1946–47.

A39 Heavy Assault Tank Tortoise

Entered service: 1946–47 (pilot models only)
Crew: 7
Weight: 79,252kg/78 tons
Dimensions: Length – 10.06m/33ft
 Height (over turret hatch) – 3.05m/10ft
 Width – 3.91m/12ft 10in
Armament: Main – 32pdr OQF (ordnance quick-firing) gun
 Secondary – 3 x Besa 7.92mm/0.312in machine-guns, 2 in AA (anti-aircraft) mount
Armour: Maximum – 225mm/8.86in
Powerplant: Rolls-Royce Meteor V12 petrol, 484.7kW/650bhp
Performance: Speed – 19kph/12mph
 Range – 81km/50 miles

A39 Heavy Assault Tank Tortoise

The last of the British attempts to produce a heavy tank during World War II was the equivalent of the Jagdtiger, a 79,252kg/78-ton monster, appropriately called Tortoise. With a 32pdr main gun having limited traverse, it had armour up to 225mm/8.86in thick and a crew of seven. Although it was first designed in 1942, work progressed slowly until 1944, when the Jagdtiger appeared and the project received extra impetus; however, the pilot models were not delivered until after the war had ended. In trials, performance and manoeuvrability were adequate, with a top speed of 19kph/12mph, but ultimately Tortoise was really too heavy to be a feasible proposition.

TOG 1 and TOG 2 Heavy Tanks

LEFT: **TOG 2** after restoration. The massive tank then mounted a 17pdr gun in the large turret that would later be fitted to the A30 Challenger.

TOG Heavy Tank

Entered service: 1940 (prototypes only)
Crew: TOG 1 – 6; TOG 2 – 8
Weight: TOG 1 – 64,555kg/63.5 tons
 TOG 2 – 81,284kg/80 tons
Dimensions: Length – 10.13m/33ft 3in
 Height (over turret hatch) – 3.05m/10ft
 Width – 3.12m/10ft 3in
Armament: Main – TOG 1 – 2pdr in turret and a 75mm/2.95in howitzer in nose
 TOG 2 – 6pdr (77mm/3.03in) or 17pdr OQF (ordnance quick-firing) gun
 Secondary – None fitted
Armour: Maximum – 75mm/2.95in
Powerplant: Paxman-Ricardo V12 diesel, 447.4kW/600bhp
Performance: Speed – 14kph/8.5mph
 Range – 81km/50 miles

The acronym TOG stands for "The Old Gang" and refers to the team set up on the outbreak of World War II to find solutions to UK tank needs. The members were all men who had been directly responsible for the very successful World War I tank programme: Stern, Wilson, Swinton, d'Eyncourt, Ricardo, Symes and Tritton. They now produced a very large, heavy tank, weighing some 81,284kg/80 tons, which was long enough to cross wide trenches and well protected against anti-tank weapons. TOG 1 had a 75mm/2.95in howitzer in its nose and a 2pdr in a Matilda II-type turret above, and would probably have been ideal to fight the largely static battles of World War I but was entirely wrong for the Blitzkrieg of World War II.

The trials of TOG 1 revealed problems with the electric transmission, and so a hydraulic transmission was tried out on TOG 2, which also mounted a larger turret and a 6pdr gun (later changed to a 17pdr). This was the heaviest British tank of World War II; however, during development the Churchill was produced, trialled and accepted, so interest in TOG waned. It became yet another failed design project, and TOG 2 (Revised) was never built.

BT Medium Tank series

This series of Soviet medium tanks owes its existence to the purchase of an American M1931 Christie tank by the Soviet Purchasing Commission. It had, like the original Christie tank, the ability to run either on its tracks or on its road wheels (four large road wheels on each side). The Soviets did their copying very thoroughly and the BT-1 was made to the same all-riveted construction as the American M1931, with a similar turret containing two machine-guns. Even the engine was a copy of the Liberty from the Christie model.

The BT-1 was only a limited production run, soon replaced by the BT-2 which had a new turret mounting a 37mm/1.46in gun and a machine-gun. This was the first major production model and weighed about a ton more than its predecessor.

The next model was the BT-3/BT-4, again very similar but with solid disc wheels rather than spoked wheels. It also had a 45mm/1.77in gun as its main armament. Production was limited, but there were conversion models: one (in 1939) which had a new turret mounting a flamethrower, while another had its gun removed and carried a folding wooden bridge – neither went into full production.

Then came the major production model, the BT-5, with a larger cylindrical turret mounting a 45mm/1.77in gun and coaxial machine-gun, better vision devices, a strengthened suspension and a new, more powerful engine. The BT-5A model was for close-support work and mounted a 76.2mm/3in howitzer instead of the 45mm/1.77in gun. There was also a command version which had an extensive frame aerial around the turret and a radio inside at the rear.

Next in line was the BT-7 which had a new conical turret (with a ball-mounted machine-gun in its rear) on all except the

earliest vehicles. It was of an all-welded construction, with a new, more powerful engine, a new gearbox, more space for extra fuel and ammunition stowage and thicker frontal armour. This model was the main type in service from the beginning of World War II until the end of 1941. Like its predecessor, there was also both a close-support version (76.2mm/3in howitzer) and a command version (BT-7-1 (V)).

Drastic redesign then took place, the BT-7M model being considerably more streamlined with more room for the new V2 diesel engine, sloped front glacis plate rather than the distinctive "V" nose and the same turret as the T-28 medium tank. It was also known as the BT-8.

Final development was the BT-IS, which was only built as a prototype, but was significantly different in design, being the first Red Army tank to have sloping side armour and front glacis.

ABOVE AND LEFT: **The BT-7 Red Army Medium Tank was the direct descendant of the BT heritage that owes its origin to the Christie M1931 from which it was copied. All had the pointed front glacis and large roadwheels, which gave them high cross-country speed. Heavier than the BT-5, it had an improved conical turret, mounting a 45mm/1.77in gun and was the main tank in Russian service during 1940–41.**

BT Medium Tank series (1, 2, 5 and 7) family				
Entered service:	BT-1	BT-2	BT-5	BT-7
		1932	1933	1935	1936
Crew: 3				
Weight: kg	10,200	11,200	11,500	13,900
tons	10	11	11.3	13.7
Dimensions:				
Length m	5.49	5.49	5.49	5.66
ft in	18	18	18	18/7
Height m	1.93	1.93	2.21	2.41
ft in	6/4	6/4	7/3	7/11
Width m	2.24	2.24	2.24	2.43
ft in	7/4	7/4	7/4	7/11.5

Armament: Main – BT-1 – 2 x machine-guns; BT-2 – 1 x 37mm/1.46in gun; BT-5 and BT-7 – 1 x 45mm/1.77in gun

Secondary – All 1 x 7.62mm/0.3in DT machine-gun, except BT-7 2 x 7.62mm/0.3in DT machine-guns

Armour: Maximum – All 13mm/0.5in, except BT-7 – 22mm/0.87in

Powerplant: All Liberty Aero V12 petrol, 298.5kW/400bhp, except BT-7 – M-15T V12 petrol, 335.8kW/450bhp

Performance:

Speed tracks – All 65kph/40mph, except BT-7 – 72kph/45mph

Speed wheels – BT-1/2 – 105kph/65mph; BT-5 – 112kph/70mph

Range tracks – All c200km/124 miles, except BT-7 – c400km/249 miles

Range wheels – All c300km/186 miles, except BT-7 – c500km/311 miles

Carro Armato M11/39 Medium Tank

LEFT: **The M11/39 Medium Tank directly evolved from the Carro Armato tank of 1935. A hundred were ordered following the Spanish Civil War which had revealed inadequacies in the small CV33 and CV35 tankettes. They proved to be no match for the British tanks in the early days of the desert war.**

At almost 11 tons, this was the start of the Italian medium tank line and evolved from lighter versions. The main armament was a 37mm/1.46in hull-mounted gun, while the manually operated turret, offset to the left, contained twin 8mm/0.315in Breda machine-guns. Although it had an adequate diesel engine and a good sprung bogie suspension, its riveted armour was very thin, giving minimal protection to its crew, so it was of very little use in battle and fell as easy prey to the British tanks when it went into action in Libya in 1940. Many were knocked out, while a few were captured and used by the Australians in the North African desert in early 1941. The M11/39 was soon withdrawn from service.

Carro Armato M11/39 Medium Tank

Entered service: 1939
Crew: 3
Weight: 11,000kg/10.8 tons
Dimensions: Length – 4.74m/15ft 6.5in
  Height (over turret hatch) – 2.3m/7ft 6.5in
  Width – 2.21m/7ft 3in
Armament: Main – 37mm/1.46in Vickers-Terni L/40 gun
  Secondary – 2 x 8mm/0.315in Breda Model 38 machine-guns
Armour: Maximum – 30mm/1.18in
Powerplant: Fiat SPA 8T V8 diesel, 78.3kW/105bhp
Performance: Speed – 32kph/20mph
  Range – 200km/124 miles

Carro Armato M13/40 Medium Tank

Developed in 1939, this tank was largely based upon the M11/39, although at almost 14 tons it was larger and had slightly thicker armour. Its main armament was a new high-velocity 47mm/1.85in gun and coaxial 8mm/0.315in Breda machine-gun, which was mounted in the turret, replacing the twin 8mm/0.315in Breda machine-guns which were now gimbal-mounted in the front hull.

It was probably the best and most widely used Italian tank of World War II, although it was still no match for its opponents. Initially in the desert it suffered from mechanical failure and had to be tropicalized (especially against the sand which got into everything mechanical), with the fitting of improved air and fuel filters. The M13/40 saw action during the first campaign in the North African desert, and despite its excellent gun, it soon proved easy meat for the British heavy infantry tanks

LEFT: **Probably the most widely used Italian tank of the war, the M13/40 was still no match for the British Matilda II. It first saw action in December 1940 in Libya, but its armoured protection proved inadequate in battle, even in 1940. This one is at the Aberdeen Proving Ground in the USA.**

(Matilda II). During the resounding defeat of the 10th Italian Army at Beda Fomm/Sidi Saleh, Libya, in February 1941, over a hundred M13/40s were captured in pristine condition. These were used to equip both the British 6th Royal Tank Regiment and the Australian 6th Cavalry as a temporary, emergency measure.

Carro Armato M13/40 Medium Tank

Entered service: 1940
Crew: 4
Weight: 14,000kg/13.8 tons
Dimensions: Length – 4.90m/16ft 1in
  Height (over turret hatch) – 2.39m/7ft 10in
  Width – 2.21m/7ft 3in
Armament: Main – 47mm/1.85in Model 37 L/32 Ansaldo gun
  Secondary – 3 x 8mm/0.315in Breda Model 38 machine-guns (one coaxial and two hull-mounted)
Armour: Maximum – 42mm/1.65in
Powerplant: SPA 8 TM40 V8 diesel, 93kW/125bhp
Performance: Speed – 32kph/20mph
  Range – 200km/124 miles

Carro Veloce 33 Tankette

In 1929 the Italians purchased some Vickers Carden-Loyd Mark VI tankettes from Britain, and at the same time obtained permission to manufacture them in Italy. A total of 25 were built under the designation Carro Veloce 29 by Ansaldo, with automotive parts from Fiat. The CV33 was directly descended from the CV29, designed and built by Ansaldo from 1931–32. There were various models over the years of this little two-man tankette. The usual armament was either one or two Breda machine-guns; however, from 1940 some vehicles were re-armed with a 20mm/0.79in Solothurn anti-tank gun while all had a stronger suspension, new tracks and better vision devices for the driver.

LEFT: **The Carro Veloce 33 – this is an early production model – was armed with either a single 6.5mm/0.256in machine-gun or twin 8mm/0.315in machine-guns. A mass of these little tankettes looked most impressive but were no real use even against light tanks with thicker armour and bigger guns.**

Carro Veloce 33 Tankette

Entered service: 1933
Crew: 2
Weight: 3,200kg/3.2 tons
Dimensions: Length – 3.18m/10ft 5in
Height (over turret hatch) – 1.3m/4ft 3in
Width – 1.42m/4ft 8in
Armament: Main – 1 x 6.5mm/0.26in or
2 x 8mm/0.32in Breda machine-guns
Armour: Maximum – 14mm/0.55in
Powerplant: FIAT-SPA CV3 4-cylinder petrol,
31kW/42bhp
Performance: Speed – 42kph/26mph
Range – 125km/78 miles

Carro Veloce L35/Lf Flamethrower Tankette

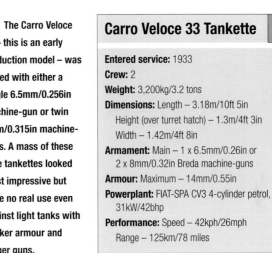

LEFT: **The flamethrowing version of the small Italian tankette was the L35/Lf, which towed a trailer full of flame fluid (later models had the fuel tank mounted in the rear of the tankette above the engine). This model is on show at the Bovington Tank Museum, Dorset. Other L35s were fitted with eight bridges: L3/35(P) – *Passarella* (Gangway).**

The Carro Veloce L35/Lf (*Lanciaflamme*) was the flamethrower variant of the CV33 tankette. It had a long-barrelled hooded flamethrower instead of the usual machine-guns. A 500-litre/110-gallon armoured fuel trailer was towed behind the *carro d'assalto lanciafiamme*. On a later model the flamethrower fuel tank was mounted on the rear of the vehicle. The range of the flamethrower was about 100m/328ft.

Carro Veloce L35/Lf Flamethrower Tankette

Entered service: 1933
Crew: 2
Weight: 3,200kg/3.2 tons
Dimensions: Length – 3.18m/10ft 5in
Height (over turret hatch) – 1.3m/4ft 3in
Width – 1.42m/4ft 8in
Armament: Main – Lanciaflamme Flamethrower
Armour: Maximum – 14mm/0.55in
Powerplant: FIAT-SPA CV3 4-cylinder petrol,
31kW/42bhp
Performance: Speed – 42kph/26mph
Range – 125km/78 miles

Char d'Assault Schneider CA1 Heavy Tank

Char d'Assault Schneider CA1 Heavy Tank	
Entered service: 1916	
Crew: 7	
Weight: 12,500kg/12.3 tons	
Dimensions: Length – 6.32m/20ft 8in	
Height (over turret hatch) – 2.3m/7ft 6in	
Width – 2.05m/6ft 9in	
Armament: Main – 75mm/2.95in gun	
Secondary – 2 x 8mm/0.315in Hotchkiss machine-guns	
Armour: Maximum – 11mm/0.43in	
Powerplant: Schneider, 4-cylinder petrol, 41kW/55bhp	
Performance: Speed – 8.1kph/5mph	
Range – 80km/49.7 miles	

LEFT: **The Schneider CA1 was the first French tank to be designed in World War I. The first of the 400 to be built were delivered in September 1916, not long after the first British tanks made their appearance. It had vertically coiled spring suspension.**

The Schneider CA1 was the first French tank to be designed and, as with many designs of the time, it was based upon the Holt tractor chassis. The first of those built was delivered in September 1916, so the French were not very far behind the British in the design and production of this new type of weapon system. The driving force was Colonel (later General) Jean Baptiste Estienne, who is reputed to have said, "Whoever shall first be able to make land ironclads armed and equipped ... will have won the war." Designed by Eugene Brille of the Schneider Company, the Char d'Assault Schneider CA1 weighed 12,500kg/12.3 tons, mounted a 75mm/2.95in gun in a sponson on the right-hand side of the tank along with two 8mm/0.315in machine-guns, one on each side. It had a crew of seven men and rear main access doors. Note also the nosepiece which acted as a wire-cutter, important for cutting barbed wire.

RIGHT: **On the left side the sponson just contained a machine-gun. This is a late-production CA1 with improved roof ventilation and larger fuel tanks.**

The Schneider was first committed to battle at Berry-au-Bac on April 16, 1917. 132 Schneider's in eight companies were organized into two columns and reached their objectives but were then subjected to heavy enemy fire and many were lost – 76 in total – with 57 being completely destroyed by artillery. The other main reason for such heavy losses was the vulnerability of the Schneider's fuel tanks to the German "K" anti-tank bullet.

Late production models attempted to solve these problems with better-protected fuel tanks and more roof ventilation than the earlier model.

Schneider also built a prototype CA2 with a turret-mounted 47mm/1.85in main gun, but this was never put into production.

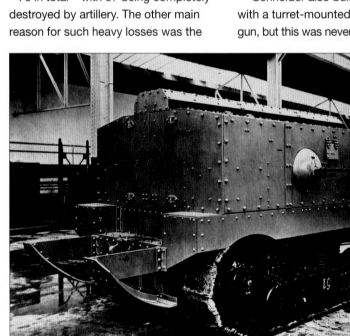

Char d'Assault Saint Chamond Heavy Tank

The second French heavy tank of World War I was the Saint Chamond, designed by a Colonel Rimailho and built in 1916 by the *Compagnie des Forges et Acieries de la Marine et d'Homércourt*, whose factory at Saint Chamond gave the tank its name. At almost 23 tons, it was heavier than the Schneider, had a large crew of nine, mounted a 75mm/2.95in gun in its nose, and also had four machine-guns, positioned two to each side of the vehicle. It was easily identified from its front hull and flat roof.

ABOVE: **Some 400 Saint Chamonds were built in 1916.** BELOW: **On later models of the St Chamond, the original gun was replaced by a regular Model 1897 field gun.**

The Saint Chamond had an electric transmission, with a 67.1kW/90bhp Panhard motor driving a dynamo which powered two electric motors – one per track, with a top speed of 12kph/7.45mph. Despite this, its cross-country performance was indifferent, as it tended to bury its nose when negotiating soft going.

By mid-range production of the vehicle, the two cylindrical cupolas were replaced by a flat pitched roof. Later models reinstalled a single, flat-topped cupola on the right for the driver, and replaced the original main gun with the regular 75mm/2.95in Model 1897 field gun.

A total of 400 Saint Chamonds were built, and the tank first saw action in early May 1917, but the design problem with the nose was insurmountable and the quest for a perfect heavy tank moved on.

Char d'Assault Saint Chamond Heavy Tank

Entered service: 1917
Crew: 9
Weight: 23,000kg/22.64 tons
Dimensions: Length – 8.83m/28ft 11.5in
  Height (over turret hatch) – 2.36m/7ft 9in
  Width – 2.67m/8ft 9in
Armament: Main – 75mm/2.95in 1897 Model field gun
  Secondary – 4 x 8mm/0.315in Hotchkiss machine-guns
Armour: Maximum – 17mm/0.67in
Powerplant: Panhard, 4-cylinder petrol 67.1kW/90bhp
Performance: Speed – 12kph/7.45mph
  Range – 60km/37.3 miles

LEFT: **Coming into service in 1935, with 40mm/1.57in of armour plate and a 75mm/2.95in gun in its belly, the Char B1 was one of the most formidable tanks in the world at that time. The Char B1-bis was even heavier, with a larger secondary armament in its turret and thicker armour. This Char B1 is on parade in Paris in 1936.**

Char B1 Heavy Tank

Entered service: 1931
Crew: 4
Weight: 30,480kg /30 tons
Dimensions: Length – 6.37m/20ft 11in
Height (over turret hatch) – 2.82m/9ft 3in
Width – 2.49m/8ft 2in
Armament: Main – 1 x 75mm/2.95in short gun in hull and 1 x 47mm/1.85in gun in turret
Secondary – 2 x 7.5mm/0.295in machine-guns (one in hull, one in turret)
Armour: Maximum – 40mm/1.57in
Powerplant: Renault, 6-cylinder petrol, 134.2kW/180bhp
Performance: Speed – 28kph/17.4mph
Range – 150km/93 miles

Char B1 Heavy Tank

The development of the Renault Char de Bataille B1 began in the 1920s when, at the request of General Estienne ("Father of the French Tank Corps"), a consortium of French companies designed a new tank under the codename *Tracteur 30*, with specifications for a vehicle with high mobility and heavy fire power. The result was the Char B1, a tank with considerable potential.

Armed with a short 75mm/2.95in gun carried in a front hull mounting, the sighting of the weapon was controlled by the driver, and corrections were made by moving the tank. The sophisticated Naeder Steering Unit, which allowed delicate and very accurate adjustment, had a double differential and hydrostatic drive, which gave the "infinitely variable steering" necessary to lay the 75mm/

2.95in gun. There was also a fixed 7.5mm/0.295in machine-gun controlled by the driver, both weapons being loaded by a crewman sitting beside him. In the turret there was a coaxially mounted 47mm/1.85in anti-tank gun and 7.5mm/0.295in machine-gun fired by the commander. This gun layout effectively halved the amount of ammunition the vehicle could carry.

Char B1-bis Heavy Tank

Char B1-bis Heavy Tank

Entered service: 1935
Crew: 4
Weight: 32,500kg/32 tons
Dimensions: Length – 6.52m/21ft 5in
Height (over turret hatch) – 2.79m/9ft 2in
Width – 2.5m/8ft 2in
Armament: Main – 1 x 75mm/2.95in short gun in hull and 1 x 47mm/1.85in gun in turret
Secondary – 2 x 7.5mm/0.295in machine-guns
Armour: Maximum – 60mm/2.36in
Powerplant: Renault, 6-cylinder petrol, 223.7kW/300bhp
Performance: Speed – 28kph/17.4mph
Range – 180km/111.8 miles

The B1-bis version evolved from the B1 and appeared in 1935. It had thicker armour, a larger gun in the turret (47mm/1.85in instead of 37mm/1.46in) and a more powerful 223.7kW/300bhp Renault aircraft engine. Again no traverse was possible for its nose-mounted 75mm/

ABOVE: **A Char B1-bis (Encore). Note the new AP x 4 turret and 47mm/1.85in gun.**

2.95in gun, so to lay in azimuth the tank had to be turned on its tracks. Of the 365 Char B1-bis built, large numbers were captured in a serviceable condition by

the Germans in France in 1940. Although one of the best armed and armoured tanks of its day, these captured B1s were not immediately issued to German fighting units, because of the limitations of the one-man turret and the tank's generally poor performance. Instead they were used as training vehicles or fitted with radio sets and used to equip second line units, mainly in the west.

Char 2C Heavy Tank

During World War I, the French had issued a specification for a heavy "breakthrough" tank, Char de Rupture C, at a weight of about 40 tons. Two prototypes, Chars 1A and 1B were produced from 1917–18. Further development then produced an even heavier tank of nearly 70 tons – and this was the Char 2C. Although it did not become operational during the war, ten were built, the last being delivered in 1922. In their day they were the most powerful tanks in the world, with a crew of twelve, a 75mm/2.95in gun in the front turret and four machine-guns (one in an auxiliary turret at the rear of the tank). One of them was converted to mount a 155mm/6.1in howitzer as well as the 75mm/2.95in gun and the four machine-guns, and this led some Intelligence circles to think that France was building large numbers of "super tanks". The Char 2C had two engines totalling 186.4kW/250bhp, driving electric generators to run a motor for each track, giving the tank a top speed of 12kph/7.5mph.

The last of these tanks were destroyed in 1940 by enemy air attack or captured, when they were being transported to the front by train.

TOP: **Ten Char 2C Heavy Tanks were produced before the end of the war in 1918, but did not see operational service until 1921. They were fitted with German engines provided as part of post-war reparations.** ABOVE: **The massive Char 2C Heavy Tank was designed by FCM and was selected as the "breakthrough" tank for the large scale offensive planned for 1919, but was never needed.** BELOW LEFT: **In 1940, the surviving six Char 2Cs were destroyed or captured by the Germans while still on railway flat cars. The 2C had a crew of 12 men. Here, one still on its flat car is under German guard.**

Char 2C Heavy Tank

Entered service: 1918
Crew: 12
Weight: 69,000kg/67.9 tons
Dimensions: Length – 10.26m/33ft 8in
    Height (over turret hatch) – 4m/13ft 1in
    Width – 2.95m/9ft 8in
Armament: Main – 75mm/2.95in
    Secondary – 4 x 8mm/0.315in Hotchkiss
    machine-guns
Armour: Maximum – 45mm/1.77in
Powerplant: 2 x Daimler or Maybach, 6-cylinder
    petrol, 387.7kW/520bhp
Performance: Speed – 12kph/7.5mph
    Range – 100km/62.1 miles

Elefant/Ferdinand Heavy Tank Destroyer

This 65,000kg/64-ton tank destroyer/ heavy assault gun mounted an 8.8cm/3.46in StuK 43/2 L/71 gun in a limited traverse mount. The monstrous Ferdinand (named in honour of its creator Ferdinand Porsche) was ideal when used as a long-range tank killer, but not nearly as effective as an assault gun because of its lack of traverse and the absence of any close-in defensive capability. At Kursk its performance was disappointing, and almost all were lost to determined Soviet tank-killer teams.

This problem was solved to a degree with the fitting of an MG34 (*Maschinengewehr 34*), but Elefant was really only at its best when fighting at long range – it is reputed to have knocked out a T-34 at a distance of 4.82km/3 miles. Another improvement to the superstructure of about half the Elefants built was the fitting of a cupola for the commander.

Elefant/Ferdinand Heavy TD	
Entered service: 1942	
Crew: 6	
Weight: 65,000kg/64 tons	
Dimensions: Length – 8.14m/26ft 8in	
Height (over turret hatch) – 2.97m/9ft 9in	
Width – 3.38m/11ft 1in	
Armament: Main – 8.8cm/3.46in gun	
Secondary – 7.92mm/0.312in machine-gun	
Armour: Maximum – 200mm/7.87in	
Powerplant: 2 x Maybach HL120TRM V12 petrol, each developing 223.7kW/300bhp	
Performance: Speed – 30kph/18.6mph	
Range – 150km/93.2 miles	

LEFT: The *Sturmgeschutz mit 8.8cm(3.46in) PaK43/2 (Sd Kfz 184),* to give its full title, was a heavy assault gun/tank destroyer, known as both Elefant and Ferdinand (the latter in honour of Dr Ferdinand Porsche). Only 90 of these massive vehicles were produced, and they first fought at Kursk, from July to August 1943.

Jagdpanzer IV Tank Destroyer

The PzKpfw IV chassis was used for a number of excellent tank destroyers, over 3,500 being produced and used to great effect in battle. The first Jagdpanzer IV replaced the StuG III in early 1944, weighing nearly 24 tons; with a 7.5cm/ 2.95in PaK39 L/48 gun and carrying 79 rounds, it was basically an improved version of its predecessor. The next development Jagdpanzer IV/70(V) and Jagdpanzer IV/70(A) followed later in the year, mounting the deadly new Vomag long-barrelled 7.5cm/2.95in PaK42 L/70 main gun, with a performance similar to that of Panther. The only difference between these two new Marks was the manufacturer – "V" for Vomag and "A" for Alkett.

Jagdpanzer IV TD	
Entered service: 1943	
Crew: 4	
Weight: 24,000kg/23.6 tons	
Dimensions: Length – 6.85m/22ft 6in	
Height (over turret hatch) – 1.85m/6ft 1in	
Width – 3.17m/10ft 5in	
Armament: Main – 7.5cm/2.95in gun	
Secondary – 1 or 2 x 7.92mm/0.312in machine-guns	
Armour: Maximum – 100mm/3.94in	
Powerplant: Maybach HL120TRM, V12 petrol, 522kW/700hp	
Performance: Speed – 40kph/24.9mph	
Range – 210km/130.5 miles	

LEFT: The Panzer IV/70(V) (*Sd Kfz 162/1*) was another German tank destroyer. It was an improved version of the Jagdpanzer IV which itself had been an improved version of the StuG III. This one is at the Aberdeen Proving Ground in the USA.

E-100 Super Heavy Tank

LEFT, BELOW AND BOTTOM LEFT: **As well as producing the massive 191,000kg/188-ton Maus, the Germans also began a parallel development in 1943 of a super-heavy series known as the E-100 and weighing 140,000kg/137.8 tons. A year later Hitler put an end to such super-heavy development and the project continued at very low priority. At the end of the war just one chassis remained without its turret, as these three photographs show (note that the chassis in the bottom photograph is on a trailer).**

In May 1945 at the Henschel tank proving ground and development centre near Kassel, an enormous experimental heavy tank was discovered by the Allied forces. It weighed approximately 138 tons, with its external features resembling the Tiger Model B tank, but with increased length and width, heavier armour plate, wider tracks and a new suspension system.

The E-100 heavy tank that the Allies had found was the most advanced of an entirely new series of tanks which the German weapons procurement department had initiated in mid-1943. Known as the E-Series, its purpose

was ultimately to replace all the current tanks with a new group of standardized vehicles (E-10, E-25, E-50, E-100), incorporating all the improvements learned from five years AFV combat. However, by the end of the war only this prototype vehicle had been built.

The E-100 was to have been armed with the same weapons as Maus in the same Krupp turret, although one was never fitted. The tank was to have been powered by a Maybach 12-cylinder "V" type engine, developing 521.9kW/700hp, though for initial testing a normal Tiger B H1 230 P30 engine was fitted. With tracks nearly 102cm/40in wide, the

E-100 had a ground pressure of nearly 1.4kg/cm² (20psi), while its suspension comprised a series of overlapping steel road wheels, with MAN disc springs – so it did indeed look very like the Tiger B.

In fact, the E-100, like the Maus, was an absurd "wonder weapon" dreamed up to keep an insane Führer happy. It was doomed from the start by its weight.

E-100 Super Heavy Tank

Entered service: 1945 (prototype only)
Crew: 5
Weight: 140,000kg/137.8 tons
Dimensions: Length – 10.27m/33ft 8in
   Height (over turret hatch) – 3.29m/10ft 10in
   Width – 4.48m/14ft 8in
Armament: Main – 17.2cm/6.77in gun
   Secondary – 7.5cm/2.95in gun and a
   7.92mm/0.312in machine-gun
Armour: Maximum – 240mm/9.45in
Powerplant: Maybach HL234, V12 petrol,
   521.9kW/700hp (for trials only)
Performance: Speed – 40kph/24.9mph
   Range – 120km/74.6 miles

FCM 36 Infantry Tank

The French FCM 36 was produced in 1936 as a light infantry support tank using welded armour. It was armed with a 37mm/1.46in low-velocity main gun and a 7.55mm/0.297in machine-gun in an octagonal turret, which had a non-rotating commander's position on the top. Powered by an 8.4-litre Berliet water-cooled diesel engine (the first French tank to be diesel powered), it had a top speed of 24kph/15mph and a radius of action of about 225km/140 miles. A distinctive feature of this vehicle was the skirting plates with mud chutes fitted over the upper half of the tracks.

When the manufacturers raised the unit price, the French Army curtailed their order to 100 vehicles, which were built between 1936–39 and saw action between May and June 1940. Combat proved it to be severely under-gunned and many were captured by the Germans who, appreciating this vehicle's range, modified them into a gun carriage, mounting the Krupp 10.5cm/4.1in leFH18 gun in an armoured superstructure on top of the original chassis.

ABOVE: **The Char FCM 36 was a French infantry support tank built in 1936, and mounting a 37mm/1.46in gun and machine-gun in an octagonal-shaped turret. It was the first French tank to be powered by a diesel engine.** BELOW: **These FCM 36s were on parade in Paris on July 14, 1939, the last Bastille Day before war came.** BOTTOM LEFT: **The diesel engine for this tank was made in France under licence from Ricardo, who had made engines for some of the first British tanks during World War I.**

FCM 36 Infantry Tank

Entered service: 1936
Crew: 2
Weight: 12,350kg/12.15 tons
Dimensions: Length – 4.22m/13ft 10m
　　　Height (over turret hatch) – 2.15m/7ft 0.61in
　　　Width – 1.95m/6ft 4.75in
Armament: Main – 37mm/1.46in gun
　　　Secondary – 7.55mm/0.297in machine-gun
Armour: Maximum – 40mm/1.57in
Powerplant: Berliet 8.4-litre, 4-cylinder diesel, 67.9kW/91hp
Performance: Speed – 24kph/15mph
　　　Range – 225km/140 miles

LEFT: **Although the Ford 3 Ton was designated as a "tank", it was designed as a machine-gun carrier. Only 15 of these tiny 3,150kg/3.1-ton tankettes were built before the Armistice cancelled further orders.**

Ford 3 Ton Tank

Entered service: 1918
Crew: 2
Weight: 3,150kg/3.1 tons
Dimensions: Length – 4.17m/13ft 8in
    Height (over turret hatch) – 1.60m/5ft 3in
    Width – 1.68m/5ft 6in
Armament: Main – 7.62mm/0.3in machine-gun
Armour: Maximum – 13mm/0.51in
Powerplant: 2 x Ford Model T 4-cylinder petrol,
    33.58kW/45hp
Performance: Speed – 13kph/8mph
    Range – Unknown

Ford 3 Ton Tank

The US Army tank battalions that saw action in France during World War I were equipped with either British heavy tanks or French light tanks. In 1918, Ford built a two-man tank using the same characteristics and basic design of the highly successful French Renault FT-17. It was the cheapest and smallest tank built in the USA and undoubtedly the most successful. It was powered by two electrically started Model T Ford engines, producing 33.58kW/45hp between them, with the driver seated at the front and the steering being controlled through variation of the gear ratios of each engine. The gunner also was positioned at the front, armed with a 7.62mm/0.3in machine-gun in a limited-traverse mount. A prototype was sent to France and arrived in time to be tested and approved before the Armistice. Although over 15,000 were originally ordered, only 15 vehicles were actually ever built.

LEFT: **The Ford 6 Ton Tank was an exact American copy of the French FT-17, although because of the difference between French and American engineering standards, they virtually had to be completely redesigned.**

Ford 6 Ton Tank (M1917)

Entered service: 1917
Crew: 2
Weight: 6,574kg/6.47 tons
Dimensions: Length – 5.0m/16ft 5in
    Height (over turret hatch) – 2.3m/7ft 7in
    Width – 1.9m/6ft 3in
Armament: Main – 1 x 37mm/1.46in cannon or
    1 x Colt 7.62mm/0.3in machine-gun
Armour: Maximum – 17mm/0.67in
Powerplant: Buda HU modified 4-cylinder petrol,
    31.34kW/42hp
Performance: Speed – 9kph/5.6mph
    Range – 48km/29.8 miles

Ford 6 Ton Tank (M1917)

Copied directly from the French Renault FT-17 tank, this vehicle's official name was the M1917, but was known initially as the 6 Ton Special Tractor for security reasons. Although nearly 1,000 of these tanks were built, only 64 had been finished before the end of the war, and of these only 10 reached France. There were numerous improvements over the French design, including replacing the steel-rimmed wooden idler wheels on the Renault with all-steel ones, fitting a self-starter to the 4-cylinder engine and constructing a bulkhead between the crew and the engine compartment.

They continued in service for many years, and like the Liberty tank (the British Mark VIII), they were given to Canada for training purposes in 1939.

Holt Gas–Electric Tank and other US experimental tanks

As soon as tanks had been used in combat and their exploits reported in the newspapers, designs for tanks of all shapes and sizes began to appear in the USA. All were private ventures, the first being the CLB 75 Tank, designed and built by the CL Best Agricultural Tractor Company and comprising one of their tractors with a simulated armoured body, surmounted by a revolving turret containing two light cannon. There were many others: the Holt's HA 36; the Holt's Gas and Electric Tank; the Steam Tank; the Skeleton Tank; the Studebaker Tank; and the One-Man Tank.

The HA 36, built by the Holt Tractor Factory in 1916, was a small one-man tank, closely resembling a British heavy tank in miniature. Powered by a motorcycle engine with link chain tracks and wooden track plates, it was "armed" with dummy guns. The Holt's Gas and Electric Tank was built by Holt's and General Electric, USA, and was based upon standard Holt tracks and suspension components. It was driven by a Holt 67.1kW/90hp engine which powered a General Electric generator that provided the current to drive two electric motors – one for each track. It was armed with a 75mm/2.95in mountain gun. The Steam Tank was produced by the US Engineer Corps in 1918, with the assistance once again of

TOP: **The Holt's Gas-Electric Tank weighed some 25,400kg/25 tons and was armed with a 75mm/2.95in howitzer. It was based upon standard Holt tracks and suspension components.** ABOVE: **The Holt's HA 36 Tank, a one-man machine, closely resembled a British heavy tank, only much smaller.**

Holt's, and had a very similar external appearance to a British Mark IV; however, the similarity ended there. Motive power was to be provided via two 2-cylinder steam engines, each with its own kerosene burning boiler. One can imagine what heat this

LEFT: **The Steam Tank, a 50,800kg/ 50-ton machine, had many of the characteristics of the British Mark IV Heavy Tank, but power was via two steam engines.** BELOW: **The smallest of the experimental tanks was this One-Man Tank which had an armoured body on top of a tractor.** BOTTOM: **The Skeleton Tank. With a crew of two men, this 9,144kg/ 9-ton vehicle was armed with just one machine-gun, but was light enough to have a good cross-country performance.**

would have generated inside the vehicle, and what would have happened to the crew if enemy fire had pierced a boiler! The Skeleton Tank was built by the Pioneer Tractor Company of Winona, and as its name implies, was built in skeleton form, with a two-man fighting compartment suspended between the track frames. The use of ordinary iron piping for the skeleton kept the weight down to less than 9,144kg/9 tons and resulted in a good cross-country performance. The Studebaker Supply Tank was of conventional design and was to have been ordered in large numbers for use in 1919, but the Armistice was signed and the contract cancelled. The One-Man Tank, as the name implies was a small track-based, lightly armoured vehicle, crewed by one man and armed with a single machine-gun.

None of these experimental models would be adopted, the US Army eventually equipping their fledgling armoured forces with British and French tanks instead.

Space does not allow for the detailed specifications of all these prototypes, so those for the Holt's Gas-Electric are included by way of example.

Holt Gas-Electric Tank

Entered service: 1918 (prototype only)
Crew: 6
Weight: 25,400kg/25 tons
Dimensions: Length – 5.03m/16ft 6in
   Height (over turret hatch) – 2.38m/7ft 10in
   Width – 2.77m/9ft 1in
Armament: Main – 75mm/2.95in Mountain Howitzer
   Secondary – 2 x 7.62mm/0.3in machine-guns
Armour: Maximum – 15mm/0.59in
Powerplant: Holt 4-cylinder petrol, generating
   67.1kW/90hp
Performance: Speed – 9.66kph/6mph
   Range – Unknown

Hotchkiss H-35 Light Tank

LEFT: **The Hotchkiss H-35 was a *char leger* (cavalry tank) and thus considered by some French infantry as unsuitable. Nevertheless, it did come into service, many seeing action in France in 1940, with large numbers being captured and used extensively by the Germans.**

**Hotchkiss H-35
Light Tank**

Entered service: 1936
Crew: 2
Weight: 10,600kg/10.43 tons
Dimensions: Length – 4.22m/13ft 10in
    Height (over turret hatch) – 2.62m/8ft 7in
    Width – 1.96m/6ft 5in
Armament: Main – 37mm/1.46in gun
    Secondary – 7.5mm/0.295in machine-gun
Armour: Maximum – 40mm/1.58m
Powerplant: Hotchkiss 1935, 6-cylinder,
    55.91kW/75hp
Performance: Speed – 27.4kph/17mph
    Range – 150km/93.2 miles

Following demands from the French Cavalry for a light tank, the Hotchkiss H-35 was designed in 1933 and entered service in 1936, at which time its role was expanded to that of an infantry support tank. In the end some 400 were manufactured, with three quarters allotted to the Cavalry and the remaining quarter to the Infantry.

However, with its short-barrelled 37mm/1.46in main gun and single machine-gun as armament and its poor speed, its combat performance was disappointing against German armour. Under-gunned and underpowered, its sole advantage was its thick cast armour in the hull and turret. Commandeered by the Germans, the remaining H-35s had their turrets removed and were used as "schleppers" – to haul artillery and munitions. The turrets were incorporated into static defence lines.

Hotchkiss H-39 Light Tank

LEFT: **A line of brand new H-39s being prepared for issue. This little light tank was a development of the H-35 but had a new engine and a long-barrelled 37mm/1.46in gun. Like the H-35, it was also captured and used by the Germans, both in Russia and the Mediterranean theatre. Some H-39s were still in use by the Israelis in 1956.**

**Hotchkiss H-39
Light Tank**

Entered service: 1939
Crew: 2
Weight: 12,100kg/11.9 tons
Dimensions: Length – 4.23m/13ft 10in
    Height (over turret hatch) – 2.16m/7ft 1in
    Width – 1.96m/6ft 5in
Armament: Main – 37mm/1.46in gun
    Secondary – 7.5mm/0.295in machine-gun
Armour: Maximum – 40mm/1.57in
Powerplant: Hotchkiss 1938, 6-cylinder petrol,
    89.5kW/120hp
Performance: Speed – 36.5kph/22.7mph
    Range – 150km/93.2 miles

Between the H-35 and H-39 there was an interim model, the H-38. It sported a new, more powerful 89.5kW/120hp petrol engine which improved its mobility but still had the same ineffectual 37mm/1.46in main gun. It was only in the final model of the series, the H-39, that the main armament, though remaining the same calibre, was upgraded to a long-barrelled variant.

This vehicle did not fare long or well against the Germans in 1940 who, as with its predecessors, removed the turret to use it as a tractor to haul artillery and munitions. Radio sets were fitted with a 2m/6ft 6in-long rod aerial mounted on a tripod on the front right-hand mudguard. It was used by the Germans both in the Russian and Mediterranean theatres.

LEFT: The first of the new breed of Soviet heavy tanks to replace the KV-1 was the Joseph Stalin 1, which mounted an 85mm/3.34in gun, although some were fitted with 100mm/3.94in guns. Here one fires at point-blank range at a German strongpoint in East Prussia, January 25, 1945.

LEFT: The first of the new breed of Soviet heavy tanks to replace the KV-1 was the Joseph Stalin 1, which mounted an 85mm/3.34in gun, although some were fitted with 100mm/3.94in guns. Here one fires at point-blank range at a German strongpoint in East Prussia, January 25, 1945.

JS-1 Heavy Tank

Entered service: 1943
Crew: 4
Weight: 46.000kg/45.3 tons
Dimensions: Length – 8.32m/27ft 3in
   Height (over turret hatch) – 2.9m/9ft 6in
   Width – 3.25m/10ft 8in
Armament: Main – 100mm/3.94in gun
   Secondary – 2 x 7.62mm/0.3in machine-guns
Armour: Maximum – 132mm/5.2in
Powerplant: V2-IS 12-cylinder diesel,
   382.8kW/510hp
Performance: Speed – 40kph/24.9mph
   Range – 250km/155 miles

JS-1 Heavy Tank

Hard on the heels of the KV-1, Russia began to develop a new tank in 1941, to cope with the new German tanks that had appeared in response to both it and the T-34 in the race for battlefield supremacy. At that time, the requirement was for a four-man tank with an 85mm/3.35in gun and sufficient armour to keep out the German 50mm/ 1.97in anti-tank gun round, but with no significant increase in weight over the KV-1 series. By the time the JS-1 appeared in 1943, the main armament had been changed from 85mm/3.34in to 100mm/3.94in. Basically an enlarged superstructure over a KV chassis enabled the fitting of a larger turret ring and turret to accommodate the larger main gun. This tank had a very good ballistic shape, a low silhouette and was very reliable. In late 1944 a small number had their 100mm/3.94in gun replaced with a 122mm/4.8in gun in a larger turret.

LEFT: Popularly known as the Victory Tank, the JS-2 was next in line, and mounted a 122mm/4.8in gun. Production began in January 1944.

JS-2 Heavy Tank

Entered service: 1944
Crew: 4
Weight: 46,000kg/45.3 tons
Dimensions: Length – 9.9m/32ft 6in
   Height (over turret hatch) – 2.73m/8ft 11in
   Width – 3.09m/10ft 2in
Armament: Main – 122mm/4.8in D-25 gun
   Secondary – 3 x 7.62mm/0.3in machine-guns
Armour: Maximum – 120mm/4.72in
Powerplant: V2-IS 12-cylinder diesel,
   382.8kW/513hp
Performance: Speed – 37kph/23mph
   Range – 240km/149 miles

JS-2 Heavy Tank

The next model in the JS series appeared in 1944, an improved model of the JS-1, but with little external difference other than the 122mm/4.8in main gun which now became standard. This made the JS-2 the most powerfully armed tank in the world at that time. It had a smaller cupola and some differences in the armour silhouette around the front hull. The JS-2 was known as the Victory Tank, and led on to the JS-3. It was undoubtedly the most advanced heavy tank of its time and had a major influence on Western tank design. The JS-2 was accepted for production at the end of December 1943, and by the beginning of 1944 some 100 were in operational service.

KV-1 Heavy Tank

The KV-1 Heavy Tank with which Russia entered World War II was, along with the T-34, the closest any Allied forces came to armour parity with the Germans at that time. It was basically a redesign of the T-100, with one its turrets eliminated. Named after the Russian defence commissar Marshal Klimenti Voroshilov, it first saw active service in the Russo-Finnish war. It was replaced a little later, in 1940, by the KV-1A, which mounted a better gun with a higher muzzle velocity and firing a larger round – the 76.2mm/3in L/41.5 Model 40. This firepower combined with thick armour stunned the Germans when they first encountered it. A special diagnostic team from Germany was rushed to the front to analyse both it and the T-34. However, it was let down by its unreliable transmission, and this, coupled with its weight, made it difficult to drive, slow and cumbersome. Production ceased in 1943.

LEFT: **The KV-1 Heavy Tank gave the Germans a shock when they first encountered it during the opening weeks of their assault on the USSR because they had summarily discounted the Red Army's heavy tanks as being both old-fashioned and obsolete. This one, having been captured in the Russo-Finnish war, still has a Finnish swastika on its turret.**

KV-1 Heavy Tank

Entered service: 1939
Crew: 5
Weight: 43,000kg/42.3 tons
Dimensions: Length – 6.68m/21ft 11in
　　Height (over turret hatch) – 2.71m/8ft 11in
　　Width – 3.32m/10ft 11in
Armament: Main – 76.2mm/3in L/41 ZiS-5 gun
　　Secondary – up to 4 x 7.62mm/0.3in
　　machine-guns
Armour: Maximum – 75mm/2.95in
Powerplant: V2K V12 diesel, 410kW/550bhp
Performance: Speed – 35kph/21.7mph
　　Range – 150km/93 miles

KV-2 Heavy Tank

KV-2 Heavy Tank

Entered service: 1940
Crew: 6
Weight: 53,963kg/53.1 tons
Dimensions: Length – 6.79m/22ft 3in
　　Height (over turret hatch) – 3.65m/12ft
　　Width – 3.32m/10ft 11in
Armament: Main – 152mm/5.98in L/20 howitzer
　　Secondary – 2 x 7.62mm/0.3in machine-guns
Armour: Maximum – 110mm/4.33in
Powerplant: V2K V12 diesel, 410kW/550bhp
Performance: Speed – 26kph/16mph
　　Range – 150km/93 miles

LEFT: **The close-support version of the KV-1 was known as the KV-2, and mounted a massive 152mm/5.98in howitzer in a large slab-sided turret. This captured KV-2 is being inspected by the Germans.**

The KV-2 was a specialized tank developed to break through fortifications similar to the Funnies being developed in the Western theatre by the British. A huge 152mm/5.98in howitzer was mounted in a gargantuan turret and could fire a special dustbin-sized anti-concrete shell to destroy bastions and pillboxes. There was an extra crew member in the turret to help operate this weapon system, pushing the crew total up to six.

The chassis and engine were the same as that of the KV-1, which made it even slower and more vulnerable than its predecessor, and the Germans quickly learned to aim for its tracks to first immobilize and then destroy it.

The No. 1 Lincoln Machine Little Willie

Designed by William Tritton (later Sir), chief executive of William Foster and Co. Ltd of Lincoln, and Lt W. G. Wilson, then an RNAS (Royal Naval Air Service) armoured car officer, the "Tritton Machine", as it was sometimes called, was designed and constructed between August 2 and September 8, 1915. It weighed 18,290kg/18 tons, and above its rectangular hull was to have been a centrally mounted turret with a 2pdr gun; however, this was never fitted and a dummy turret of the correct weight was used when the machine was tested.

The machine had Bullock tracks, brought from America, where they had been developed commercially from an original British design. Tail wheels helped the cross-country performance and aided steering.

The first version prototype of the No. 1 Lincoln Machine suffered from track problems, through a lack of grip and an inclination for the tracks to come off when crossing trenches. Speed was between 3.2–4.8kph/2–3mph. It could just about cross a 1.2m/4ft wide trench and mount a 0.61m/2ft vertical step.

ABOVE: **The very first tank to be built in the world – "Little Willie", the No. 1 Lincoln Machine – which was designed and completed in 1915.** RIGHT: **This was the No. 1 Lincoln Machine as designed by Tritton and Wilson, utilizing Bullock tracks and a dummy turret. It was modified to become "Little Willie" by using different tracks. Note also the rear steering wheels.**

In order to meet new War Office revised requirements to cross a 1.52m/5ft trench and climb a 1.37m/4.5ft step, the No. 1 Lincoln Machine had to be rebuilt, using the original hull and engine (a 6-cylinder Daimler petrol engine, developing 78.29kW/105bhp), but with completely redesigned tracks. The new tracks had their frames increased in length and comprised cast steel plates riveted to links which had guides engaging with rails on the side of the track frames. This pattern of track construction was used for all British tanks up to 1918 to improve cross-country performance. The simulated turret was also removed, and "Little Willie" was completed early in December 1915. (Presumably the name had some ribald connection with Kaiser Wilhelm II.)

The No. 1 Lincoln Machine "Little Willie"

Entered service: 1915 (prototype only)
Crew: 4–6
Weight: 18,290kg/18 tons
Dimensions: Length – 5.53m/18ft 2in
   Height (over turret hatch) – 3.1m/10ft 2in
   Width – 2.85m/9ft 4in
Armament: Main – 2pdr (40mm/1.57in) gun
   Secondary – 1 x 7.7mm/0.303in Maxim
   machine-gun and up to 3 x 7.7mm/0.303in
   Lewis machine-guns
Armour: Maximum – 6mm/0.24in
Powerplant: Daimler 6-cylinder petrol, generating
   78.29kW/105bhp
Performance: Speed – 3.2kph/2mph
   Range – Unknown

LK I Light Tank

LEFT: **The LK I was a relatively simple tank, with a Daimler car chassis and axles for its suspension. It was only ever produced in prototype form in mid-1918.**

LK I Light Tank

Entered service: 1918 (prototype only)
Crew: 3
Weight: 7,000kg/6.89 tons
Dimensions: Length – 5.49m/18ft
    Height (over turret hatch) – 2.48m/8ft 2in
    Width – 2m/6ft 7in
Armament: Main – 1 x 7.92mm/0.312in machine-gun
    Secondary – None
Armour: Maximum – 8mm/0.31in
Powerplant: 4-cylinder petrol, 44.7kW/60bhp
Performance: Speed – 13kph/8mph
    Range – 64km/40 miles

The German light tank LK I (*Leichte Kampfwagen I*) was designed in mid-1918 by Joseph Vollmer, who had also worked on the A7V. He advocated the use of simple, light tanks that were easy and cheap to produce in preference to large, heavy and expensive ones. The LK I only reached prototype stage before the Armistice. Using a Daimler car chassis as well as other automotive parts (such as axles for the sprocket and idler wheels), it followed the normal layout of an automobile, weighed nearly 7 tons, had a three-man crew and was armed with one 7.92mm/0.312in machine-gun.

LK II Light Tank

LEFT: **The *Leichte Kampfwagen II* was produced from the LK I. It had thicker armour and a 57mm/ 2.24in gun, but was still a relatively simple tank. Two prototypes were built, but the subsequent order for 580 never materialized, because World War I ended. The design was passed to Sweden and used as the basis of their Strv M/21 Light Tank.**

LK II Light Tank

Entered service: 1918
Crew: 3
Weight: 8,890kg/8.75 tons
Dimensions: Length – 5.1m/16ft 9in
    Height (over turret hatch) – 2.49m/8ft 2in
    Width – 1.98m/6ft 6in
Armament: Main – 1 x 57mm/2.24in gun or
    2 x 7.92mm/0.312in machine-guns
Armour: Maximum – 14mm/0.55in
Powerplant: Daimler-Benz, 4-cylinder petrol, 44.7kW/60hp
Performance: Speed – 12kph/7.5mph
    Range – 64.4km/40 miles

An LK II was then designed from the LK I, mounting a larger 57mm/ 2.24in main gun and weighing almost 2,000kg/2 tons more due to its thicker armour, but otherwise being similar to its predecessor. It also did not get further than prototype stage. A variant carrying two 7.92mm/0.312in machine-guns in a traversing turret was also proposed but never built, for although two gun-armed LK II prototypes were manufactured, the planned production run of 580 was terminated by the Armistice of November 1918. After 1918, the LK II drawings were passed to Sweden and used to manufacture their Strv M/21 of 1921.

Medium B Whippet

The shape of the Medium B was more like that of the heavy tank than its predecessor, the Medium A Whippet, but with a large fixed turret mounted on top at the front of the hull. The Medium B weighed 18,289kg/18 tons and was longer and wider than the Medium A, but not so tall. The engine, a 6-cylinder 74.57kW/100hp Ricardo, was mounted in a separate compartment, with a bulkhead to divide it from the crew of four – the first tank ever to have this feature.

BELOW LEFT: **Built in 1918, the shape of the Medium B Whippet reverted back to the earlier rhomboidal design. The Armistice led to the cancellation of the order; however, 17 of the 45 built were sent to Russia in 1919, to support the White Russians against the Bolsheviks.**

Medium B Whippet

Entered service: 1918
Crew: 4
Weight: 18,289kg/18 tons
Dimensions: Length – 6.93m/22ft 9in
   Height (over turret hatch) – 2.59m/8ft 6in
   Width – 2.69m/8ft 10in
Armament: Main – 4 x 7.7mm/0.303in Hotchkiss
   machine-guns
Armour: Maximum – 14mm/0.55in
Powerplant: Ricardo 6-cylinder petrol,
   74.57kW/100hp
Performance: Speed – 12.7kph/7.9mph
   Range – Approximately 64km/40 miles

Medium C Hornet

Although it was designed in late 1917, none of the 45 Medium Cs built actually left the factory until after the Armistice. They remained in service until 1925, and proved to be remarkably effective tanks, with a better performance than any of the previous Mediums.

The Medium C had a fixed turret armed with four Hotchkiss 7.7mm/0.303in machine-guns, and a rotating commander's cupola. At 20,320kg/20 tons, its rear-mounted 111.8kW/150hp Ricardo engine gave it a power-to-weight ratio of 7.5, while its fuel tanks held 682 litres/150 gallons – over double that of the Medium A. Top speed was still only 12.9kph/8mph and its radius of action was 121km/75 miles.

The very last tank to be designed in World War I was the Medium Mark D, which never got further than the design stage. However, various modified models were produced after the war, the Johnson Light Infantry Tank being based on the Medium D design. It also had a fixed turret with three ball-mounted machine-guns sited ahead of the driver who sat at the rear above the gunners' stations, steering by means of a small conning tower. There was also a new wire rope suspension system to improve its speed.

LEFT: **Designed by Tritton in late 1917, the Hornet, as the Medium C was also called, resembled the Medium B (engine at rear), but incorporated all the wartime experience of the tank crews, so it was considerably improved.**

Medium C Hornet

Entered service: 1918
Crew: 4
Weight: 20,320kg/20 tons
Dimensions: Length – 7.92m/26ft
   Height (over turret hatch) – 3.00m/9ft 6in
   Width – 2.54m/8ft 4in
Armament: Main – 4 x 7.7mm/0.303in Hotchkiss
   machine-guns
Armour: Maximum – 14mm/0.55in
Powerplant: Ricardo 6-cylinder petrol,
   111.8kW/150hp
Performance: Speed – 12.9kph/8mph
   Range – 121km/75 miles

Medium A Whippet

Designed by Sir William Tritton in November 1916, the Medium A, also known as the Whippet or the Tritton Chaser, was the only British medium tank to see action during World War I. Construction began in December 1916 at William Foster's factory in Lincoln, and trials were held on February 11, 1917, after which an order was placed for 200 tanks four months later.

The tank ran on two 33.6kW/45hp 4-cylinder Tyler lorry engines – one for each track, with dual ignition. It also had twin four-speed gearboxes and clutches, making it very difficult to handle and seriously increasing servicing time. Gentle steering, such as on roads, was by means of a column which controlled the throttle on each engine – and thus each track, accelerating one and retarding the other automatically. For serious turning, especially on cross-country, the gearboxes had to be used.

Seventy gallons of fuel was carried, contained in a drum-shaped tank in the front of the machine (under armour-plating) and was fed to the engines by an autovac system. The tracks were half-round, like those on "Little Willie". There was no unditching beam, but instead there were two towing shackles, and oak spuds were provided. For observation, there were three rotary peephole covers and three periscope openings.

ABOVE: **The Tank Museum's Whippet. This was the tank, nicknamed Caesar, on which Lt Sewell won his Victoria Cross on April 29, 1918.** LEFT: **One of Sewell's No. 9 Section, 3rd (Light) Tank Battalion, which he commanded in 1918.**

The first Whippets to see action did so on March 26, 1918, at Hebuterne, during the Second Battle of the Somme. They continued to perform sterling work right up to the Armistice; indeed, one of the Tank Corps Victoria Crosses was awarded to Lieutenant Cecil Sewell while he was commanding his Whippet, Caesar II, A 253, which is now on show at the Tank Museum, Bovington, England.

The official account of his action says, "This officer displayed the greatest gallantry and initiative in getting out of his own tank and crossing open ground under heavy shell and machine-gun fire to rescue the crew of another Whippet of his section which had side-slipped into a large shell hole, overturned and taken fire." After releasing the crew, Sewell then dashed back across open ground to assist one of his own crew, and a few minutes later he was hit again, this time fatally, while dressing his driver's wounds. He showed "utter disregard for his own personal safety".

ABOVE LEFT: **Good view of the open rear door of a 3rd Battalion Whippet. Two hundred of these 14,225kg/14-ton tanks were built.** ABOVE: **A quartet of Medium A Whippets take part in the Armistice Day parade in Central London as part of a large tank column.** BELOW: **The lighter, faster Whippet was ideal for exploiting the successes of the heavy tanks – a sort of armoured cavalry.**

Medium A Whippet	

Entered service: 1917
Crew: 3
Weight: 14,225kg/14 tons
Dimensions: Length – 6.10m/20ft
  Height (over turret hatch) – 2.74m/9ft
  Width – 2.62m/8ft 7in
Armament: 4 x 7.7mm/0.303 Hotchkiss
  machine-guns
Armour: Maximum – 14mm/0.55in
Powerplant: 2 x Taylor JB4 petrol, each developing
  33.6kW/45hp
Performance: Speed – 12.9kph/8mph
  Range – 64.4km/40 miles

Mark I Heavy Tank "Mother"

Even while "Little Willie" was being built, Tritton and Wilson were working on a new design, which had a much longer track length in order to improve its cross-country performance and – to be sure of meeting the new War Office requirements – to cross a 1.52m/5ft trench and climb a 1.22m/4ft step. It had been worked out that this could be achieved by a wheel 1.83m/6ft in diameter, so the length of the track on the ground and its shape had to be the same as the lower curve of a wheel of that size. This meant raising the height of the front horns, and gave

rise to the now familiar rhomboidal shape common to all of the British World War I heavy tanks. In order to keep the centre of gravity low, it was decided to mount the tank's main armament – two naval 6pdr guns – in side sponsons. During her life, "Mother" had various names such as "Big Willie" and "HMLS Centipede", but as the very first battle tank she was rightly called "Mother" – despite her Male armament (Female tanks had two extra machine-guns instead of 6pdrs so they were about a ton lighter).

ABOVE: **"Clan Leslie" a British Heavy Tank Mark I (Male). Note the long-barrelled 6pdr naval gun in its side sponson. A total of 150 of these tanks were built, the basic design being exactly the same as for "Mother".**
LEFT: **Mark I Male tank D7 (No. 742) commanded by Lt Enoch pauses after the Flers Battle.**

The building of the first batch of 100 Mark I tanks began in February 1916, following the same basic design as "Mother". They were called "tanks" for security reasons, to disguise their true purpose. Half of the first batch was Male tanks with 6pdr guns, the rest Female with two machine-guns in each sponson.

It was not until after the first tank versus tank engagement in April 1918 that the danger of having a tank with no effective weapon capable of penetrating an enemy tank was realized, and thereafter hermaphrodite tanks with one 6pdr sponson and one dual machine-gun sponson were introduced. The Mark I was recognizable by its tail wheels to assist with steering, the unshortened barrel on its ex-Naval 6pdr guns and the anti-grenade "roof" made of chicken wire.

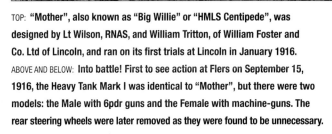

TOP: **"Mother", also known as "Big Willie" or "HMLS Centipede", was designed by Lt Wilson, RNAS, and William Tritton, of William Foster and Co. Ltd of Lincoln, and ran on its first trials at Lincoln in January 1916.**
ABOVE AND BELOW: **Into battle! First to see action at Flers on September 15, 1916, the Heavy Tank Mark I was identical to "Mother", but there were two models: the Male with 6pdr guns and the Female with machine-guns. The rear steering wheels were later removed as they were found to be unnecessary.**

Mark I Heavy Tank "Mother" (Male)	
Entered service: 1916	
Crew: 8	
Weight: 28,450kg/28 tons	
Dimensions: Length – 9.9m/32ft 6in	
Height (over turret hatch) – 2.41m/7ft 11in	
Width – 4.19m/13ft 9in	
Armament: Main – 2 x 6pdr (57mm/2.24in) guns	
Secondary – 7.7mm/0.303in Hotchkiss machine-gun	
Armour: Maximum – 12mm/0.47in	
Powerplant: Daimler 6-cylinder petrol, 111.8kW/150bhp	
Performance: Speed – 5.95kph/3.7mph	
Range – 35.4km/22 miles	

Mark I Medium Tank

Following on from the Medium D, this Vickers-built 12,192kg/12-ton tank was originally called Light Tank Mark I and was the first British tank designed after World War I, with production models coming into service in 1924. It was later reclassified as Mark I Medium Tank and

was the first British tank to have all-round traverse capability and geared elevation for the main gun, a 3pdr (47mm/1.85in), a 94mm/3.7in howitzer being fitted in the close-support tanks. Two Vickers machine-guns were ball-mounted in the hull sides, while there were four Hotchkiss machine-guns carried in the turret for dismounted use. The crew was five (commander, driver, radio-operator and two gunners). Spring suspension enabled it to achieve a higher speed than previous designs, the 67.1kW/90hp air-cooled Armstrong Siddeley V8 engine giving it a top speed of 24kph/15mph. Production of the Mark I and II amounted to some 160 in total.

LEFT: **Mediums on training. The Mark I remained in operational service until 1938 and was thereafter only used for training.**

ABOVE: **The Mark I Medium Tank was the first British tank to be designed after World War I, and to reach production. It had a fully traversing turret and its main armament could be elevated. This rear view has the turret traversed rear and the rear door open.**

Mark I Medium Tank	

Entered service: 1924
Crew: 5
Weight: 12,192kg/12 tons
Dimensions: Length – 5.33m/17ft 6in
    Height (over turret hatch) – 2.82m/9ft 3in
    Width – 2.79m/9ft 2in
Armament: Main – 3pdr (47mm/1.85in) gun
    Secondary – 2 x 7.7mm/0.303in Vickers machine-guns and 4 x Hotchkiss 7.7mm/0.303in machine-guns
Armour: Maximum – 8mm/0.315in
Powerplant: Armstrong-Siddeley V8 petrol, developing 67.1kW/90hp
Performance: Speed – 24kph/15mph
    Range – 241km/150 miles

Mark II and Mark III Heavy Tanks

In all, some 150 Mark I Heavy Tanks were produced and delivered to the Army. As a result of their impact upon the battlefield, the Commander-in-Chief Field-Marshal Sir Douglas Haig ordered a further 1,000 tanks to be built. First of these were 50 Mark IIs – 25 Male and 25 Female. They were almost identical to the Mark I apart from minor alterations resulting from the limited battle experience of the Mark Is on the Somme.

The tail wheels were discarded, there was a revised hatch on top, and a wider track shoe at every sixth track link in order to improve traction. Armour on these early tanks had to be cut and drilled as soft steel and then hardened to inhibit hostile fire. The front plates were 10mm/0.394in thick, the sides 8mm/0.315in. The tank was built by riveting sheets of armour plate to butt straps and angle iron. Inevitably, there were gaps,

which allowed molten metal to penetrate inside when a joint was hit by small arms fire. This "splash", as it was called, meant that the crew had to wear small

steel masks with a chain-mail visor hanging down over the face, to reduce injury. However, they were uncomfortable to wear and made it much more difficult to observe, so the crews would hang blankets inside to absorb the splash.

The Mark III Heavy Tank was virtually identical to the Mark II except that it had slightly thicker armour. Fifty Mark IIIs (half of them Male and half Female) were built. The later Males were armed with the short-barrelled 6pdr gun because naval guns proved too long for land use, banging into trees or becoming buried in the mud. Guns could fire either High-Explosive or Armour-Piercing shot.

BELOW: Apart from having slightly thicker armour, the Mark III was identical to the Mark II. Only 50 were built (half Male and half Female).

Mark III Heavy Tank (Male)

Entered service: 1917
Crew: 8
Weight: 28,450kg/28 tons
Dimensions: Length – 9.9m/32ft 6in
  Height (over turret hatch) – 2.41m/7ft 11in
  Width – 4.19m/13ft 9in
Armament: Male – 2 x 6pdr (57mm/2.24in) guns
  Female – 2 x Hotchkiss 7.7mm/0.303in machine-guns
Armour: Maximum – 12mm/0.47in
Powerplant: Daimler 6-cylinder petrol, developing 111.8kW/150bhp
Performance: Speed – 5.95kph/3.7mph
  Range – 35.4km/22 miles

Mark II Medium Tank

The Mark II Medium Tank shared many features with the Mark I Medium, using the same basic chassis, engine and armament. They also both had the sprung "box bogie" suspension which gave the Mark II a speed of 40–48kph/ 25–30mph, far in advance of its theoretical design speed of around 29kph/18mph. However, the extra weight of the Mark II reduced the top speed to around 24kph/15mph. Armament comprised the 3pdr gun, plus two Vickers machine-guns in the hull sides and three Hotchkiss machine-guns projecting out around the turret.

There were other differences between the Marks. Externally, the Mark IIs appeared much bulkier, the armour was thicker, the superstructure was a little higher, and the driver's hood stood proud of the hull top. Also, the driver's glacis was steeper, the headlights larger and the Mark IIs had suspension skirts. The major mechanical difference was in the steering, with the Mark II having Rackham Steering, with an additional epicyclic gearbox between the main gearbox and the differential cum cross-shaft.

ABOVE: **A line of Mediums firing on the Gunnery School Ranges at Lulworth, Dorset. This is still the "home" of tank gunnery, now as part of the British Army Armour Centre.** BELOW: **The Tank Museum's Vickers Mark II* Medium Tank. Entering service in 1926, the Royal Tank Corps was pleased to receive these modern tanks, although they probably did not realize that they would stay in active service until after the beginning of World War II!**

In 1932, modifications were made to the Medium Mark II, resulting in the Marks II* and II**. In the former, the three Hotchkiss machine-guns in the turret were replaced by a single coaxial Vickers, while the commander's cupola was set further back in the turret roof. A lead counterweight was added at the back of the turret. In the latter, the wireless was placed in an armoured container and attached at the back of the turret.

A total of 160 Mark II Mediums were built and were used for training after war was declared, but never saw action. Latterly, some of those in Egypt were buried up to their turrets at Mersa Matruh as static pillboxes. The Tank Museum's Mark II* was restored to full running order by Vickers Defence Systems in the 1980s.

Mark II Medium Tank	

Entered service: 1925
Crew: 5
Weight: 14,224kg/14 tons
Dimensions: Length – 5.33m/17ft 6in
    Height (over turret hatch) – 2.69m/8ft 10in
    Width – 2.79m/9ft 2in
Armament: Main – 3pdr (47mm/1.85in) gun
    Secondary – 3 x 7.7mm/0.303 Vickers
    machine-guns (1 x coaxial replacing 3 x Hotchkiss)
Armour: Maximum – 12mm/0.47in
Powerplant: Armstrong-Siddley 8-cylinder petrol,
    developing 67.1kW/90hp
Performance: Speed – 24kph/15mph
    Range – 193km/120 miles

Mark II and Mark III Light Tanks

B ritish light and medium tank development began with the Whippet, which was created to provide a fast cavalry or pursuit tank to exploit any opportunity or breakthrough by the heavy tanks. Later, after the war, light tanks or tankettes were built to help mechanize the infantry. However, with the advent of these small, fast and low-silhouette vehicles, a new concept for

their use was found, namely to provide reconnaissance for the heavier tanks. Turreted versions of the Carden-Loyd were developed and known as Patrol Tanks Marks I and II.

During the mid-1930s and after having taken over Carden-Loyd, Vickers-Armstrong spent much time and effort in the development of light tanks. Initially a series of two-man machines (Marks I–IV)

mounting a single Vickers machine-gun, they were later enlarged into three-man light tanks armed with two machine-guns in a two-man turret. These light AFVs were perfect for patrolling the border provinces of the far-flung British Empire.

The Mark II was based on the Mark I, with the same hull, but having a larger rectangular turret, the No. 1 Mark I, and with a new, more powerful Rolls-Royce 6-cylinder engine replacing the Meadows of its predecessor. It was fitted with Horstmann spring coil suspension.

The next two Marks – the IIA and IIB – were fitted with the No. 1 Mark II turret, modified with air louvers on the sides for hot climates. A difference between the two was that the Mark IIA had an extra fuel tank fitted and the Mark IIB a single large-capacity tank of the same capacity as the Mark IIA. Entering service in 1933, the Mark III was the same as its predecessors other than having an extended rear superstructure to accommodate a modified Horstmann suspension system which had evolved from a two-pair to four-pair type.

LEFT: **Entering service in 1933, the Mark III Light Tank was similar in layout to the Mark II, but had its superstructure extended rearwards and was fitted with a modified Horstmann suspension.**

Mark II Light Tank	

Entered service: 1931
Crew: 2
Weight: 4572kg/4.5 tons
Dimensions: Length – 3.58m/11ft 9in
    Height (over turret hatch) – 2.01m/6ft 7in
    Width – 1.91m/6ft 3in
Armament: Main – 7.7mm/0.303in Vickers
    machine-gun
Armour: Maximum – 10mm/0.39in
Powerplant: Rolls-Royce 6-cylinder, 49.2kW/66bhp
Performance: Speed – 48.3kph/30mph
    Range – 209.2km/130 miles

Mark III Valentine Infantry Tank

The prototype of the Valentine was produced by Vickers on February 14, 1940, hence its name. Over 8,000 Valentines were built in 11 different Marks, as well as various specialized variants, and it remained in production until 1944, being supplied to Russia and built under licence in Canada. This accounts for approximately a quarter of all British wartime tank production.

Over the course of its service life the Valentine's construction changed from being riveted to welded, and its power source from petrol to diesel – the AEC petrol and diesel engines being finally replaced with the more reliable GMC two-stroke diesel. It also had a variety of main armaments, beginning with the 2pdr, giving way to the 6pdr and then to the 75mm/2.95in on the final model. The Valentine saw most of its active service in the North African theatre, where extra fuel tanks attached to the rear increased its range, although it was also used by Commonwealth troops in the Pacific and Asian theatres.

Variants included a bridgelayer, flail and snake explosive-charge mine-sweepers, self-propelled guns, a flame-thrower and also an amphibious version.

ABOVE: **A modern photograph of the Bovington Tank Museum's Infantry Tank Mark III Valentine in desert colours. Developed by Vickers, it proved to be both strong and reliable.** BELOW LEFT: **In April 2004 Ex Smash was held at Studland Bay in Dorset, during which Mr John Pearson's wonderfully restored Valentine DD (Duplex Drive) went into the water from a landing craft to commemorate the loss of six crewmen of 4/7 DG back in 1944. The DD was also on show at the Tank Museum's "Tankfest" on May 23, 2004.**

Mark III Valentine Infantry Tank

Entered service: 1940
Crew: 3
Weight: 17,272kg/17 tons
Dimensions: Length – 5.89m/19ft 4in
  Height (over turret hatch) – 2.29m/7ft 6in
  Width – 2.64m/8ft 8in
Armament: Main – 2pdr (40mm/1.58in) or 6pdr (57mm/2.24in) or 75mm/2.95in gun
  Secondary – 7.92mm/0.312in Besa machine-gun
Armour: Maximum – 65mm/2.56in
Powerplant: AEC 6-cylinder diesel, 97.73kW/131bhp; or AEC 6-cylinder petrol, 100kW/135bhp; or GMC diesel, 100kW/135bhp
Performance: Speed – 24kph/14.9mph
  Range – 145km/90 miles

Mark IV Light Tank

Mark IV Light Tank

Entered service: 1934
Crew: 2
Weight: 4,674kg/4.6 tons
Dimensions: Length – 3.40m/11ft 2in
   Height (over turret hatch) – 2.13m/7ft
   Width – 2.06m/6ft 9in
Armament: 1 x 7.7mm/0.303in and
   1 x 12.7mm/0.5in machine-guns
Armour: Maximum – 12mm/0.47in
Powerplant: Meadows 6-cylinder petrol,
   65.6kW/88bhp
Performance: Speed – 56kph/35mph
   Range – 201km/125 miles

LEFT: **Built in the 1930s and based on the "Indian Pattern" light tanks, this Mark IV Light Tank now resides at the Tank Museum. The principal change to the Mark III was its suspension.**

The Mark IV Light Tank was based on the Vickers experimental "Indian Pattern" vehicles of 1933, being produced the following year. It was the first light tank that used the hull as a chassis, with its automotive parts then bolted on to it. The hull was lengthened, its armour thickened and it consequently had a higher superstructure with the turret set further back than other light tanks. The Horstmann suspension was modified to dispense with the idler wheel by re-spacing the bogies, which gave the vehicle a distinctive track path. The turret itself was similar to that of the Mark III Light Tank, but certain modifications were made, with a cupola variant for those vehicles bound for service in India.

Mark V Light Tank

Mark V Light Tank

Entered service: 1935
Crew: 3
Weight: 4,217kg/4.15 tons
Dimensions: Length – 3.68m/12ft 1in
   Height (over turret hatch) – 2.21m/7ft 3in
   Width – 2.06m/6ft 9in
Armament: 1 x 7.7mm/0.303in and
   1 x 12.7mm/0.5in Vickers machine-guns
Armour: Maximum – 12mm/0.5in
Powerplant: Meadows 6-cylinder petrol, developing
   65.6kW/88bhp
Performance: Speed – 51kph/32mph
   Range – 200km/125 miles

LEFT: **This Mark V Light Tank is being inspected by a visiting German delegation during the 1930s. It was the first of the light series to have a three-man crew (two men in the turret).**

Entering service in 1935, the Mark V Light Tank had a longer hull than its predecessor in order to accommodate a turret ball-race and then a larger two-man turret – the first on a light tank – raising the crew total to three. It was armed with Vickers 7.7mm/0.303in and 12.7mm/0.5in coaxial machine-guns and had a circular commander's cupola. With its heavier weight of 4,217kg/4.15 tons, its handling and characteristics were a big improvement on earlier Marks.

However both the Mark IV and Mark V were obsolete at the start of World War II. A few remained, mostly used for training, though two chassis were used for experiments with anti-aircraft mounts in 1940.

Mark IV Heavy Tank

Designed in October 1916, the Mark IV was put into production between March and April 1917. More Mark IVs were built than any other model – a total of 1,220 – of which 205 were tank tenders with specially boosted 93.2kW/125bhp Daimler engines. The tenders were fitted with square box-like sponsons and used to carry tank supplies into battle.

The Mark IV had various improvements, including an armoured 273-litre/60-gallon petrol tank mounted outside the tank between the rear horns. This was much safer than the earlier internal tanks, which were located on either side of the driver. Sponsons were hinged so that they could be swung

TOP: **More Mark IV Heavy Tanks were built than any other model – a total of 1,220 in all. This is the Tank Museum's "HMS Excellent", which was restored to full running order in 1971 by 18 Command Workshop, REME.** ABOVE: **This Mark IV Heavy Tank bears the letters "WC" for "Wire Cutter", but is being used as an observation platform, having lost part of its right-hand track.** BELOW LEFT: **Male Tank No. 2341 bore the "Chinese Eye" on its sides as it was paid for by Mr Eu Tong Sen of the Malay States. This custom is still retained today by the tanks and other AFVs of 1 RTR.**

inside during rail journeys, instead of having to be removed and carried separately. The size of the sponsons was also reduced so that the lower edges were not so close to the ground. In both versions, the Vickers and Hotchkiss machine-guns were replaced by Lewis guns, but these proved a great disappointment and later had to be replaced with modified Hotchkiss machine-guns. Thicker steel was used in the construction of the Mark IV – 12mm/0.47in in front and on the sides, decreasing to 8mm/0.315in elsewhere. This made it bullet-proof against the German anti-tank rifle. The first Mark IVs went into action on June 7, 1917, at the Battle of Messines Ridge.

However, it would be during the Battle of Cambrai on November 20, 1917, that they really showed their prowess, many of the 476 tanks taking part being heavy Mark IVs, whose silhouette now forms an indispensable part of

both the RTR cap and arm badges, while November 20 is celebrated every year as the RTR Regimental Day.

Many of the tank crews fighting at Cambrai had been trained with the invaluable help of the Royal Navy Gunnery Training Establishment at Whale Island, Portsmouth, so Mark IV Heavy Tank No. 2324 was presented to HMS *Excellent* in recognition on May 1, 1919. Twenty years later it was restored to full serviceability and allocated to the RN defence battalion, patrolling Portsmouth during air raids, until it damaged a private car and had to be confined to barracks!

ABOVE: "Any more for the Skylark?" A crowd of footsore infantrymen cadge a lift on this Mark IV (Female), those at the rear resting their feet on the underclothing beam. BELOW: Without its weapons fitted, this Mark IV Heavy Tank is recognizable as a Female by its smaller sponsons. The steel plate was proof against German armour-piercing "K" rounds.

In 1971 it was decided to hand back the historic old tank to the Army and before doing so, 18 Command Workshop, REME at Bovington, spent three years carefully restoring it to full running order.

Mark IV Heavy Tank (Male)

Entered service: 1917
Crew: 8
Weight: 28,450kg/28 tons
Dimensions: Length – 8.03m/26ft 4in
  Height (over turret hatch) – 2.49m/8ft 2in
  Width – 3.91m/12ft 10in
Armament: Main – 2 x 6pdr (57mm/2.24in) guns
  Secondary – 4 x 7.7mm/0.303in Lewis machine-guns
Armour: Maximum – 12mm/0.47in
Powerplant: Daimler 6-cylinder petrol, developing 74.57kW/100bhp
Performance: Speed – 6kph/3.7mph
  Range – 40km/25 miles

Mark V Heavy Tank

The major step forward achieved with the Mark V, designed in August 1917 and in the hands of troops in May 1918, was that one man could drive the tank by himself. This was because it was fitted with a four-speed epicyclic gearbox designed by W. G. Wilson, replacing the change-speed gearing of earlier models. The engine was a purpose-built Ricardo, developing 111.85kW/150hp. The tank also had better observation and ventilation, while the 273 litres/60 gallons of petrol contained in armoured fuel tanks at the tail gave a radius of action of 72.4km/45 miles compared with 38.6km/24 miles of the early Marks and 40km/25 miles of the Mark IV. A total of 200 Males and 200 Females were built between December 1917 and June 1918. One device that could be fitted to the Mark IV or Mark V was the Tadpole Tail – a device which lengthened the tank by about 2.74m/9ft to improve its performance. However, this lacked both rigidity and lateral stability.

The most ideal solution came with the Mark VA, when an additional 1.83m/6ft of armour was added between the sponson opening and the epicyclic gear housing, allowing additional storage space to carry up to 25 men. As a result, the weight went up from 29,465kg/29 tons to 33,530kg/33 tons and, because the engine power was not increased, the tank was much less manoeuvrable and slower than the standard Mark V.

TOP: **The Mark V Heavy Tank, which is in immaculate running order, belonging to the Tank Museum. The major advance with the Mark V was the fact that it could be driven by one man and thus did not require secondary gearsmen to change gear.** ABOVE: **A Mark V Heavy Tank demonstrates how the underditching beam is used – attached to the tracks by chains, tracks then rotate, bringing the beam down until it can get some purchase so as to assist in egress.**

Mark V Heavy Tank No. 9199, now at the Tank Museum and still in full running order, was issued to the 8th Battalion, Tank Corps, in July 1918. They were the first battalion to receive the Mark V. Crew H 41 were the first to see action in 9199, the commander, Lt H. A. Whittenbury, writing afterwards, "8th August 1918. Commenced the attack at 8:20am preceding the infantry by about 100yds ... enemy gun flashes observed ... Drove on zig-zag course ... Both six pounders had picked up targets and were firing ... Drove down steep slope into ravine ... opened fire with both six pounders firing HE and case shot at 40yds range into trenches and dugouts. Also fired a good many rounds with front Hotchkiss and observed many casualties."

At 10:15am, after a fierce battle, H 41 returned unscathed, having expended 87 6pdr HE, 18 case shot and 1,960 Hotchkiss rounds. Whittenbury would be awarded a Military Cross for his gallant action.

The following month, with a different commander, H 41 preceeded an infantry attack on the village of Estrees and was hit by shellfire which damaged its left track, but they managed to get back to the rallying point before the track broke.

From 1918–19 No. 9199 was used for training at Bovington, then in 1921 it went to the 4th Battalion, Tank Corps at Wogret Camp near Wareham until 1925, when it returned to Bovington. During World War II it was used for towing and recovery by the Camp Workshops and the Driving and Maintenance School, then in 1949 it was donated to the Tank Museum.

ABOVE: **Mark V Heavy Tank No. 9199 at the Bovington Tank Museum, painted in its World War I colours. The white/red/white stripes on the nose were British tank recognition markings that were still being used at the start of World War II in the Western Desert.** LEFT: **This Mark V has really got itself stuck in a very deep hole and will need more than an unditching beam to free itself!** BELOW: **The Mark V* had an additional 1.82m/6ft of armour added between the sponson housing and the epicyclic gear housing. Not only did this improve its trench-crossing ability, it also gave much more storage room inside (e.g. it could carry 25 men or the equivalent weight in stores).**

Mark V Heavy Tank (Male)

Entered service: 1918
Crew: 8
Weight: 29,465kg/29 tons
Dimensions: Length – 8.03m/26.4ft in
 Height (over turret hatch) – 2.49m/8ft 2in
 Width – 3.91m/12ft 10in
Armament: Main – 2 x 6pdr (57mm/2.24in) gun
 Secondary – 4 x 7.7mm/0.303in Hotchkiss machine-guns
Armour: Maximum – 12mm/0.47in
Powerplant: Ricardo 6-cylinder petrol, 111.85kW/150hp
Performance: Speed – 7.4kph/4.6mph
 Range – 72.4km/45 miles

Mark VI Light Tank

The Mark VI Light Tank was similar to the Mark V Light Tank, except for its turret which was redesigned to allow room for a wireless. This tank was produced in a number of versions, the main two being the Mark VIA and VIB. The Mark VIA had a single return roller removed from the top of the leading bogie and attached to the hull sides, and an octagonal cupola fitted with two lookouts.

The differences in the Mark VIB were to simplify production, and included a one-piece armoured louvre over the radiator (rather than two pieces) and a plain circular commander's cupola, replacing the faceted one of the Mark VIA, fitted with glass block lookouts.

The Light Tank Mk VI series entered production in 1936, and a thousand were in service worldwide with the British Army at the outbreak of World War II. In 1940, both in Europe and North Africa, the Light Mark VI formed a major part of the British tank strength. When the British Expeditionary Force (BEF) sailed for France in 1940, this tank was to be found in all divisional cavalry regiments and in the cavalry light tank regiments of 1st Armoured Division. Unfortunately, it was widely used in roles other than that for which it was designed (reconnaissance) and suffered heavy losses when used in a front-line role, especially when confronted by the better-armed and armoured German

TOP: **The immaculately restored Mark VIB Light Tank is in full running order at the Tank Museum, Bovington. It entered production in 1936, and over a thousand were in worldwide service when war began.** ABOVE: **Equipped with flotation gear, this Mark VI Light Tank carried out successful swimming trials.**

tanks. However, the Mark VI served with distinction not only in France, but in the Western Desert, Greece, Malta, Crete and Syria (with the Australians), and took part in the siege of Tobruk.

It was, however, woefully under-armoured (10mm/0.39in maximum armour thickness) and under-gunned (just machine-guns). In fact, some of the Light Mark VIs that were rushed

ABOVE: **Speeding across the training area at Bovington, Dorset, this Mark VIB Light Tank could reach a speed of 56kph/35mph on roads.** RIGHT: **The last of the series – the Mark VIC Light Tank had its Vickers machine-guns replaced by one 7.92mm/0.312in Besa and one 15mm/0.59in Besa air-cooled machine-gun. It also had wider suspension wheels and broader tracks.** BELOW: **Good photograph of a Vickers Mark VIA Light Tank. The commander wears the badge of the 3rd The King's Own Hussars who were part of 1st (Light) Armoured Brigade.**

over to France to support the BEF did not even have their machine-guns because they were still packed in grease in their crates on board ships that had yet to arrive! No wonder the commander of 1st Armoured Division, Maj Gen Roger Evans, would later write of it as: "this travesty of an armoured division". Thus, the tank crews had just their pistols as their tanks' only offensive weapons!

Mark VIB Light Tank	
Entered service: 1937	
Crew: 2	
Weight: 5,080kg/5 tons	
Dimensions: Length – 4.01m/13ft 2in	
Height (over turret hatch) – 2.26m/7ft 5in	
Width – 2.08m/6ft 10in	
Armament: Main – 1 x 12.7mm/0.5in or	
1 x 15mm/0.59in machine-gun	
Secondary – 1 x 7.7mm/0.303in Vickers or	
1 x 7.92mm/0.312in Besa machine-gun	
Armour: Maximum – 10mm/0.394in	
Powerplant: Meadows 6-cylinder, 65.6kW/88bhp	
Performance: Speed – 56kph/34.78mph	
Range – 200km/124.2 miles	

Mark VIII Heavy Tank

Instead of just improving on existing Marks, the Mark VIII Heavy Tank was an entirely new design. The "International", as it was called, was the largest, heaviest and most powerful of all the British World War I heavy tanks. It had a Ricardo V12 (or Liberty V12) engine, producing 223.7kW/300hp at 1,250rpm. At 37,593kg/37 tons it was a good 9,144kg/9 tons heavier than the Mark I, with roughly double the power-to-weight ratio. This was to have been a joint Anglo-American venture to build in all some 4,450 tanks "to win the war in 1919", along with 2,000 Mark Xs which never reached a full design stage.

Before the war ended, the British sent one of the few Mark VIIIs they had constructed over to the USA so that they could replicate it – although the Americans decided to fit their own Liberty V12 engine in place of the British Ricardo.

However, the Armistice rapidly put paid to their grandiose ideas and, although about 100 Mark VIIIs were built by the Americans after the war, only five were ever completed by

ABOVE: **Moving the Tank Museum's International. After spending many years outside in all weathers, the Mark VIII was moved under cover into the new "George Forty Hall", together with all the other priceless World War I exhibits, during the mid-1980s.** RIGHT: **Cutaway drawing of the Mark VIII, showing its main components.**

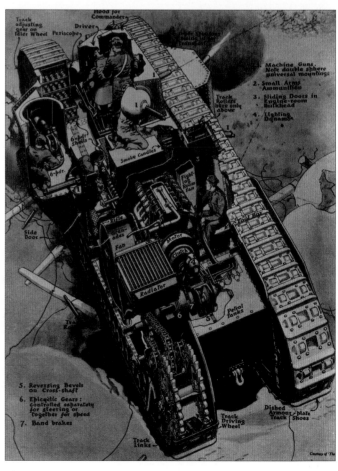

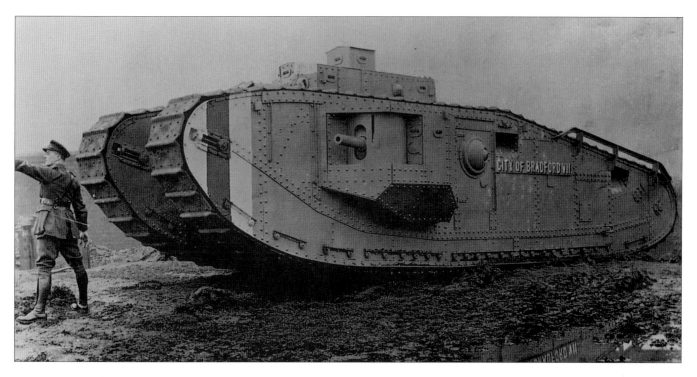

the British before the Armistice, and only three of these reached the troops. Armed with two 6pdrs, seven machine-guns, and a separate engine compartment (the first heavy tank to have one), it had great potential and would undoubtedly have been a battle-winner.

In 1940 the US Army sent some of the Mark VIIIs to Canada to help train the newly forming Canadian armoured units (they also sent a number of the Ford 6 Ton version of the Renault FT-17).

Not shown here, because it was a troop/cargo carrier rather than a tank, is the Mark IX, the very last British design of World War I to go into action. It had four large oval doors (two on each side) instead of gun sponsons, and could carry 10 tons of stores or 30 fully equipped infantrymen inside its capacious interior and thus under armour. One of its prototypes was even made amphibious by attaching large air drums to its sides, and was being tested on Armistice Day!

TOP, ABOVE AND BELOW: **This selection of all-round views of the Mark VIII give an excellent impression of the entirely new design of the International – so named because it was going to be built by Britain and the USA as a joint venture "to win the war in 1919". The Armistice put paid to that, with only some 100 of the proposed 4,500 being built. Only five were completed, and only three reached troops before the war ended.**

Mark VIII Heavy Tank

Entered service: 1918
Crew: 8
Weight: 37,593kg/37 tons
Dimensions: Length – 10.41m/34ft 2in
   Height (over turret hatch) – 3.12m/10ft 3in
   Width – 3.76m/12ft 4in
Armament: Main – 2 x 6pdr (57mm/2.24in) guns
   Secondary – 7 x 7.7mm/0.303in machine-guns
Armour: Maximum – 16mm/0.63in
Powerplant: Ricardo or Liberty V12 petrol, 223.7kW/300bhp
Performance: Speed – 9.7kph/6mph
   Range – 88km/55 miles

M1 and M2 Combat Cars

ABOVE: **A close-up of M1 Combat Cars belonging to the 1st Cavalry Regiment. Here the commanders man their pintle-mounted anti-aircraft machine-guns with air-cooled barrels.**

At the beginning of World War II, the United States had four closely related basic types of light AFV. The Infantry had Light Tanks M2A2 and M2A3, while the Cavalry, who were not allowed to have tanks, called theirs Combat Cars M1 and M2. The simplest way of telling them apart was that the light tanks had twin turrets, earning themselves the nickname of "Mae Wests" (for obvious anatomical reasons)!

The Combat Cars had single octagonal turrets with two machine-guns, one 12.7mm/0.5in and one 7.62mm/0.3in calibre, mounted coaxially. All had a second 7.62mm/0.3in machine-gun in the hull, and a third for anti-aircraft defence – the first recorded instance of this provision on any AFV.

Both the M1 and M2 had a crew of four, two in the turret and two in the hull. However, it must be said that both these vehicles were totally inadequate for operating on the modern battlefield of the time, except in a scouting role, and fortunately they never had to prove themselves in battle.

The Combat Car M2 was the first to be fitted with the distinctive trailing idler wheel, which increased the vehicle's footprint and aided traction and therefore

ABOVE LEFT: **What's in a name? These little light tanks were called Combat Cars because the US Cavalry were not allowed to have tanks!** ABOVE: **A company of M1 and M2 Combat Cars under a very special commander, Major Ernie Harmon, who would go on to become one of the US Army's star armoured battlefield commanders during World War II.**

overall performance. It also had its power plant changed from a Continental petrol engine to a Guiberson diesel radial engine. In 1940, with the formation of the American Armored Force, the need for the "Combat Car" subterfuge became unnecessary and Combat Cars M1 and M2 became known as the M1A1 and M1A2 Light Tanks.

M1 Combat Car

Entered service: 1935
Crew: 4
Weight: 8,528kg/8.39 tons
Dimensions: Length – 4.14m/13ft 7in
  Height (over turret hatch) – 2.36m/7ft 9in
  Width – 2.39m/7ft 10in
Armament: Main – 12.7mm/0.5in machine-gun
  Secondary – 3 x 7.62mm/0.3in machine-guns
Armour: Maximum – 16mm/0.63in
Powerplant: Continental W-670 7-cylinder petrol, 186.4kW/250hp
Performance: Speed – 72.4kph/45mph
  Range – 161km/100 miles

LEFT: **A "Mae West" (so called because it had twin turrets!) fords a stream during training. Note that no armament is installed.** ABOVE: **This M2A4, the very first US-built tank to arrive in the UK, is seen here being inspected by General (later Field Marshal) Alexander.**

M2 Light Tank series

As World War II approached, the Americans still had four basic types of light armoured vehicle, all of which were closely related because all had been developed from the T2 tank series. The two infantry tanks were known as the M2A2 and M2A3. The M2A2 had numerous development models with a mixture of petrol and diesel engines, modified suspensions and other features. These were all of a similar size, weight, crew and armament, and all had twin turrets. The best was probably the M2A2E3, developed in 1938, which had a modified suspension with a trailing idler.

BELOW: **An M2A2 Light Tank being driven up a loading ramp onto a rail flat car. One turret contains a 12.7mm/0.5inch machine-gun, the other a 7.62mm/0.30 inch machine-gun.**

The M2A3 was an improved version of the M2A2, and appeared during 1938. Not only did it have slightly thicker frontal armour, better engine cooling and improved engine access, but it also had a longer track base, which necessitated repositioning the bogie units. Last of the development models of the M2A3s was the M2A3E3, which had a reworked suspension with a trailing idler wheel, giving it a better cross-country performance.

The M2A4 represented the last model of the M2 Light Tank series and was perhaps the most important and best of them all. For the first time it had a main armament larger than a machine-gun, the 37mm/1.46in M5 tank gun which had an armour-piercing capability. This was housed in a single turret with an all-round

manual traverse. One hundred and three rounds were carried on board for the gun which, even though it did not have much hitting power (it could only penetrate 25.4mm/1in of armour at 914m/1,000 yards), was just coming into service as the US Army's standard anti-tank gun.

The pilot model of the M2A4 was completed at Rock Island Arsenal in early 1939. The single turret had been found to be greatly superior to the twin "Mae Wests", while the tank had thicker armour on the front and hull sides (up to 25mm/0.98in), which increased the weight up to 12,193kg/12 tons and reduced its top speed accordingly. Nevertheless, the M2A4 was undoubtedly the best of the early American light tanks and would lead directly on to the M3 light – the famous Honey.

M2A4 Light Tank

Entered service: 1940
Crew: 4
Weight: 12,193k/12 tons
Dimensions: Length – 4.45m/14ft 7in
Height (over turret hatch) – 2.52m/8ft 3in
Width – 2.54m/8ft 4in
Armament: Main – 37mm/1.46m gun
Secondary – 4 x 7.62mm/0.3in machine-guns
Armour: Maximum – 25mm/0.98in
Powerplant: Continental 7-cylinder radial, 186.6kW/250hp
Performance: Speed – 54.7kph/34mph
Range – 209km/130 miles

M3 General Lee Medium Tank and variants

The British called the standard M3 the "General Lee", after the Civil War General Robert E. Lee. Its main armament was the sponson-mounted 75mm/2.95in gun which only had a limited traverse. In the fully rotating turret on the top of the tank was a 37mm/1.46in gun and coaxial machine-gun. There were up to three more machine-guns – one in the commander's cupola and either one or two fixed machine-guns firing through the front plate (the earlier production models had two).

M3 General Grant Medium Tank

The British version of the M3 was purchased under Lend-Lease by a special Tank Commission and modified for British Army service. It differed from the General Lee in having a larger turret with a bulge at the rear to take a radio set. This meant that the operator could also act as loader for the 37mm/1.46in gun, and one crew member fewer was needed to man the "General Grant", as the British version was called (after General

RIGHT: **A British-crewed M3 Medium Grant is admired by some local boys in Tunisia. The Grant had no commander's cupola, so it was lower. It also had a larger turret with room for the radio in the bustle.**

Ulysses S. Grant). The commander's cupola was also dispensed with, thus reducing the overall height by some 101mm/4in. The General Grant made a significant impact in the Western Desert and was later used in Europe and the Far East, where it did excellent work, "bunker-bashing" and supporting infantry.

The Lee had a seven-man crew – commander, 37mm/1.46in gunner, 37mm/1.46in loader, 75mm/2.95in

ABOVE: **The American M3 Medium Tank, known to the British as the "General Lee". It was then specially modified for British service, their model being known as the "General Grant". This Lee belongs to the Budge Collection and was taking part in an Open Day at the Tank Museum, Bovington. There is no commander's cupola on this particular M3 Lee.**

gunner, 75mm/2.95in loader, radio operator and driver. In the Grant, the 37mm/1.46in loader doubled up as a radio operator.

LEFT: **On show at the Bovington Tank Museum is this General Grant, as supplied to the British. It differs from the Lee by not having a commander's cupola, and with an enlarged turret bustle in the top turret for the wireless, thus saving one crewman.**

ABOVE: **This shows a T5 Phase III Medium Tank, photographed at the Rock Island arsenal in 1938. It was the prototype of the standard M2 Medium Tank and the forerunner of the M3.**
ABOVE RIGHT: **This M3A1 is a Lee with the additional commander's cupola and a cast hull. Later production models had no side door or escape hatch in the floor.** RIGHT: **This is the M3A2, again a Lee, but with an all-welded hull.**

M3 in combat

The first M3s to see action were those sent with British Eighth Army in the Western Desert in 1942. Rommel wrote in his diary of them: "The advent of the new American tank has torn great holes in our ranks. Our entire force now stood in heavy and destructive combat with a superior enemy."

M3 Grant Canal Defence Light

When the M3 was replaced by the Sherman M4, a number of British Grants were fitted with a Canal Defence Light similar to that which had been previously installed in the Matilda CDL. The turret was removed and replaced with an armoured searchlight housing, sporting a dummy wooden gun, but also containing a machine-gun.

M3 General Grant Medium Tank

Entered service: 1941
Crew: 6 (7 on the Lee)
Weight: 27,219kg/26.7 tons
Dimensions: Length – 5.64m/18ft 6in
　　Height (over turret hatch) – 3.12m/10ft 3in
　　Width – 2.72m/8ft 11in
Armament: Main – 75mm/2.95in M2 or M3 gun
　　Secondary – 37mm/1.46in M5 or M6 cannon,
　　4 x 7.62mm/0.3in machine-guns
Armour: Maximum – 57mm/2.24in
Powerplant: Continental R-975-EC2 radial petrol,
　　253.5kW/340hp
Performance: Speed – 42kph/26mph
　　Range – 193km/120 miles

M4 Sherman Medium Tank

Of all the tanks ever built, the M4 Sherman was undoubtedly the most widely used by all the Allies, a staggering 49,234 Sherman guns tanks being produced in the USA, more than half the entire American wartime tank production and equal to the total combined wartime output of Great Britain and Germany! Add to this the vast number of variants and the figure becomes even more impressive.

The M4 Medium was the logical successor to the M3 Medium Tank Lee/Grant, and about the same time as the latter was first going into production, the Ordnance Committee directed that work should begin on its successor because they appreciated that the M3 was only a stopgap. This resulted in the construction of the Medium Tank T6 (the prototype M4) at the Aberdeen Proving Ground in early 1941. Clearly there was British and Canadian input into the design, which bore a striking resemblance to the Canadian Ram Medium Tank.

At about the same time, the Rock Island Arsenal built a second pilot model and, in September 1941, the new tank was quickly standardized, entering service on September 5, 1941, as the Medium Tank M4. Interestingly, one of the new tank factories to build the Sherman had first to be built from scratch near Detroit – in just three months from breaking earth to rolling out the first tank! Full-scale production would end in early 1944, by which time six basic models of the gun tank, designated M4 through to M4A6 (less M4A5), had been built.

The Sherman, as it was soon called, would first see active service with the British 8th Army in North Africa in October 1942. Two months later, it was first used in action by American troops in Tunisia in early December 1942. The M4 was an extremely robust and reliable tank which used the same basic chassis as the M3 Medium; it therefore had vertical volute spring suspension, a rear engine and front drive. There were six

TOP: **The Canadian-built "Grizzly I" is virtually identical to the M4 Sherman, apart from having different drive sprockets and tracks. Nearly 50,000 Shermans were built during World War II.** ABOVE: **This immaculate Sherman M4A1E8 (76) is privately owned by the Indiana Military Museum in Vincennes, USA. The "Easy Eight" had an improved suspension and mounted the 76mm/2.99in gun.**

basic Marks of Sherman produced in three main tank factories in the USA. Initially armed with the 75mm/2.95in gun, there were also two models with close-support 105mm/4.13in howitzers, four with the improved 76mm/2.99in gun and "Wet" stowage (ammunition in water-protected racks below the turret) and, finally, a heavily armoured assault version nicknamed "Jumbo".

The main change from the M3 Medium was the fact that Sherman had a fully rotating turret instead of its main gun being in a side sponson. Not only did this give the gun all-round traverse, but also meant that the crew could be reduced to five: three in the turret (commander, gunner and loader/operator) and two in the hull (driver and co-driver/hull gunner). The Sherman was a very user-friendly AFV, and well able to deal with most terrain. Unfortunately, however, it had a tendency to catch fire easily when struck by enemy shells – the Allies nicknamed it the "Ronson Lighter" because it was guaranteed to light first time, while the Germans called it the "Tommy Cooker" – hence the wet stowage arrangement when the tank was re-gunned, plus the addition of appliqué armour and even sandbags, to increase protection. A continuing shortage of the initial R-975 Continental air-cooled radial aircraft engine led to the forced adoption of no fewer than four further engines, both petrol and diesel, including the remarkable Chrysler multi-bank 30-cylinder petrol engine.

The Sherman was adapted to perform a wide range of specialized tasks with conversion to swimming tanks (the addition of a flotation screen in the highly secret Sherman DD swimming tank, used most effectively during the D-Day landings), engineer/dozer vehicles, tank recovery vehicles, beach recovery vehicles, armoured personnel carriers, assault bridge-carriers, flamethrower tanks, mine-clearing tanks (including flails, rollers and explosives – even a mine-resistant vehicle), self-propelled guns, howitzer, anti-aircraft gun and rocket platforms, and as tank destroyers to name but a few! The British had their own designations for the wide range of variants, which included the most effective Sherman to see wartime action – the Firefly, which mounted a highly effective 17pdr gun.

The Sherman's versatility was immense and did not end when war finished. After 1945, the Sherman was used by many armies worldwide, especially by the Israelis who, in their own inimitable way, adapted the tank for a wide variety of uses and prolonged its life as a gun tank by refitting with improved engine, main armament and armour.

ABOVE: **This massive rocket array, mounted on top of a sandbagged Sherman, was known as the Rocket Launcher T 34 "Calliope". It consisted of 60 x 117mm/4.6in rocket tubes and saw limited combat during World War II.**
BELOW: **US Marines hitch a ride. Tank-borne infantry moving up to occupy Ghuta on Okinawa. There are at least 18 "passengers" hitching a ride, which is fine until the tank has to use its guns.**

RIGHT: **A Sherman fords a canal near Nancy, France, September 12, 1944. Note the foliage cut as camouflage to break up the tank's unmistakable outline, and also the heavy 12.7mm/0.5in Browning Heavy AA machine-gun on top of the turret.**

M4 Sherman Medium Tank (mid-production)

Entered service: 1941
Crew: 5
Weight: 30,339kg/29.86 tons
Dimensions: Length – 5.88m/19ft 4in
  Height (over turret hatch) – 2.74m/ 9ft
  Width – 2.68m/8ft 10in
Armament: Main – 75mm/2.95in M3 gun
  Secondary – 2 x 7.62in/0.3in and
  1 x 12.7mm/0.5in AA (anti-aircraft) machine-guns
Armour: Maximum – 75mm/2.95in
Powerplant: Continental R-975C1 Petrol, 9-cylinder
  4-cycle radial, 298.5kW/400hp
Performance: Speed – 39kph/24.2mph
  Range – 192km/119.3 miles

M3 Light Tank series

The M2A4 was effectively a prototype for the next light tank, the M3, which had many of its features, such as the single rotating seven-sided turret and 37mm/1.46in gun. The M3 was designed in the spring of 1940, the main requirement being for thicker armour which increased the weight to 12,904kg/ 12.7 tons combat-loaded, and required stronger suspension. Nicknamed the Honey, the M3 first saw action with the British Army in the Western Desert, where it was officially known as the Stuart I in British Army nomenclature.

The first production models of the M3 were of a riveted construction, but they were soon followed in the series with increasing proportions with welded armour. There were also petrol and diesel engine variants. With the M3A1, the side sponson machine-guns were soon removed because they could not be properly aimed and must have wasted a great deal of ammunition. There was also now no commander's cupola; instead the turret had a basket and a power traverse.

The final model of the M3 series was the M3A3 (Stuart V in British parlance). It had a larger turret and no side sponsons, which created space for extra fuel tanks and ammunition stowage. An experimental model, which had twin Cadillac engines, a turret basket and other modifications, was the prototype for the M5 Light Tank.

ABOVE: **The M3A1 Light Tank was so well liked by its crews that they called it the Honey when it first came into British service in the Western Desert in 1941. Their experience led to modifications such as the removal of the two sponson machine-guns.**

M3A1 Light Tank Stuart Mk III

Entered service: 1940
Crew: 4
Weight: 12,904kg/12.7 tons
Dimensions: Length – 4.52m/14ft 10in
    Height (over turret hatch) – 2.31m/7ft 7in
    Width – 2.24m/7ft 4in
Armament: Main – 37mm/1.46in M6 gun
    Secondary – 3 x 7.62mm/0.3in machine-guns
Armour: Maximum – 51mm/2.01in
Powerplant: Continental W-670, 7-cylinder radial petrol, 186.4kW/250hp
Performance: Speed – 58kph/36mph
    Range – 113km/70 miles

M5 Light Tank

ABOVE: **The end of the Honey tank line was the M5 that came off the assembly line in March 1942. This beautifully restored M5A1 belongs to Judge Jim Osborne of the Indiana Military Museum, Vincennes, Indiana.**

The end of the Honey line was the M5 – they missed out the "M4" designation so as not to cause confusion with the M4 Sherman. It shared the same weapon systems as the M3, and first came off the assembly line in March 1942, with the British calling it the Stuart VI. It weighed 14,936kg/14.7 tons and was powered by two Cadillac engines, giving the vehicle a top speed of 60kph/37mph.

M5 Light Tank

Entered service: 1942
Crew: 4
Weight: 14,936kg/14.7 tons
Dimensions: Length – 4.34m/14ft 3in
    Height (over turret hatch) – 2.31m/7ft 7in
    Width – 2.26m/7ft 5in
Armament: Main – 37mm/1.46in M6 gun
    Secondary – 3 x 7.62mm/0.3in machine-guns
Armour: Maximum – 64mm/2.52in
Powerplant: 2 x Cadillac Series 42 V8, each developing 82kW/110hp
Performance: Speed – 60kph/37mph
    Range – 161km/100 miles

M6 Heavy Tank

Until the start of World War II the USA had shown little interest in heavy tanks, one major reason being the difficulty of transporting them, especially overseas. However, the success of German armour and the obvious vulnerability and lack of firepower of the standard light and medium tanks led to a recommendation to develop a heavy tank in the 50,800kg/50-ton class.

Designed in 1940, the M6 Heavy Tank weighed almost 45 tons and was armed with a 76.2mm/3in main gun, plus a 37mm/1.46in gun mounted coaxially, and a total of four machine-guns (two 12.7mm/0.5in and two 7.62mm/0.3in). Its armour was up to 133mm/5.24in thick and it had a top speed of 35kph/22mph. When it appeared in 1942 it was the most powerful tank in the world.

However, the Armored Force were not impressed with the new tank and, after testing, concluded that it was too heavy, did not have a large enough main armament and suffered from transmission problems. Some 40 vehicles were built, but they were only ever used for trial purposes.

LEFT: **This M6A2 Heavy Tank weighed 45,316kg/44.6 tons and was armed with a 76.2mm/3in gun. Originally designed as the heavy counterpart to the M3/M4 Mediums, only 40 were ever built of all models, and it never saw operational service.**

M6 Heavy Tank

Entered service: 1942
Crew: 5
Weight: 45,316kg/44.6 tons
Dimensions: Length – 8.43m/27ft 8in
   Height (over turret hatch) – 3.23m/10ft 7in
   Width – 3.23m/10ft 7in
Armament: Main – 1 x 76.2mm/3in gun and
   1 x 37mm/1.46in gun
   Secondary – 2 x 12.7mm/0.5in and
   2 x 7.62mm/0.3in machine-guns
Armour: Maximum – 133mm/5.24in
Powerplant: Wright Whirlwind G-200 9-cylinder
   radial, 690kW/925hp
Performance: Speed – 35kph/22mph
   Range – 161km/100 miles

M26 Pershing Heavy Tank

The M26 Pershing was developed from the T26 series – the outcome of reclassifying the T25 as a heavy tank in June 1944. Weighing about 41 tons, with a 90mm/3.54in main gun, 102.6mm/4in armour on the front of the turret and a top speed of 48kph/30mph, the new tank was just about a match for the German Tiger I, produced some years

earlier. There were also attempts to further upgrade the main armament, such as the T15E1 gun, and to increase the armour by welding extra plates on the front of the hull. It was the most powerful American tank to see combat in World War II. Wartime production of the M26 totalled 1,436. It went on to see service in the Korean War.

M26 Pershing Heavy Tank

Entered service: 1944
Crew: 5
Weight: 41,861kg/41.2 tons
Dimensions: Length – 8.61m/28ft 3in
   Height (over turret hatch) – 2.77m/9ft 1in
   Width – 3.51m/11ft 6in
Armament: Main – 90mm/3.54in M3 gun
   Secondary – 1 x 12.7mm/0.5in and
   2 x 7.62mm/0.31in machine-guns
Armour: Maximum – 102.6mm/4in
Powerplant: Ford GAF, 373kW/500hp
Performance: Speed – 48kph/30mph
   Range – 161km/100 miles

LEFT: **The M26 Pershing was the most powerful and best all-round American tank of World War II, but was only standardized and entered service in 1944. Its 90mm/3.54in main gun was almost on a par with the German 8.8cm/3.46in. It went on to do well following World War II, seeing service in the Korean War (1950–53).**

M10 Wolverine Tank Destroyer

This was the first really successful tank destroyer in the US Army. With a five-sided open topped turret it had a crew of five, a 76mm/2.99in main gun and could carry 54 rounds of ammunition. It had a top speed of 48kph/30mph and weighed 29,059kg/28.6 tons – with a counterweight needed to the rear of the turret to balance the gun. A total of 5,000 M10s were built between September 1942 and December 1943, initially using the Lee/Grant M3 standard chassis, then the M4 Sherman chassis.

ABOVE: **The M10 Wolverine was a well-liked and effective American tank destroyer, armed with a 76mm/2.99in M7 gun. The M10 was based on the M3 medium chassis, and the M10A1 was based on the M4 Sherman.**

M10 Achilles Tank Destroyer
The British up-gunned some of the M10s they received from America by fitting their highly lethal 17pdr. The result was known as "Achilles", with a similar open-topped turret to Wolverine and its counterweight situated at the end of the gun barrel

just behind the muzzle brake. Fast and hard-hitting, it was one of the best Allied tank killers of World War II.

M10 Wolverine TD	
Entered service: 1942	
Crew: 5	
Weight: 29,059kg/28.6 tons	
Dimensions: Length – 5.82m/19ft 1in	
Height (over turret hatch) – 2.49m/8ft 2in	
Width – 3.05m/10ft	
Armament: Main – 76mm/2.99in M7 gun	
Secondary – 12.7mm/0.5in machine-gun	
Armour: Maximum – 37mm/1.46in	
Powerplant: 2 x GMS6-71 diesel	
Performance: Speed 48kph/30mph	
Range – 322km/200 miles	

LEFT: **Most effective of the M10s was the British conversion, known as "Achilles", which mounted the Ordnance quick-firing 17pdr Mark 5 in place of the 76mm/2.99in gun. This was the same gun as mounted on the Sherman Firefly and the Challenger A30.**

M18 Hellcat Tank Destroyer

The Hellcat was also very fast, with a top speed of 80–89kph/50–55mph. Its lower silhouette from a redesigned turret and good cross-country performance made it liked by its crews and an excellent hit-and-run hunter-killer. Similar to the Wolverine, it mounted a 76mm/2.99in main gun and a 12.7mm/0.5in machine-gun for close defence.

LEFT: The M18 Hellcat was well liked by its crews and it knocked out many enemy AFVs in north-west Europe and Italy, where it was widely used. It was light (18,187kg/17.9 tons) and fast, and it carried a lethal punch with its 76mm/2.99in M1 gun. It also had an excellent cross-country performance and a good turn of speed. The 76mm/2.99in gun (as fitted in later Shermans) had a maximum range of 14,721m/16,100yds and used APCBC/HE-T.

M18 Hellcat TD

Entered service: 1943
Crew: 5
Weight: 18,187kg/17.9 tons
Dimensions: Length – 6.66m/21ft 10in
  Height (over turret hatch) – 2.57m/8ft 5in
  Width – 2.97m/9ft 9in
Armament: Main – 76mm/2.99in M1 gun
  Secondary – 12.7mm/0.5in machine-gun
Armour: Maximum – 12mm/0.47in
Powerplant: Continental R-975, 9-cylinder radial, 298.5kW/400hp
Performance: Speed – 89kph/55mph
  Range – 241km/150 miles

M36 Gun Motor Carriage

Most effective of all American tank destroyers was the M36, which mounted a 90mm/3.54in main gun that was the most powerful on the battlefield to date. The only problem was the weight of the new gun which necessitated the creation of a new rounded turret. Standardized in July 1944, the first of these new TDs arrived in Europe in August 1944 and were immediately in action.

Demand for the M36 Gun Motor Carriage increased enormously after the battles in Normandy which had shown that this was the best US weapon to deal with enemy tanks.

M36 Gun Motor Carriage

Entered service: 1944
Crew: 5
Weight: 28,145kg/27.7 tons
Dimensions: Length – 6.15m/20ft 2in
  Height (over turret hatch) – 2.72m/8ft 11 in
  Width – 3.05m/10ft
Armament: Main – 90mm/3.54in M3 gun
  Secondary – 12.7mm/0.5in machine-gun
Armour: Maximum – 50mm/1.97in
Powerplant: Ford GAA V8, 373kW/500hp
Performance: Speed – 48kph/30mph
  Range – 241km/150 miles

RIGHT: The M36 Gun Motor Carriage mounted a 90mm/3.54in gun in an attempt to be able to knock out the large, better-armed enemy tanks such as Tiger and Panther. Over 1,500 were built and reached north-west Europe in September 1944.

M22 Locust Light Tank

LEFT: **Out of a total of just over 800 Locusts, the British took delivery of several hundred, issuing them to the 6th Airborne Armoured Reconnaissance Regiment to supplement the Tetrarchs carried in Hamilcar gliders. They saw action during the Rhine Crossing in March 1945. One M22 was rebuilt as the T10 Light Tractor (airborne) designed to carry five men, but this project was suspended in 1943.**

M22 Locust Light Tank

Entered service: 1941
Crew: 3
Weight: 7,417kg/7.3 tons
Dimensions: Length – 3.94m/12ft 11in
   Height (over turret hatch) – 1.73m/5ft 8in
   Width – 2.24m/7ft 4in
Armament: Main – 37mm/1.46in M6 gun
   Secondary – 7.62mm/0.3in machine-gun
Armour: Maximum – 25mm/0.98in
Powerplant: Lycoming 0-435T 6-cylinder radial, 121kW/162hp
Performance: Speed – 64kph/40mph
   Range – 217km/135 miles

Designed as an airborne tank in 1941 by the charismatic J. Walter Christie, the M22 Locust only saw operational service with the British Army, who deployed it in small numbers with the 6th Airborne Reconnaissance Regiment during the Rhine Crossing. The Locust was transported by a Hamilcar glider, which had been specially designed to carry the British light airborne tank, the Tetrarch. The Locust was armed with a 37mm/1.46in gun and a coaxial machine-gun but it really proved too light to be of any great consequence on the battlefield.

M24 Chaffee Light Tank

Undoubtedly the best light tank of World War II was the M24 Chaffee, named after General Adna Chaffee, the "Father of the US Armored Force". It was a five-man tank, but was normally manned by only four men due to manpower shortages. The main armament was a powerful 75mm/2.95in gun which had been adapted from the heavy aircraft cannon as used in the B-25G Mitchell bomber. Although no match for the bigger German tanks, the M24 was remarkably effective against smaller targets. It remained the standard US light tank long after the end of the war and was modified to anti-aircraft and mortar carriage variants. The M24 Chaffee also saw service in Korea in the 1950s.

M24 Chaffee Light Tank

Entered service: 1944
Crew: 4 or 5
Weight: 18,289kg/18 tons
Dimensions: Length – 5.49m/18ft
   Height (over turret hatch) – 2.46m/8ft 1in
   Width – 2.95m/9ft 8in
Armament: Main – 75mm/2.95in M6 gun
   Secondary – 1 x 12.7mm/0.5in and
   2 x 7.62mm/0.3in machine-guns
Armour: Maximum – 38mm/1.5in
Powerplant: 2 x Cadillac 44T24 V8, each developing 82kW/110hp
Performance: Speed – 55kph/34mph
   Range – 282km/175 miles

LEFT: **Named after the "Father" of the Armored Force, General Adna R. Chaffee, the M24 was not a great success as a gun tank either during World War II or in the early part of the Korean War, when it was outgunned by the North Korean T-34/85. Variants included the M19 GMC, an AA tank mounting twin 40mm/1.58in guns, and the M41 HMC, mounting a 155mm/6.1in M1 howitzer.**

M1931 Christie

Tank development between the wars owed much to the brilliant, but unpredictable American engineer J. Walter Christie, who was the advocate of light, fast tanks that could move cross country at amazing speeds on his unique suspension system, or equally well without their tracks, just on their road wheels. His designs proved very influential in the burgeoning world of armour design beyond his native country, but closer to home in the USA he was regarded as a difficult man to deal with.

Based on his M1928 vehicle, the M1931 was modified to include a turret as well as various automotive improvements so that it was reputed to have had a top speed on its tracks of 74kph/46mph, while on its wheels on roads it could supposedly reach 113kph/70mph.

Although the US Army did not adopt his designs to a significant extent, other countries showed far more interest. Two of these tanks were purchased by the Russians and became the models for the BT series, while in the UK it was to influence British Cruiser tank development.

LEFT: **This is another of Christie's modern, streamlined tanks – the M1936 Airborne tank. Christie and his son are inside. Despite lack of interest in the USA, his revolutionary suspension was adopted by the British, the Poles and, most importantly, by the Soviet Union in their BT series.**

TOP: **Designed by the brilliant but irascible J. Walter Christie, the T3 Medium Tank was also called the Convertible and the 1928 Tank. It led on to the M1931 Medium Tank, which had a turret with a 37mm/1.46in gun.**
ABOVE: **The M1931 tank could run on its tracks, as seen here, or on its wheels.**

M1931 Christie

Entered service: 1931 (prototype only)
Crew: 2
Weight: 10,668kg/10.5 tons
Dimensions: Length – 5.43m/17ft 10in
    Height (over turret hatch) – 2.21m/7ft 3in
    Width – 2.24m/7ft 4in
Armament: Main – 37mm/1.46in gun
    Secondary – 7.62mm/0.3in machine-gun
Armour: Maximum – 16mm/0.63in
Powerplant: Liberty, 12-cylinder petrol, 252kW/338hp
Performance: Speed – 64kph/40mph (tracks), 113kph/70mph (wheels)
    Range – 274km/170 miles

Neubaufahrzeuge V and VI

Tank production developed very rapidly in pre-World War II Nazi Germany. In addition to light and medium tanks, some interest was also shown in designing a heavy tank to follow on from the Grosstraktor. This new vehicle was simply called Neubaufahrzeuge (NbFz)

(New Construction Vehicle) and weighed about 24,385kg/24 tons. Five prototypes were built by Krupp and Rheinmetall, the former building the Model A, armed with coaxial 7.5cm/2.95in and 3.7cm/1.46in

guns, and the latter the Model B, mounting a 10.5cm/4.13in howitzer and a 3.7cm/1.46in gun. Both Models also had a second subsidiary turret in front of the main one, mounting two coaxial 7.62mm/0.3in machine-guns.

Ordered in 1934–35, the tanks were originally designated PzKpfw V and VI, but, as neither was put into production, these designations were passed on to the Panther and Tiger tanks. The prototype NbFzs were initially located at the tank training school at Putlos until early in 1940, when three were used in Norway. One was destroyed there and the other two returned to Germany towards the end of that year, where they returned to the panzer training school to be used as parade ornaments in the camp.

ABOVE AND BELOW LEFT: **As a direct result of the experience gained from the *Grosstraktor* (cover name for a heavy tank secretly produced in the late 1920s), Krupp and Rheinmetall were each asked to produce prototype heavy tanks *Neubaufahrzeuge* (New Construction Vehicle) Model A (NbFz VI) and Model B (NbFz V) respectively. Both were multi-turreted. Three were sent to Oslo, Norway, in April 1940 and saw action there, one being destroyed and the other two returning to Germany.**

Neubaufahrzeuge V/VI

Entered service: 1934
Crew: 6
Weight: 24,385kg/24 tons
Dimensions: Length – 7.32m/24ft
   Height (over turret hatch) – 2.72m/8ft 11in
   Width – 3.05m/10ft
Armament: Main – 7.5cm/2.95in gun or 10.5cm/4.13in howitzer and 1 x 3.7cm/1.46in coaxial gun
   Secondary – 3 x 7.92mm/0.312in machine-guns (2 x coaxial in subsidiary turret)
Armour: Maximum – 70mm/2.76in
Powerplant: 6-cylinder petrol, 372.9kW/500hp
Performance: Speed – 35.4kph/22mph
   Range – 140km/87 miles

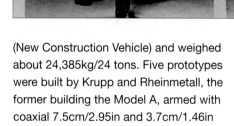

PzKpfw Maus Super-Heavy Tank

Hitler's obsession with heavy tanks reached its zenith with the production of the super-heavies, of which only two models were actually ever built – Maus and the E-100 – although a number of others were talked about and some even reached the design stage. Clearly certain influential members of the German armaments industry shared Hitler's enthusiasm for super-heavy tanks, initially anyway, and foremost among them was Dr Porsche.

What is clear is that the time and energy spent on designing and producing these behemoths wasted a vast amount of precious design and production effort, which Germany could ill afford to spare. Guderian described the Maus as "this gigantic offspring of the fantasy of Hitler and his advisers" which originally started life under the more appropriate codename of Mammut (Mammoth).

The heaviest tank ever built, Maus weighed an incredible 191,000kg/188 tons – too heavy to cross any bridge or move anywhere off level ground on its own. Only one Maus was completed to the stage where it had a turret and armament, consisting of one 12.8cm/5.04in L/55 gun and one coaxial 7.5cm/2.95in L/36.5 gun. It is now in the Russian Tank Museum.

ABOVE AND BELOW LEFT: **Super-Heavy German Tank, Maus, which at 191,000kg/188 tons was the largest and heaviest tank ever built during World War II. It was designed to out-gun and outperform all Allied AFVs. With a 12.8cm/5.04in gun and immensely thick frontal armour, two prototypes were constructed in late 1943, but although five more were ordered, they were never completed. Maus did at least have its turret fitted, unlike E100. The tank is crammed with complicated machinery so it would have been difficult to maintain. It was intended to be submersible to a depth of 8m/26ft!**

PzKpfw Maus Super-Heavy Tank

Entered service: 1945 (prototype only)
Crew: 5
Weight: Approximately 191,000kg/188 tons
Dimensions: Length – 10.09m/33ft 1in
    Height (over turret hatch) – 3.66m/12ft
    Width – 3.67m/12ft 0.5in
Armament: Main – 12.8cm/5.04in and
    7.5cm/2.95in coaxial gun
    Secondary – 7.92mm/0.312in machine-gun
Armour: Maximum – 200mm/7.87in
Powerplant: Mercedes-Benz MB509 V12 petrol,
    783kW/1,080hp
Performance: Speed – 20kph/12.4mph
    Range – 186km/115.6 miles

PzKpfw I Light Tank

The PzKpfw I Ausf A was the first German tank to go into mass production. It had the same hull and suspension as its predecessor, the PzKpfw I Ausf A *Ohne Aufbau* (literally "without turret") which had been produced without a turret and weapon system to bypass the Treaty of Versailles that prevented Germany from building tanks. Weighing just over 5 tons, with a crew of two and mounting two 7.92mm/ 0.312in machine-guns, it was soon outclassed on the battlefield and was withdrawn from active service in 1941. The Ausf B had a slightly longer chassis than the Ausf A (just under 0.5m/8in longer) and a more powerful engine.

The modification increased its weight to 5,893kg/5.8 tons. It was also phased out of service in 1941.

There was also a command version of the PzKpfw I, which was used at company, battalion, regimental and brigade level in the headquarters of panzer units from the mid-1930s up to the early war years. A radio transmitter was included in addition to the radio receiver normally only fitted in the PzKpfw I. The superstructure had to be raised in height to make room for the radio and its operator.

Some versions of the Ausf B had an odd-looking cable-operated arm which could drop a demolition charge over the

ABOVE: **The PzKpfw I Ausf B was the second production model and entered service in 1935, being slightly longer than the Ausf A. It was armed with two machine-guns.** BELOW LEFT: **The Tank Museum's Kleinerbefelswagen I, the command version of the PzKpfw IB. It has a fixed turret and was for use by unit commanders.**

rear end of the tank. This could be placed near obstacles and then set off remotely.

The final development of the PzKpfw I was a 21,337kg/21-ton infantry assault tank, which had very thick armour. Thirty were built in 1942, and a few were taken to Russia for combat testing. However, as a result of these tests, further orders were cancelled.

PzKpfw I Ausf B Light Tank	

Entered service: 1934
Crew: 2
Weight: 5,893kg/5.8 tons
Dimensions: Length – 4.42m/14ft 6in
    Height (over turret hatch) – 1.72m/5ft 8in
    Width – 2.06m/6ft 9in
Armament: Main – 2 x 7.92mm/0.312in machine-guns
Armour: Maximum – 13mm/0.51in
Powerplant: Maybach NL38TR, 6-cylinder petrol, 74.5kW/100hp
Performance: Speed – 40kph/24.9mph
    Range – 153km/95.1 miles

PzKpfw II Light Tank

The next model in the German light tank family was the PzKpfw II, weighing nearly 10 tons, with a crew of three, mounting a 2cm/0.79in cannon capable of firing both high-explosive and armour-piercing ammunition, along with a coaxial MG34 machine-gun. First manufactured in 1936, it underwent an initial development cycle of three versions – A, B and C, by which time the suspension had changed from one very similar to the PzKpfw I to five independently sprung, larger roadwheels and four top rollers. The A version is distinguishable from later models by the periscope on the turret top placed centrally behind the guns. With the B and C models only minor variations were made, which included extra bolted-on armour plate, improvements in vision devices and the addition of a turret cupola.

The PzKpfw II series then continued up to the Ausf L, with its armament remaining the same but with constant changes to its chassis, superstructure and automotive systems, as well as increases in armour thickness. PzKpfw IIs

saw action in all theatres and were later modified into a number of variants, including having the turret removed to become an artillery and ammunition "Schlepper". There was also the "Flamingo" flamethrower variant, which had two flamethrowers mounted on the front corners of the tank's superstructure.

The final model of this series was the Panzerspahwagen II Light Recce tank, called the *Luchs* (Lynx) and was

ABOVE: **PzKpfw II Ausf F. This was the final model of the normal PzKpfw II series. The major difference was that the hull was made from one flat 35mm/1.38in plate.**

designed and developed as a reconnaissance tank. It had a crew of four and weighed 13,208kg/13 tons. Its main armament was a 2cm/0.79in KwK38 gun, with a coaxially mounted MG34. About 100 were built in late 1943 and saw service in both Russia and Europe.

BELOW: **PzKpfw II Ausf L was also known as the *Luchs*. It was a light reconnaissance tank with a crew of four and weighed 13,208kg/13 tons. This one is in the Tank Museum, Bovington.**

PzKpfw II Ausf F Light Tank

Entered service: 1935 (Ausf A), 1941 (Ausf F)
Crew: 3
Weight: 9,650kg/9.5 tons
Dimensions: Length – 4.81m/15ft 9in
    Height (over turret hatch) – 2.15m/7ft 0.5in
    Width – 2.28m/7ft 8in
Armament: Main – 2cm/0.79in cannon
    Secondary – 7.92mm/0.315in machine-gun
Armour: Maximum – 35mm/1.38in
Powerplant: Maybach HL62TR, 6-cylinder petrol, 104.4kW/140hp
Performance: Speed – 40kph/24.9mph
    Range – 200km/124.3 miles

PzKpfw III Medium Tank

The backbone of the German Panzer Divisions was their medium tanks in the 15,240–20,320kg/15–20-ton range. Tracing its original development as far back as 1935, the PzKpfw III was a vital tank produced up until 1943. There were versions ranging from Ausf A–N (minus I and K), but with other variants including flamethrower, submersible, various command versions, and a turret-less ammunition carrier. The chassis was also the foundation of the StuG assault-gun series.

The early models mounted a KwK 3.7cm/1.46in gun, plus twin machine-guns in the turret and a third in the hull, manned by the radio operator. Ausf As were issued first in 1937, but withdrawn from service in early 1940 because their armour thickness, at only 15mm/0.59in, was found to be inadequate. By the time of the Ausf E, the tank still mounted the same armament, but its armour was now up to 30mm/1.18in and its weight had increased accordingly to over 19 tons.

The first model to mount the new KwK 5cm/1.97in gun (necessitating a turret redesign) was the Ausf F. First ordered in 1939, it saw service in Poland and France, when it was quickly realized that more armour and bigger guns were needed. The problem with the PzKpfw III was that it could not accept a gun larger than 5cm/1.97in because of the restrictive size of the turret ring. Six hundred Ausf G models were produced from April 1940 onwards, with their weight now just over 20,320kg/ 20 tons.

The Ausf L mounted the 5cm/1.97in KwK39 L/60 gun and once again had thicker armour on the front of the turret, now 57mm/2.24in. Ausf M came fitted with *Schürzen* (skirts) to protect from HEAT (High-Explosive Anti-Tank) weapons such as the bazooka and the PIAT.

TOP: **The Tank Museum's PzKpfw III Ausf L, which mounts a long-barrelled 5cm/1.97in KwK39 L/60 gun, the second model to do so. The Ausf L first saw action in USSR in 1942.** LEFT: **The Tank Museum's PzKpfw III going through its paces during a Tankfest. As can be seen, it is still in excellent running order.**

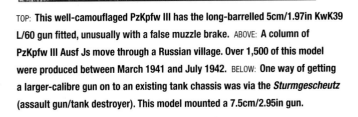

Variants included: a specially designed artillery OP tank (*Artillerie Panzerbeobachtungwagen*) to enable the Forward Observation Officer to accompany a panzer formation (the turret space normally taken up by the main armament being replaced by an artillery plotting board and extra radios); a command tank (*Panzerbefelswagen*); an armoured recovery vehicle (*Bergepanzer III*); a supply carrier (*Schlepper III*); and an engineer vehicle (*Pionerpanzer*). However, more remarkable was the *Tauchpanzer* (literally "diving tank") which was completely waterproofed so that it could operate at depths of 15m/50ft and remain submerged for up to 20 minutes. Designed for use in 1940 for the aborted invasion of England, they were later used to great effect for the crossing of the River Bug on June 22, 1941, at the start of the invasion of Russia.

TOP: **This well-camouflaged PzKpfw III has the long-barrelled 5cm/1.97in KwK39 L/60 gun fitted, unusually with a false muzzle brake.** ABOVE: **A column of PzKpfw III Ausf Js move through a Russian village. Over 1,500 of this model were produced between March 1941 and July 1942.** BELOW: **One way of getting a larger-calibre gun on to an existing tank chassis was via the *Sturmgescheutz* (assault gun/tank destroyer). This model mounted a 7.5cm/2.95in gun.**

PzKpfw III Ausf F Medium Tank

Entered service: 1937
Crew: 5
Weight: 19,500kg/19.2 tons
Dimensions: Length – 5.38m/17ft 8in
    Height (over turret hatch) – 2.45m/8ft 0.5in
    Width – 2.91m/9ft 7in
Armament: Main – 3.7cm/1.46in KwK gun (early models)
    Secondary – 2 x 7.92mm/0.312in machine-guns
Armour: Maximum – 30mm/1.18in
Powerplant: Maybach HL120 TRM, V12 petrol,
    223.7kW/300hp
Performance: Speed – 40kph/24.9mph
    Range – 165km/102.5 miles

PzKpfw IV Medium Tank

Undoubtedly the best German medium tank was the PzKpfw IV, and it was the only German battle tank to remain in production throughout World War II, being constantly up-armoured and up-gunned. The PzKpfw IV was a well-made robust tank with a satisfactory cross-country performance and a large turret ring that enabled it to take more powerful guns.

The early models mounted a 7.5cm/2.95in L/24 low-velocity, short-barrelled gun in its role as an infantry support tank. Versions Ausf A–E had increased armour and therefore increased weight and the hull machine-gun, omitted on both the Ausf B and C, was again fitted from the Ausf D onwards.

In 1941 plans were laid to improve the firepower of PzKpfw IV by fitting a long-barrelled 7.5cm/2.95in gun. The Ausf F was the first to be so fitted, and stowage arrangements had to be modified to accept the larger rounds. When it first appeared in mid-1942, it was more than a match for any of the contemporary Allied tanks

The Ausf G was very like the Ausf F, with minor variations, including thicker side armour. More of the Ausf H was produced than any other model and had better transmission, thicker armour and a new idler. It was the penultimate model in the PzKpfw IV range.

Last of the line was the Ausf J, which weighed 25,401kg/ 25 tons, had a range of over 300km/186 miles and a top speed of 38kph/23.6mph. It was also fitted with *Schürzen* (skirts) to

TOP: **The Tank Museum's PzKpfw IV which, together with the PzKpfw III, was the backbone of the *Panzerwaffe*, remaining in quantity production from 1937 to 1945.** ABOVE: **A striking photograph of a PzKpfw IV Ausf C that appeared in *SIGNAL*, the German propaganda magazine.**

protect against HEAT (High-Explosive Anti-Tank) weapons and had extra "stand-off" armour around the turret. Its long-barrelled 7.5cm/2.95in gun had an excellent performance against enemy armour.

LEFT: **Early model PzKpfw IVs break through a wall into woodland during training prior to the invasion of the Low Countries in 1940.** BELOW LEFT: **A column of PzKpfw IV Ausf Hs make their way up to the Orel battle front in August 1943. Note the add-on "stand-off" armour around the turret to guard against bazooka-type weapons (also side plates to similarly protect the suspension).** BELOW: **These GIs of 35th US Infantry Division make their way carefully in this ruined town, skirting a knocked-out and abandoned PzKpfw IV.** BOTTOM: **An early model PzKpfw IV armed with the short-barrelled support 7.5cm/ 2.95in KwK37 L/24 gun waits to engage an enemy strongpoint while a Russian soldier crawls to safety – but was it staged for propaganda purposes?**

Like the PzKpfw III, the IV also had many variants in addition to the more obvious ones. There was a range of assault gun/ tank destroyers, including StuG IV, Jagdpanzer IV, Panzer IV 70(V) and Panzer IV 70(A), on up to *Hornisse* which mounted an 8.8cm/3.46in anti-tank gun. Then there was a range of AA guns (*Flakpanzer*) and numerous self-propelled howitzers and various types of bridges. However, probably the most unusual was the ammunition carrier for the SP heavy siege mortar *Karlgerät* that could carry four of its massive 60cm/23.61in rounds in specially designed racks above the engine compartment!

PzKpfw IV Ausf F2 Medium Tank

Entered service: 1942
Crew: 5
Weight: 22,350kg/22 tons
Dimensions: Length – 6.63m/21ft 9in
    Height (over turret hatch) – 2.68m/8ft 9.5in
    Width – 2.88m/9ft 5.5in
Armament: Main – 7.5cm/2.95in KwK40 L/43 gun
    Secondary – 2 x 7.92mm/0.312in machine-guns
Armour: Maximum – 50mm/1.97in
Powerplant: Maybach HL120 TRIM, V12 petrol, 223.7kW/300hp
Performance: Speed – 40kph/24.9mph
    Range – 209km/129.9 miles

PzKpfw V Panther Heavy Tank

As World War II progressed, the Germans maintained their tank superiority by bringing the PzKpfw V and VI heavy tanks into service in the 40,640–60,960kg/40–60 ton range, well ahead of the Allies. PzKpfw V, or Panther as it is more commonly known, owes much of its design to a detailed study undertaken of the Russian T-34 which had proved to be greatly superior to the PzKpfw III and IV. The Ausf D model Panther, appearing in 1943, weighed 43,690kg/43 tons, mounted a 7.5cm/2.95in KwK42 L/70 gun and had a crew

of five. With a top speed of about 45kph/28mph, and a radius of action of 200km/124.3 miles, it was a formidable opponent.

A total of 850 of the Ausf D model were built, and it was the first to go into service despite the fact that the next model following it was called Ausf A! Some 2,000 Ausf As were built between August 1943 and May 1944. It had various improvements over its predecessor, including better running gear, thicker armour and a new commander's cupola.

The Ausf G was produced as a result of combat experience with the Ausf D

ABOVE: **This Panther is in the show ring at the French Armour School, Saumur – still in good running order.** BELOW: **A peasant family in their ancient horse-drawn cart pass a knocked-out Panther Ausf G in an Italian village.**

and A. Over 3,000 Ausf Gs were built between March 1944 and April 1945. The hull was redesigned, now without the driver's vision visor – which must have been a vulnerable spot. Variants included command and observation tanks and also the ARV (Armoured Recovery Vehicle) Bergepanther.

PzKpfw V Ausf G Heavy Tank

Entered service: 1944
Crew: 5
Weight: 45,465kg/45.5 tons
Dimensions: Length – 8.87m/29ft 1in
Height (over turret hatch) – 2.97m/9ft 9in
Width – 3.43m/11ft 3in
Armament: Main – 7.5cm/2.95in KwK42 L/70 gun
Secondary – 2 x 7.92mm/0.312m machine-guns
Armour: Maximum – 100mm/3.94in
Powerplant: Maybach HL230P30 V12 petrol, 522kW/700hp
Performance: Speed – 46kph/28.75mph
Range – 200km/125 miles

Jagdpanther Heavy Tank Destroyer

Of the various special adaptations of Panther, the Jagdpanther Heavy Tank Destroyer was perhaps the most famous. It mounted an 8.8cm/3.46in PaK43/3 L/71 gun which could penetrate 182mm/7.17in of armour at 500m/1,640ft. It was a well-protected, fast (46kph/ 28.6mph) and effective tank destroyer.

According to the official German handbook, the Jagdpanther was designed as a *Schwerpunkt* (literally "centre of gravity") weapon for the destruction of enemy tank attacks, and its employment as a complete battalion was considered to be the primary consideration towards achieving success. Production began in January 1944, and the first Jagdpanthers entered service in June 1944. Nearly 400 were built between January 1944 and March 1945. The Jagdpanther was undoubtedly the most important variant of the Panther.

ABOVE: **The Jagdpanther, sporting an unusual camouflage pattern. This tank destroyer mounted the fearsome 8.8cm/3.46in PaK43/3 L/71. Probably the largest concentration of Jagdpanthers was assembled for the Ardennes offensive in December 1944.** BELOW LEFT: **This abandoned Jagdpanther – note the unfired ammunition alongside the track – may well be badly damaged on the far side; certainly the idler wheel and track guard seem to have sustained a strike. 392 Jagdpanthers were built, the prototype being shown to Hitler in December 1943.**

Jagdpanther Heavy TD

Entered service: 1944
Crew: 5
Weight: 46,000kg/45.3 tons
Dimensions: Length – 9.9m/32ft 8in
  Height (over turret hatch) – 2.72m/8ft 11in
  Width – 3.42m/11ft 2.6in
Armament: Main – 8.8cm/3.46in anti-tank gun
  Secondary – 2 x 7.92mm/0.312m machine-guns
Armour: Maximum – 100mm/3.94in
Powerplant: Maybach HL230P30, V12 petrol, 522kW/700hp
Performance: Speed – 46kph/28.6mph
  Range – 160km/99.4 miles

PzKpfw VI Ausf E Tiger 1 Heavy Tank

The most famous of all German World War II tanks was the Tiger, although only approximately 1,360 were ever produced – compared with 6,000 Panthers. Tiger production began in July 1942 and first saw action in Russia in August 1942.

Weighing 56,900kg/56 tons, the Tiger's main armament was the dreaded 8.8cm/3.46in KwK36 L/56 gun that could penetrate 110mm/4.33in of armour at 2,000m/6,561ft. To the average Allied soldier, the Tiger became the symbol of the invincibility of German armour – to a degree which completely outweighed its true capabilities – although when introduced, it was undoubtedly the world's most powerful tank. It did have weak points, however, one of them being its very low-gear turret traverse, which made bringing the main gun to bear on a target very slow.

ABOVE: **Probably the most famous tank of World War II was the German PzKpfw VI Ausf E, Tiger I. This was the first one ever captured complete by the British in North Africa, and is now in running order at the Tank Museum, Bovington.** BELOW: **Question: "When is a Tiger not a Tiger?" Answer: "When it has been specially made for the movies!". This excellent replica "Tiger I" was built using a T-34 chassis for the film** *Saving Private Ryan.* **It is seen here at a Bovington Tankfest in 2002. It is much smaller than the original but otherwise looks remarkably similar, apart from the running gear.**

PzKpfw VI Ausf E Tiger 1 Heavy Tank	

Entered service: 1942
Crew: 5
Weight: 56,900kg/56 tons
Dimensions: Length – 8.45m/27ft 8.5in
  Height (over turret hatch) – 3m/9ft 10in
  Width – 3.56m/11ft 8in
Armament: Main – 8.8cm/3.46m KwK36 L/56 gun
  Secondary – 2 or 3 x 7.92mm/0.312in
  machine-guns
Armour: Maximum – 100mm/3.94in
Powerplant: Maybach HL210P45 V12 petrol,
  522kW/700hp
Performance: Speed – 37kph/22.9mph
  Range – 195km/121 miles

PzKpfw VI Ausf B Tiger 2 Heavy Tank

The *Königstiger* (Royal or King Tiger) or Tiger 2, as it was called, was a formidable tank that could deal with any of its opponents on the battlefield with ease. It weighed over 69,090kg/68 tons, was armed with a long-barrelled 8.8cm/3.46in KwK43 L/71 gun which could penetrate 132mm/5.19in of armour at 2,000m/6,561ft. It was thus able to deal effortlessly with the heaviest Allied tanks. However, its sheer weight and bulk gave it a relatively poor cross-country performance and made for problems in maintenance and reliability. Only 489 King Tigers were built, and they were used mainly in the defensive battles as the Allies advanced deep into Germany.

RIGHT: **This King Tiger has the much more streamlined Porsche turret, and is on show at the Tank Museum, Bovington. The King Tiger mounted the more powerful, longer-barrelled KwK43 L/71 8.8cm/3.46in gun.**

PzKpfw VI Jagdtiger Heavy Tank Destroyer

This monster tank destroyer, weighing 70,000kg/68.9 tons, mounted a 12.8cm/5.04in PaK44 L/55 gun and was undoubtedly the largest and most powerful armoured fighting vehicle to see combat service in World War II, its gun out-ranging most others. The 77 Jagdtigers that were built saw service in the Ardennes and later in the defence of the German "Fatherland".

PzKpfw VI Jagdtiger Heavy TD

Entered service: 1944
Crew: 6
Weight: 70,000kg/68.9 tons
Dimensions: Length – 10.65m/34ft 11.5in
 Height (over turret hatch) – 2.95m/9ft 8in
 Width – 3.63m/11ft 11in
Armament: Main – 12.8cm/5.04in anti-tank gun
 Secondary – 2 x 7.92in/0.3in machine-guns
Armour: Maximum – 250mm/9.8in
Powerplant: Maybach HL230P30 V12 petrol, 522kW/700hp
Performance: Speed – 38kph/23.6mph
 Range – 170km/105.6 miles

LEFT: **Largest and heaviest of the Tiger conversions was the Jagdtiger, which mounted a massive 12.8cm/5.04in PaK44 L/55 gun that could penetrate 157mm/6.18in of armour at 1,500m/4,921ft. I once saw a Jagdtiger that had knocked out nearly an entire regiment of Shermans, but had then been knocked out itself by a *Jabo* (fighter-bomber).**

Renault FT-17 Light Tank and derivatives

Designed by Louis Renault, with the support of the irrepressible General Estienne, the Char Mitrailleuse Renault FT-17 was a remarkable little tank, a true milestone in design which lasted right up to the outbreak of World War II, and was adapted and produced by many countries all over the world. The American Ford 6 Ton Tank, for example, was in essence an American-built Renault FT.

A very large number of FT-17s were built, in seven different models, including a cast turret version. One unique aspect of the tank was its fully revolving turret – the first tank in the world to have all-round traverse. Armed with an 8mm/0.315mm Hotchkiss machine-gun, the two-man tank weighed just over 6 tons, was powered by a 26.1kW/35hp Renault engine and had vertical coil suspension. Later the Hotchkiss was replaced with a new 7.5mm/0.295in machine-gun.

The Renault factory received its first order for 150 F-17s in March 1917 and the first tanks appeared on the battlefield on May 31, 1918, at the Forest of Retz.

FT-17 in American Service

Renault FT-17 tanks were used by the US Army to equip the 344th and 345th Light Tank Battalions. Armed with a 37mm/1.46in gun in the turret and a machine-gun in the hull, they first saw action on September 12, 1918, under the command of Lieutenant Colonel George S. Patton, in an attack against the St Mihiel Salient, France.

TOP: **The most important French tank of World War I was the FT-17, and it was later copied by many other nations, including the Americans, Russians and Italians.** LEFT: **Armed with an 8mm/0.315in Hotchkiss machine-gun, the tiny 6,604kg/6.5-ton Char Mitrailleuse Renault FT-17, to give its full title, was the first tank in the world to have a fully traversing turret.**

FT-17 in Russian Service

Although the Russians now claim that they invented the tank, the first Russian tanks were actually 32 British Mark Vs and Medium Cs, plus 100 French Renault FT-17s, bought in 1918 by the Imperial Government, many of which were later captured by the Bolsheviks. They then acquired even more when the small British force withdrew from Russia and had to leave its tanks behind. The first Russian-built tank was a copy of the Renault FT-17, the KS (*KrasnoSormova*), after the place where it was built, but was also called the Russki-Renault. It would set the pattern for Soviet tank development over the next decade.

RIGHT: **A later post-war derivative of the FT-17 was this Soviet-designed and built MS-2 Light Tank, which had an entirely new sprung suspension and transverse engine. It mounted both a 37mm/1.46in gun and two machine-guns.**

ABOVE: **Another version of the ubiquitous little French tank had a moulded turret. FT-17s were still in service at the start of World War II, and some were still being used by the Vichy French in North Africa against Operation "Torch" (November 1942).** RIGHT: **An FT-17 in British Army service. The British used these small tanks for command and liaison work, normally (as here) with the gun removed.**

LEFT: **This version of the FT-17 mounted a 37mm/ 1.46in Puteaux gun. Some 1,830 of this model were built and, as can be seen, many are still in existence as monuments.**

Renault FT-17 Light Tank

Entered service: 1917
Crew: 2
Weight: 6,604kg/6.5 tons
Dimensions: Length – 4.09m/13ft 5in
    Height (over turret hatch) – 2.13m/7ft
    Width – 1.70m/5ft 7in
Armament: Main – 8mm/0.315in machine-gun or
    37mm/1.46 gun
Armour: Maximum – 22mm/0.87in
Powerplant: Renault 4-cylinder petrol, 26.1kW/35hp
Performance: Speed – 7.7kph/4.8mph
    Range – 35km/21.7 miles

Ram Mark I Cruiser Tank

In early 1941 it was decided to produce a tank in Canada based largely on the US M3 Medium Tank, but better suited to Canadian needs. It was to have a Canadian-produced turret and main armament, together with a redesigned hull to avoid the excessively tall silhouette of the M3. The Ram I went into production in late 1941, mounting a 2pdr gun.

RIGHT: **The Tank Museum's Ram Mark II which mounts a 6pdr gun instead of the original 2pdr on the Ram Mark I. These Canadian-built medium tanks were mainly shipped to the UK during 1943 and used for training.**

Ram Mark II Cruiser Tank

After only 50 Ram Is had been produced, the main armament was changed to a 6pdr equipped with stabilization. More than 1,000 were produced and used for training in Canada and the UK. However, the only Rams to see action were those with their turrets removed and converted to Armoured Personnel Carriers (APCs) known as Ram Kangaroos. These were very successful in a variety of roles – hauling ammunition and artillery, as well as carrying troops and a variety of other weapon systems.

The arrival of the US Sherman M4 rendered the Ram unnecessary, as the new tank incorporated most of the features which had been found lacking in the M3.

Canada did go on to build their own version of the Sherman M4A1, known as the Grizzly, which had certain minor alterations to make it more suitable for UK and Canadian use.

ABOVE: **The earlier Ram 1 Cruiser Tank was armed with just a 2pdr. It incorporated all the latest American, British and Canadian ideas on firepower, protection and mobility, and was built ahead of the advent of the British 6pdr.** LEFT: **The British took the turrets off some of the Canadian Ram tanks, "gutted" them and used them as armoured personnel carriers for infantry sections. This one is badged for the 79th Armoured Division.**

Ram Mark II Cruiser Tank

Entered service: 1942
Crew: 5
Weight: 29,484kg/29 tons
Dimensions: Length – 5.79m/19ft
  Height (over turret hatch) – 2.67m/8ft 9in
  Width – 2.77m/9ft 1in
Armament: Main – 6pdr (57mm/2.24in) gun
  Secondary – 3 x 7.62mm/0.3in machine-guns
Armour: Maximum – 87mm/3.43in
Powerplant: Continental R-975 9-cylinder petrol, 298kW/400bhp
Performance: Speed – 40.2kph/25mph
  Range – 232km/144 miles

Renault Char D2 Infantry Tank

The D2 came in to service in 1934 and was essentially the same as the D1 but with thicker armour which increased the weight to 19,305kg/19 tons. To cope with the heavier weight, a bigger 6-cylinder 111.9kW/150hp engine was fitted and there were improvements to the transmission and suspension.

The armament remained the same. A distinctive feature of this vehicle was the large aerial mounted on the right of the rear deck behind the turret.

Renault began deliveries in 1934, but their D series was to lose out to the SOMUA Medium Tank, which was selected in preference by the French Army.

In the end only about 50 D2s were taken into service and their automotive unreliability and slow speed ensured a fairly dismal combat record. Most were deployed in North Africa as static defences and a few captured ones were incorporated into the Atlantic Wall by the Germans.

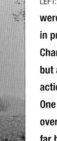
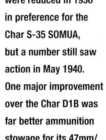

LEFT: **Orders for D2 were reduced in 1936 in preference for the Char S-35 SOMUA, but a number still saw action in May 1940. One major improvement over the Char D1B was far better ammunition stowage for its 47mm/ 1.85in main gun – from 35 to 108 rounds. In most other respects it was disappointing.**

Renault Char D2 Infantry Tank

Entered service: 1934
Crew: 3
Weight: 19,305kg/19 tons
Dimensions: Length – 4.81m/15ft 9.5in
    Height (over turret hatch) – 2.4m/7ft 10.5in
    Width – 2.16m/7ft 1in
Armament: Main – 47mm/1.85in SA34 gun
    Secondary – 2 x 7.5mm/0.295in machine-guns
Armour: Maximum – 50mm/1.97in
Powerplant: Renault, 6-cylinder petrol, delivering
    111.9kW/150hp
Performance: Speed – 22.5kph/14mph
    Range – 90km/55.9 miles

Renault FT Kegresse–Hinstin M24/25 Light Tank

In 1924, the well-known French automotive engineer Adolphe Kegresse received financial backing from M. Hinstin to work on improving the highly successful little Renault FT-17 in order to produce a quieter, faster tank. His new running-gear employed a suspension comprising eight small road wheels plus a standard-sized sprocket and idler, both at ground level, together with rubber track bands (for

quietness). Additionally, there were more rollers on outriggers both at the front and rear, designed to assist in trench crossing. The French Army bought a number of these "wheel cum tracks" and shipped them over to Morocco in 1925 when the Riffs invaded, where they were used in combat. A number were also sold to overseas buyers, including the Americans, who bought them for evaluation.

In 1925, an improved version was produced, which modified the suspension, strengthened the rubber tracks with metal pads and did away with the front rollers, but retained those at the rear. Unfortunately, there were no buyers, and this innovative AFV was shelved.

Renault FT Kegresse-Hinstin M24/25 Light Tank

Entered service: 1924
Crew: 2
Weight: 6,600kg/6.5tons
Dimensions: Length – 5.00m/16ft 5in
    Height (over turret hatch) – 2.14m/7ft
    Width – 1.83m/6ft
Armament: Main – 37mm/1.46in gun or
    8mm/0.315in machine-gun
Armour: Maximum – 22mm/0.866in
Powerplant: Renault 4-cylinder petrol,
    26.1kW/35bhp
Performance: Speed: – 12kph/7.5mph
    Range – 35km/21.7 miles

LEFT: **A Renault FT M24/25 climbs a concrete step during trials with the US Army circa 1925, clearly showing its innovative suspension. Some of these interesting little tanks saw action in North Africa in 1925 against the Riffs in Morocco.**

Renault R–35 Light Tank

Following on from the disappointing AMC 34, Renault produced their AMC 35 model, which was very similar, but with a more powerful liquid-cooled 4-cylinder engine, an upgraded bell-crank scissors suspension system and improved vision devices. The hull was of riveted construction made with rolled steel plates. The turret armament remained the short-barrelled high-velocity 47mm/1.85in main gun, although some of the late models were fitted with a long-barrelled 25mm/0.98in Hotchkiss anti-tank gun and had a crew of three. The R-35 was the most numerous of the

French tanks to fight in 1940, but fared badly because it was found to have a high fuel consumption which limited its range. It was also out-gunned by the German AFVs.

ABOVE: **Most numerous of the French tanks to fight in May/June 1940 were the light infantry support Renault R-35, armed with a short-barrelled 37mm/1.46in gun. This one is taking part in the annual demonstration at the French Armour School, Saumur.** LEFT: **On parade in Paris pre-war, the Char Leger R-35, Renault Type ZM Light Tank had a crew of only two, so the commander also had to act as gunner traversing the turret by hand.** BELOW LEFT: **A file of R-35 light infantry support tanks on training. Some 2,000 were built, many of which were exported to Poland, Turkey and Romania. The Germans also used captured R-35s and gave some to Italy.**

Renault R-35 Light Tank

Entered service: 1935
Crew: 2 or 3
Weight: 14,500kg/14.3 tons
Dimensions: Length – 4.55m/14ft 11in
    Height (over turret hatch) – 2.3m/7ft 6.5in
    Width – 2.2m/7ft 2.5in
Armament: Main – 37mm/1.46in gun
    Secondary – 7.5mm/0.295in machine-gun
Armour: Maximum – 45mm/1.77in
Powerplant: Renault, 4-cylinder petrol,
    134.2kW/180hp
Performance: Speed – 42kph/26.1mph
    Range – 160km/99.4 miles

Sentinel AC1, AC2, AC3 and AC4 Cruiser Tank

In late 1940, given the fragile state of supply between Britain and its colonies, it was decided to design a tank which could be produced in Australia, using easily obtainable items, such as truck engines. The Sentinel, as the result was called, was a tremendous achievement for a nation with such a small industrial base. It was initially produced in two versions, the first of these being the AC1, the most striking feature of this model being the very large sleeve for the bow machine-gun which was situated in the

centre of the hull. It also mounted a 2pdr main gun and had two Vickers machine-guns. The cast hull and turret were mounted on a suspension system which resembled the French Hotchkiss design, while various parts such as the final drives and transmission were copied from the American M3 Medium Tank.

Production began in 1942, and more than 60 tanks were built. However, these were only ever used for training. The second Sentinel model, the AC2, was not developed, so the next Sentinel to

reach the prototype stage was the AC3, which mounted a 25pdr howitzer in a larger turret. The triple engines (three Cadillac V8s) were now given a single crankcase. The AC3 did not progress further than testing. The next Sentinel model to be produced, the AC4, mounted a 17pdr, and this prototype was completed in 1943. However, with ample supplies of American tanks now being available, no further Sentinel production was required.

TOP: **A remarkable achievement for the infant Australian tank industry was the production of the Sentinel Cruiser Tank in 1942, seen here at the Tank Museum, Bovington. The AC1 was armed with a 2pdr gun.** LEFT: **Some prototype Sentinels were fitted with twin 25pdrs in order to simulate the recoil of an even larger weapon, like the 17pdr which was then tried in AC4 but never went into production.**

Sentinel AC1 Cruiser Tank

Entered service: 1942
Crew: 5
Weight: 28,489kg/28 tons
Dimensions: Length – 6.32m/20ft 9in
    Height (over turret hatch) – 2.57m/8ft 5in
    Width – 2.77m/9ft 1in
Armament: Main – 2pdr (40mm/1.58in) or
    25pdr (AC3) or 17pdr (AC4)
    Secondary – 2 x 7.62mm/0.3in machine-guns
Armour: Maximum – 65mm/2.56in
Powerplant: 3 x Cadillac V8 petrol, 87kW/117bhp
Performance: Speed – 48.3kph/30mph
    Range – 319km/198 miles

7TP Light Tank

In addition to the Carden-Loyds, another British export was the ubiquitous Vickers-Armstrong 6 Ton Mark E model, which was bought and copied by the Poles, who then in turn produced the 7TP – a 9,550kg/9.4-ton plus twin-turreted light tank with thicker armour than its progenitor. It was crewed by three men – the driver and one man in each turret, each armed with a 7.92mm/0.312in machine-gun (various models – Maxim, Browning and Hotchkiss – were tried). It was powered by a Polish-built Swiss-patterned Saurer 82kW/110hp 6-cylinder diesel engine.

The twin turrets of the first model were soon replaced by a single-turret variant, 7TP 2, still mounting a Bofors 37mm/1.46in gun. The final model, 7TP 3, came into production in 1937, with about 160 being built. It had thicker welded armour and now weighed 11,177kg/11 tons, a new engine and also a new turret produced in Sweden, which overhung to the rear, mounting the 37mm/1.46in Bofors high-velocity anti-tank gun, along with a coaxial 7.92mm/0.312in machine-gun. This was certainly the best tank the Poles had in service when the Germans invaded, with a few being modified and pressed into service by the Germans following their capture. Its Bofors gun was widely used by both sides in the war.

TOP: **The Poles developed the British Vickers Armstrong 6 Ton Tank first as a twin-turreted model, but then as a single, mounting a 37mm/1.46in, which then went into production in 1937.**

LEFT: **The improved model of the 7TP Light Tank had better armour up to 40mm/1.58in thick and weighed 11,177kg/11 tons.**

7TP Light Tank

Entered service: 1937
Crew: 3
Weight: 9,550kg/9.4 tons
Dimensions: Length – 4.6m/15ft 1in
  Height (over turret hatch) – 2.02m/6ft 7.5in
  Width – 2.16m/7ft 1in
Armament: Main – 37mm/1.46in anti-tank gun
  Secondary – 1 or 2 x 7.92mm/0.312in machine-guns
Armour: Maximum – 17mm/0.67in
Powerplant: Saurer 6-cylinder diesel, 82kW/110hp
Performance: Speed – 32kph/19.9mph
  Range – 160km/99.4 miles

SMK Heavy Tank

Two multi-turreted heavy tanks were designed by leading Soviet tank designer Kotin in 1938, each with three turrets, which were later reduced to two. They were designated as the T-100 and the SMK (the latter initials standing for Sergei Mironovich Kirov). They were almost identical in appearance, both having a an upper central turret mounting a 76.2mm/3in gun with all-round traverse and a lower front turret mounting a 45mm/1.77in gun which had 180-degree traverse only.

ABOVE AND BELOW: **The SMK (Sergei Mironovich Kirov) was another multi-turreted Soviet heavy tank that followed on after the T-35 and T-100. It closely resembled the T-100 and was used in the Russo-Finnish War, but proved to be lacking in both protection and firepower. It was abandoned in favour of the KV-1, which proved much more successful.**

The SMK, which at 45,722kg/45 tons was 11,177kg/11 tons lighter than the T-100, had a new torsion bar suspension, with eight independently sprung, smallish road wheels on either side (with resilient rubber-bushed hubs) with four upper return rollers. The tracks were of a new design, with heavily spudded, small-pitch links. (Spuds are part of the metal track that juts out and provides traction.) The tank was constructed of cast armour, both on hull and turrets, that was designed to give protection against at least 37mm/1.46in anti-tank round at all ranges and was up to 60mm/2.36in thick.

A small number were used in Finland, but were not successful in combat, being difficult to manoeuvre and lacking both firepower and armour, so the project was abandoned in favour of the KV-1.

SMK Heavy Tank	
Entered service: 1939	
Crew: 7	
Weight: 45,722kg/45 tons	
Dimensions: Length – 9.66m/31ft 6in	
Height (over turret hatch) – 3.3m/10ft 10in	
Width – 3.45m/11ft 4in	
Armament: Main – 76.2mm/3in L11 and	
45mm/1.77in gun	
Secondary – 4 x 7.62mm/0.3in machine-guns	
Armour: Maximum – 60mm/2.36in	
Powerplant: AM-34 diesel	
Performance: Speed – 36kph/22.4mph	
Range – 150km/93.2 miles	

Skoda LT-35 Medium Tank

Developed in 1934 and in production the following year, the Skoda LT-35 was the main battle tank of the Czech Army during the years immediately preceding the German invasion, and was also sold to Romania. It had riveted armour, and its main 37mm/1.46in gun was developed from the Skoda anti-tank gun of the same calibre, renowned for its accuracy. There were also two 7.92mm/0.312in machine-guns, one mounted coaxially. Although generally reliable, it suffered from a few mechanical faults in its early life, which somewhat sullied its reputation. However, the proof of this vehicle's pedigree is that the Germans took over 200 into service, although they modified it and renamed it the PzKpfw 35(t).

They also continued to have it produced within Axis Europe until 1941, and it saw action in various theatres including Poland 1939, France 1940 and on the central Russian front up to 1941, where it reached the end of its front-line life and was thereafter relegated to secondary roles such as artillery tractor – *Artillerie Schlepper* 35(t).

BELOW: **The LT-35 in German service – now known as the PzKpfw 35(t).**

ABOVE: **This small Czech tank, the LT-35, was taken into service by the Germans and designated as the PzKpfw 35(t). Over 200 were acquired from the Czechs in March 1939. This model is at the Aberdeen Proving Ground in the USA.** LEFT: **The LT-35 was also in service with Romania and Slovakia pre-war, who purchased them in 1936–37 from the Czechs, as well as being in Czech service, as here.**

Skoda LT-35 Medium Tank

Entered service: 1935
Crew: 4
Weight: 10,670kg/10.5 tons
Dimensions: Length – 4.9m/16ft 1in
    Height (over turret hatch) – 2.21m/7ft 3in
    Width – 2.16m/7ft 1in
Armament: Main – 37mm/1.46in
    Secondary – 2 x 7.92mm/0.312in machine-guns
Armour: Maximum – 25mm/0.98in
Powerplant: Skoda T11 6-cylinder petrol, 89.5kW/120bhp
Performance: Speed – 35kph/22mph
    Range – 190km/118 miles

Skoda LT-38 Medium Tank

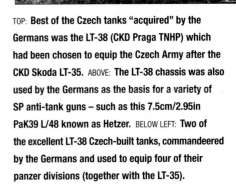

The Skoda LT-38 follows a similar history to that of the Skoda LT-35, although its quality was far superior to its predecessor, being reliable, hard-wearing and easy to maintain. Originally built for the export market by CKD, it was chosen by the Czech Army as the successor to the Skoda LT-35, with both companies co-producing the vehicle. The war then intervened, and the Germans were quick to pick up on the Skoda LT-38's value and pressed it into service for themselves.

By removing some of its ammunition and making room for a loader, they freed the vehicle's commander from that role and thereby still further improved the tank's overall performance. Later models had extra riveted armour, and following the vehicle's withdrawal from active service in 1942, the excellent chassis was used as the basis for both the Marder and Hetzer tank destroyers, as well as many others, one even mounting an 8.8cm/ 3.46in PaK43 (prototype only).

TOP: **Best of the Czech tanks "acquired" by the Germans was the LT-38 (CKD Praga TNHP) which had been chosen to equip the Czech Army after the CKD Skoda LT-35.** ABOVE: **The LT-38 chassis was also used by the Germans as the basis for a variety of SP anti-tank guns – such as this 7.5cm/2.95in PaK39 L/48 known as Hetzer.** BELOW LEFT: **Two of the excellent LT-38 Czech-built tanks, commandeered by the Germans and used to equip four of their panzer divisions (together with the LT-35).**

Skoda LT-38 Medium Tank

Entered service: 1938
Crew: 4
Weight: 9,400kg/9.25 tons
Dimensions: Length – 4.60m/15ft 1in
    Height (over turret hatch) – 2.4m/7ft 10in
    Width – 2.11m/6ft 11in
Armament: Main – 37mm/1.46in or 37mm/1.46in
    KwK L/40 or 37mm/1.46in L/45 gun
    Secondary – 2 x 7.92mm/0.312in machine-guns
Armour: Maximum – 25mm/0.98in
Powerplant: Praga EPA 16-cylinder petrol,
    93kW/125bhp
Performance: Speed – 42kph/26.1mph
    Range – 250km/155.3 miles

SOMUA S-35 Medium Tank

The SOMUA (its name an acronym of its producers: *Societe d'Outillage Mecanique d'Usinage d'Artillerie*) was the first tank with an all-cast construction of both hull and turret (which also had an electrically powered traverse), the thick armour providing excellent protection.

In the turret, the main armament was a long-barrelled high-velocity 47mm/1.85in gun, with a coaxial machine-gun alongside. The 141.7kW/190hp engine gave the S-35 a top speed of 40kph/25mph and a radius of action of 257km/160 miles. Fast and reliable, it was actually better armed and better armoured than its German opponents in 1940, but they were

not available in sufficient numbers, and, given the speed of the German attack, could not have made that much difference to the immediate outcome of events.

Some 500 of these 20-ton tanks were built and, like all contemporary French armour, were captured in large numbers

by the Germans and then pressed into their own service. As the tide of World War II turned, some came back once again into (Free) French hands, and they remained in service with the French Army for a considerable time after the end of the conflict.

ABOVE AND BELOW: **This French tank was probably one of the best medium tanks of the 1930s, with its 47mm/1.85in gun and 40mm/1.58in thick armour. This one belongs to the Bovington Tank Museum.**
ABOVE LEFT: **SOMUA S-35s like these fought in France in the 1940s, and captured models were used by both the Germans and Italians.**

SOMUA S-35 Medium Tank

Entered service: 1935
Crew: 3
Weight: 19,500kg/19.2 tons
Dimensions: Length – 5.38m/17ft 7.8in
　　　Height (over turret hatch) – 2.62m/8ft 7in
　　　Width – 2.12m/6ft 11.5in
Armament: Main – 47mm/1.85in gun
　　　Secondary – 7.5mm/0.295in machine-gun
Armour: Maximum – 40mm/1.58in
Powerplant: V8 petrol, 141.7kW/190hp
Performance: Speed – 40.7kph/25.3mph
　　　Range – 257km/160 miles

LEFT: Designed by the German tank designer Joseph Vollmer, who was responsible for the German LK I and LK II, the Swedish M/21 looked very similar to them. It had many new innovations, for example, the command version had a two-way radio, while the others just had receivers. In 1929 the engine was replaced with a more powerful Scania-Vabis.

Strv M/21 Light Tank

Entered service: 1920
Crew: 4
Weight: 9,850kg/9.7 tons
Dimensions: Length – 5.71m/18ft 9in
   Height (over turret hatch) – 2.51m/8ft 3in
   Width – 2.06m/6ft 9in
Armament: Main – 6.5mm/0.256in machine-gun
Armour: Maximum – 14mm/0.55in
Powerplant: Daimler 4-cylinder petrol,
   41.8kW/55hp
Performance: Speed – 16kph/9.9mph
   Range – 150km/93.2miles

Strv M/21 and M/29 Light Tanks

Despite the fact that Sweden has not taken part in any war since the beginning of the 20th century, they have still kept pace with the development of armoured fighting vehicles, having begun in 1921 with a copy of the German *Leichte Kampfwagen*. This is hardly surprising, as it was designed by Joseph Vollmer, the German engineer who designed and built the LK I and LK II and moved to Sweden after World War I. The Strv (*Stridsvagn* – "tank") M/21 was built in 1921 and was powered by a 4-cylinder 41.8kW/55hp Daimler engine. It had a crew of four and was armed with a single 6.5mm/0.256in machine-gun. The Strv M/29, produced in 1929, underwent a rebuild, having a more powerful Scania-Vabis 6-cylinder 59.7kW/80hp engine and heavier armour fitted, though the armament remained the same.

Strv M/31 Light Tank

By the late 1920s the Swedes had, with German assistance, established their own tank factory, the AB Landsverk Company at Landskrons. Their first design, which appeared in 1931, was a wheeled and tracked vehicle, with duplicate running gear. Two years later they produced the Strv M/31, which had a design that was well ahead of other nations, the turret and hull both being of welded construction.

The main armament of this four-man tank was a rapid-fire high-velocity 37mm/1.46in gun housed in a two-man turret with a coaxial machine-gun. The driver operated a second machine-gun.

It had a German Bussing V6 petrol engine, two-way radio communications, high-quality optical, sighting and vision devices.

Strv M/31 Light Tank

Entered service: 1931
Crew: 4
Weight: 11,500kg/11.3 tons
Dimensions: Length – 5.18m/17ft
   Height (over turret hatch) – 2.23m/7ft 4in
   Width – 2.13m/7ft
Armament: Main – 37mm/1.46in gun
   Secondary – 2 x 6.5mm/0.256in machine-guns
Armour: Maximum – 9mm/0.35in
Powerplant: Bussing V6, petrol, 104.4kW/140hp
Performance: Speed – 40kph/24.9mph
   Range – 200km/124.3 miles

LEFT: Development continued with the AB Landsverk company producing a series of designs. This one, the Strv M/31 (L-10), was well ahead of its time. It weighed 11,500kg/11.3 tons, had a crew of four and mounted a 37mm/1.46in gun and two machine-guns.

Strv M/40, M/41 and M/42 Light Tanks

The Strvs of the early 1940s were another series of well designed light tanks from the Swedish AB Landsverk Company that can trace their ancestry back to the original Czech design. The Strv M/40 was the first to be produced in quantity. It was powered by a Scania-Vabis 105.9kW/142hp 6-cylinder engine, giving it a speed of just under 48.3kph/ 30mph, had a crew of three, and was armed with a 37mm/1.46in gun with two coaxial 8mm/0.315in machine-guns.

The Strv M/41, though similarly armed, had slightly thicker armour than its predecessor. To cope with the inevitable increase in weight, it was powered by an uprated Scania-Vabis 108kW/145hp engine.

The M/41 continued in service with the Swedish Army until the 1950s, when many were modified for use as armoured personnel carriers. The Strv M/42 was the first Swedish tank to mount a 75mm/ 2.95in main gun. Entering service in 1944, it weighed 22,353kg/22 tons and had a four-man crew. In the late 1950s the M/42 was rebuilt as the Strv 74, with a more powerful gun and thicker armour.

ABOVE: **Built to the basic design of the L/60 Light Tank, the M/40 L was the first Swedish tank to reach quantity production. This model is held at the Tank Museum, Bovington Camp.** LEFT: **The Strv M/42. This extremely modern-looking tank was designed by the Swedes in 1941–42. It was the first Swedish tank to be armed with a 75mm/2.95in gun. In 1958–60 it was modernized and rebuilt as the Strv 74.**

Strv M/41 Light Tank

Entered service: 1942
Crew: 3
Weight: 10,500kg/10.3 tons
Dimensions: Length – 4.57m/15ft
    Height (over turret hatch) – 2.37m/7ft 9in
    Width – 2.13m/7ft
Armament: Main – 37mm/1.46in gun
    Secondary – 2 x 6.5mm/0.256 machine-guns
Armour: Maximum – 25mm/0.98in
Powerplant: Scania-Vabis 6-cylinder petrol, 108kW/145hp
Performance: Speed – 45kph/28mph
    Range – 200km/124.3 miles

LEFT: **In the early 1920s the Americans built a number of prototype medium tanks – the M1921, the M1922 and the T1 of 1925. The latest model of the 1925 series was the T1E2, seen here, which had a crew of four and mounted a 57mm/2.24in gun. However, none of these models were put into production due to the demise of the Tank Corps and the upper weight limit of 15,240kg/ 15 tons being applied. The T1E2 weighed 22,352kg/22 tons and had a speed of 22.53kph/14mph, so it was well over the upper weight limit of 15,240kg/15 tons imposed by the War Department.**

T1 and T2 Medium Tanks

Three prototype medium tanks were built by the USA in the early 1920s: the Medium A of 1921; the Medium A2 of 1922; and the T1 of 1925. The main armament of the T1 was either a 57mm/2.24in gun or a 75mm/2.95in gun. It also had two 7.62mm/0.3in machine-guns.

Further development continued, with the next medium tank – designated the T2 – appearing in 1930. This had a semi-automatic 47mm/1.85in gun and a 12.7mm/0.5in machine-gun in the turret, plus a 37mm/1.46in and a 7.62mm/0.3in machine-gun in the right front of the hull. This dual mounting was later replaced by a single 7.62mm/0.3in machine-gun.

The T1 had weighed nearly 20 tons. The T2, however, had to conform to the new weight limit of 15 tons, as laid down by the US War Department. It weighed just 14 tons combat-loaded and was powered by a 252kW/338hp Liberty engine. The armament included a semi-automatic 57mm/2.24in main gun with a coaxial 12.7mm/0.5in Browning machine-gun plus two 7.62mm/0.3in machine-guns in sponsons. It had good cross-country performance and externally looked quite similar to the British Vickers Medium Mark II.

Three more prototypes were built – T3, T3E2 and T4 – all of which were based upon the designs of Walter Christie. They were all fast and reliable, but only lightly armoured, and none ever saw action.

T1 Medium Tank

Entered service: 1925
Crew: 4
Weight: 19,912kg/19.6 tons
Dimensions: Length – 6.55m/21ft 6in
  Height (over turret hatch) – 2.88m/9ft 5.5in
  Width – 2.44m/8ft
Armament: Main – Either 57mm/2.24in
  or 75mm/2.95in gun
  Secondary – 2 x 7.62mm/0.3in machine-guns
Armour: Maximum – 9.5mm/0.37in
Powerplant: Liberty V12 petrol, 252kW/338hp
Performance: Speed – 22.5kph/14mph
  Range – 56km/35 miles

ABOVE: **Next in line was the T2 Medium Tank, which bore a strong resemblance to the British Vickers Medium. It weighed only 14,225kg/14 tons, having been deliberately designed to conform with the US War Department's 15,240kg/15-ton weight limit.**

LEFT: **Yet another foreign tank based upon the British export Vickers 6 Ton Tank was the Soviet T-26 Light Tank series. This one (in Finnish colours) is the T-26B, which mounted a 37mm/1.46in high velocity gun.**

T-26-S Light Tank	
Entered service: 1935	
Crew: 3	
Weight: 10,460kg/10.3 tons	
Dimensions: Length – 4.8m/15ft 9in	
Height (over turret hatch) – 2.33m/7ft 7.5in	
Width – 2.39m/7ft 10in	
Armament: Main – 45mm/1.77in L/46 gun	
Secondary – 2 or 3 x 7.62mm/0.3in machine-guns	
Armour: Maximum – 25mm/0.98in	
Powerplant: GAZ t26 8-cylinder petrol, 67.9kW/91hp	
Performance: Speed – 28kph/17.4mph	
Range – 200km/124.3 miles	

T-26 Light Tank

The T-26 was a version of the Vickers 6 Ton Light Tank built under licence using an all-riveted construction and either a single or twin turrets mounting 7.62mm/0.3in machine-guns. Early versions were exact copies of the original Vickers design, apart from a progression of armament changes ranging from a 12.7mm/0.5in machine-gun to a 27mm/1.06in gun, and then a 37mm/1.46in long-barrelled gun in the right-hand turret. From 1933 onwards, production of the twin turret version ceased, and instead a single round turret version (T-26/B-1) was introduced, mounting firstly a 37mm/1.46in, then later a 47mm/1.85in main gun.

The early models in the series weighed in the region of 8,636kg/8.5 tons, had a crew of three, a top speed of 35.4kph/22mph and saw action in Spain during the Civil War, against the Japanese in Manchuria in 1939 and in the Russo-Finnish War of 1939–40. Disappointing reports from the first two of these wars prompted a redesign with thicker, better-sloped armour, a lower silhouette and a new semi-conical turret. Known as the T-26S and made of welded construction throughout, it weighed 10,460kg/10.3 tons and mounted a 45mm/1.77in main gun plus two 7.62mm/0.3in machine-guns.

T-28 Medium Tank

The T-28 weighed 28,509kg/28 tons, had a 76.2mm/3in gun in the main turret and two separate machine-guns in subsidiary turrets with a crew of six and was powered by a 373kW/500hp engine, allowing a top speed of 37kph/23mph. The T-28A was an improved production model with thicker front armour (30mm/1.18in), while most of the next model, the T-28B, were armed with the longer, more powerful, 76.2mm/3in L/26 gun, which also had a turret basket and better vision for the driver. The final model was the T-28C, which had thicker armour – up to 80mm/3.15in on the front of the tank and high armour screens around the turret which mounted a longer L/26 gun. The T-28C was first used against the *Panzerwaffe* in 1941.

T-28 Medium Tank	
Entered service: 1933	
Crew: 6	
Weight: 28,509kg/28 tons	
Dimensions: Length – 7.44m/24ft 5in	
Height (over turret hatch) – 2.82m/9ft 3in	
Width – 2.81 m/9ft 2.5in	
Armament: Main – 76mm/3in gun	
Secondary – 3 x 7.62mm/0.3in machine-guns	
Armour: Maximum – 30mm/1.18in	
Powerplant: M17 V12 petrol, 373kW/500hp	
Performance: Speed – 37kph/23mph	
Range – 190km/118.1 miles	

LEFT: **Another multi-turreted tank to appear in the Red Army was the Soviet T-28 (note that the machine-guns are missing out of the front auxiliary turrets).**

T-37 Amphibious Light Tank

The T-37 was based on the Carden Loyd amphibious tank, again bought from the British. However, it used a GAZ AA engine and an improved suspension derived from that of the French AMR Light Tank and floated with aid of flotation pontoons. It weighed 3,200kg/ 3.15 tons, had a crew of two and was armed with a single 7.62mm/0.3in machine-gun in its small cylindrical turret located on the right-hand side of the vehicle. Some T-37s had an all-welded turret like that used on the T-35 or T-28 instead of the usual type.

Finally, towards the end of the production run in 1936, the hull was redesigned, most noticeably in the driver's area, and the flotation pontoons on the side of the hull were dispensed with. A total of approximately 1,200 T-37s were manufactured between 1933 and 1936.

T-37 Amphibious Light Tank

Entered service: 1933
Crew: 2
Weight: 3,200kg/3.15 tons
Dimensions: Length – 3.75m/12ft 3.5in
   Height (over turret hatch) – 1.82m/5ft 11.5in
   Width – 2.1m/6ft 10.5in
Armament: Main – 7.62mm/0.3in machine-gun
Armour: Maximum – 4mm/0.157in
Powerplant: GAZ AA 4-cylinder, 48.5kW/65hp
Performance: Speed – 56.3kph/35mph
   Range – 185km/115 miles

LEFT: **T-37 Amphibious Light Tank. The Russians developed these small, light, amphibious tanks after purchasing a number of Carden-Loyd tankettes. They were designed purely for reconnaissance.**

T-40 Amphibious Light Tank

The T-40 was built as a replacement for the T-37. Main armament was still one machine-gun like its predecessor (although of a larger calibre), but the T-40 anticipated the later T-30 series in having flotation tanks built into its hull and in being powered in the water by a single, four-bladed propeller.

The first version had a squared-off blunt nose, but later models were more streamlined. There was also an attempt to redress the T-37's flaw – its thin armour. However, an increase in armour thickness was at the expense of the vehicle's amphibious capability – and so development soon left the T-40 behind.

T-40 Amphibious Light Tank

Entered service: 1941
Crew: 2
Weight: 5,900kg/5.8 tons
Dimensions: Length – 4.11/13ft 6in
   Height (over turret hatch) – 1.95m/6ft 5in
   Width – 2.33m/7ft 7.5in
Armament: Main – 12.7mm/0.5in machine-gun
Armour: Maximum – 14mm/0.55in
Powerplant: GAZ 202 6-cylinder petrol,
   336kW/450hp
Performance: Speed – 65kph/40.4mph
   Range – 320km/198.8 miles

LEFT: **The T-40 amphibian was a replacement for the T-37 and other earlier models. The small 5,900kg/5.8-ton tank had a 12.7mm/0.5in machine-gun and a crew of two. The later T-40S had thicker armour, but had its rear propeller removed so it was non-amphibious. The photograph shows a T-40A, which had a streamlined, pointed nose and a folding trim vane.**

T–34/76A Medium Tank

One of the most unpleasant surprises experienced by the Germans in Russia came some five months after the launching of Operation "Barbarossa" in the shape of a new tank which inflicted heavy losses upon the PzKpfw IIIs and IVs. General Guderian was so impressed with the new Russian tank that he thought the quickest way for the Germans to deal with the situation would be to copy it! It was, of course, the T-34, one of the most important single elements in the eventual Russian victory.

Using a Christie-type suspension and mounting a 76.2mm/3in gun, the 31,390kg/30.9-ton tank had a crew of four and a top speed of 40kph/25mph. Well-armoured, robust and devoid of any frills, it was easily mass-produced – another vital factor in its favour. The next in the series, the T-34/76D, had a new hexagonal turret, with no overhang as on the previous models. This did away with the "bullet trap" which the overhang had created, and also made it more difficult for enemy soldiers who had climbed on to

the back to wedge Teller mines under the rear of the turret overhang. The T-34/76 was a critical tank at a critical time, and it helped the USSR stem and then turn the tide of World War II in their favour.

ABOVE: **Undoubtedly one of the best tanks of World War II was the Soviet T-34/76 Medium Tank, based upon the earlier T-32. It became the main Russian medium tank of the war.** BELOW LEFT: **These T-34/76Ds are advancing through the forests of Byelorussia. Note the entirely new hexagonal turret on this much improved production model.**

T-34/76A Medium Tank

Entered service: 1940
Crew: 4
Weight: 31,390kg/30.9 tons
Dimensions: Length – 6.09m/20ft
   Height (over turret hatch) – 2.57m/8ft 5in
   Width – 2.88m/9ft 5.5in
Armament: Main – 76.2mm/3in L41 gun
   Secondary – 2 x 7.62mm/0.3in machine-guns
Armour: Maximum – 65mm/2.56in
Powerplant: V234 V12 diesel, developing
   373kW/500hp
Performance: Speed – 40kph/25mph
   Range – 430km/267.2 miles

T-34/85 Medium Tank

Towards the end of 1943 the T-34 was made even more lethal by the fitting of a new 85mm/3.35in gun in an enlarged turret. The new gun had an effective range of 1,000m/3,281ft and could penetrate the frontal armour of both the Tiger and Panther at that range – or so the Russians claimed. The German MBTs probably had the edge over their Soviet counterparts, but in the end the Russian tanks were available in far larger numbers, and this would be the decisive factor – quantity to overwhelm all opposition.

ABOVE: **The T-34/85 was a much-improved model, giving it better firepower so as to match later German tanks. This one was photographed at Bovington.** ABOVE RIGHT: **The up-gunned version of the T-34 mounted the 85mm/3.35in gun in an enlarged turret. It is seen here at the Aberdeen Proving Ground in the USA.**

BELOW LEFT AND RIGHT: **Internal views of the T-34/85 at the Tank Museum. The first shows the driver's seat, instruments and one of his steering levers. The other shows the breech end of the main armament.**

T-34/85 Medium Tank

Entered service: 1944
Crew: 5
Weight: 32,000kg/31.5 tons
Dimensions: Length – 8.15m/26ft 9in
  Height (over turret hatch) – 2.74m/9ft
  Width – 2.99m/9ft 9.5in
Armament: Main – 85mm/3.35in ZiS S53 gun
  Secondary – 2 x 7.62mm/0.3in machine-guns
Armour: Maximum – 90mm/3.54in
Powerplant: V234 12-cylinder diesel, 373kW/500hp
Performance: Speed – 55kph/34.2mph
  Range – 300km/186.4 miles

Turan I and II Medium Tanks

The first tanks in Hungary were Italian CV33 tankette imports in the 1930s. When World War II broke out, the government then attempted to purchase tanks from Czechoslovakia, but with their total production taken up by Germany, the Czechs could not oblige. Instead, Hungary obtained the rights to one of the latest Skoda tanks – the T-21 – which it then modified to suit its own military and industrial requirements. Powered by a Hungarian 8-cylinder 194kW/260hp

engine, equipped with leaf spring suspension and with the original two-man turret replaced with a three-man version equipped with radio communications, the Turan I mounted a Skoda 40mm/1.58in main gun and two 8mm/0.315in machine-guns – one of them coaxial and one in the hull – and had a crew of five. The Turan II had an upgraded 75mm/2.95in main gun mounted in a modified turret, but was otherwise the same as its predecessor.

ABOVE: **The Turan I Medium Tank was a 16,257kg/ 16-ton tank built under licence in Hungary and based on a Czech design.** BELOW: **Another Hungarian Turan Medium Tank, this time a Mark II, negotiates an ad hoc wooden bridge. The Mark II mounted a 75mm/2.95in gun instead of the original 40mm/ 1.58in.** BELOW LEFT: **This Turan Mark II has plenty of passengers. Its place in the Hungarian Armoured Corps was taken by German PzKpfw III and PzKpfw IVs.**

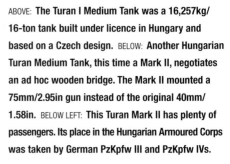

Turan II Medium Tank

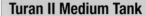

Entered service: 1943
Crew: 5
Weight: 18,500kg/18.2 tons
Dimensions: Length – 5.69m/18ft 8in
  Height (over turret hatch) – 2.33m/7ft 7.5in
  Width – 2.54m/8ft 4in
Armament: Main – 75mm/2.95in gun
  Secondary – 2 x 8mm/0.315in machine-guns
Armour: Maximum – 50mm/1.97in
Powerplant: Weiss V8 petrol, 194kW/260hp
Performance: Speed – 47kph/29.2mph
  Range – 165km/102.5 miles

Type 3 Ka-Chi Amphibious Tank

The Japanese had long been interested in amphibious armoured vehicles for use by their Imperial Navy. Based upon the Chi-He design, the Ka-Chi was of an all-welded construction and had two detachable floats, one at the bow and one at the stern, that gave the tank its buoyancy while in the water and once ashore could be discarded. It was driven through the water by means of two propellers working off the main engine, while the commander steered via twin rudders which he operated from his turret. Powered by a 179kW/240hp V12 diesel engine and operated by a crew of seven, the Ka-Chi mounted a 47mm/1.85in main gun along with two 7.7mm/0.303in machine-guns – one of them mounted coaxially in a turret which was surmounted by a cylindrical chimney, providing an escape hatch for the crew.

Type 3 Ka-Chi Amphibious Tank

Entered service: 1942
Crew: 7
Weight: 28,700kg/28.3 tons
Dimensions: Length – 10.3m/33ft 9.5in
　　Height (over turret hatch) – 3.82m/12ft 6.5in
　　Width – 3m/9ft 10in
Armament: Main – 47mm/1.85in gun
　　Secondary – 2 x 7.7mm/0.303in machine-guns
Armour: Maximum – 50mm/1.97in
Powerplant: Mitsubishi 100 V12 diesel,
　　179kW/240hp
Performance: Speed – 32kph/19.9mph
　　Range – 319km/198.2 miles

LEFT: **The Type 3 Ka-Chi Amphibious Tank, seen here out of the water after its capture by the Americans. Weighing 28,700kg/28.3 tons, mainly due to its large, detachable pontoons, it was developed by the Japanese Navy after the Army lost interest in amphibians. Note the submarine-type escape hatch on the top of the turret.**

Type 5 To-Ku Amphibious Tank

Largest of the Japanese amphibious tanks was the Type 5 To-Ku, the increase in size enabling an increase in firepower. It mounted a 47mm/1.85in main gun and a machine-gun in the front of its hull with a further 25mm/0.98in naval cannon and a coaxial machine-gun in its turret. However, the vehicle never reached full production before the end of World War II.

Type 5 To-Ku Amphibious Tank

Entered service: 1945
Crew: 7
Weight: 29,465kgkg/29 tons
Dimensions: Length – 10.81m/35ft 5.5in
　　Height (over turret hatch) – 3.00m/9ft 10in
　　Width – 3.38m/11ft 1 in
Armament: Main – 47mm/1.85in gun and
　　25mm/0.98in cannon
　　Secondary – 2 x 7.7mm/0.303in machine-guns
Armour: Maximum – 50mm/1.97in
Powerplant: Type 100 V12 diesel, 179kW/240hp
Performance: Speed – 32kph/20mph
　　Range – 319km/198 miles

LEFT: **The Type 5 To-Ku Amphibious Tank was the largest of the Japanese amphibious tanks and mounted a 47mm/1.85in gun and a machine-gun in its front hull, while in the turret was a naval 25mm/0.98in cannon and another machine-gun. It weighed 29,465kg/29 tons with its pontoons. On this model the escape tower had been done away with.**

Type 95 Ha-Go Light Tank

Speedy and reliable, the Ha-Go was one of the best tanks to be built by the Japanese, and it saw action in China and then throughout the Far East in World War II. It was powered by an advanced 6-cylinder 89.5kW/120hp diesel engine giving it a speed of 45kph/28mph, steered by the clutch and brake method with front drive sprockets and had a sliding transmission allowing four forward and one reverse gear. Its small turret was offset to the left and

mounted a 37mm/1.46in gun as its main armament, with another coaxial 7.7mm/0.303in machine-gun alongside. The somewhat bulbous superstructure protruded out over the tracks with an extra prominence for the bow 7.7mm/0.303in machine-gun.

The tank had a crew of three and suffered from the disadvantage of having the bow machine-gunner seated next to the driver in the hull leaving the commander to load, aim and fire the

ABOVE LEFT: **Undoubtedly the most-used small Japanese tank of the war. The Type 95 Ha-Go saw action in China and then throughout the Far East.**
ABOVE: **An excellent photograph of a Japanese tank commander standing proudly in front of his three-man Ha-Go.** BELOW LEFT: **The main armament of the Ha-Go was a 37mm/1.46in gun, and it also had two machine-guns. With a crew of three, it had a top speed of 45kph/28mph.**

turret guns by himself. There was also an amphibious version based on the Ha-Go that was known as the Type 2 Ka-Mi and intended for Japanese Navy use. Some 1,350 Ha-Go were built between 1935–43.

Type 95 Ha-Go Light Tank

Entered service: 1935
Crew: 3
Weight: 7,400kg/7.28 tons
Dimensions: Length – 4.38m/14ft 4.5in
　　Height (over turret hatch) – 2.18m/7ft 2in
　　Width – 2.06m/6ft 9in
Armament: Main – 37mm/1.46in gun
　　Secondary – 2 x 7.7mm/0.303in machine-guns
Armour: Maximum – 12mm/0.47in
Powerplant: Mitsubishi NVD 6-cylinder diesel, 89.5kW/120hp
Performance: Speed – 45kph/28mph
　　Range – 242km/150.4 miles

Type 89B Ot-Su Medium Tank

Entered service: 1936 (designed in 1929)
Crew: 4
Weight: 13,000kg/12.8 tons
Dimensions: Length – 5.73m/18ft 9.5in
    Height (over turret hatch) – 2.56m/8ft 5in
    Width – 2.13m/7ft
Armament: Main – 57mm/2.24in gun
    Secondary – 2 x 6.5mm/0.256in machine-guns
Armour: Maximum – 17mm/0.67in
Powerplant: Mitsubishi 6-cylinder diesel,
    89.5kW/120hp
Performance: Speed – 26kph/16.2mph
    Range – 170km/105.6 miles

LEFT: **The Type 89 Ot-Su Medium Tank was developed from the British Vickers Medium. Its main armament was a 57mm/2.24in gun.**

Type 89B Ot-Su Medium Tank

Having obtained a Vickers Medium C from Britain, the Japanese Osaka Arsenal produced a modified version in the Type 89 Light Tank of just under 10,160kg/10 tons, mounting a 57mm/2.24in main gun and two machine-guns. They were so delighted with this design that they used it as the basis for a heavier medium tank (Type 89) which was standardized in 1929. From 1936, a diesel version of this tank, the Type 89B, was developed by Mitsubishi and remained in service during most of World War II.

There were two versions; the first had a one-piece front plate, the driver being located on the left. Main armament was a Type 90 57mm/2.24in gun and there was a 6.5mm/0.256in machine-gun at the rear of the turret, plus another one on the right of the front plate. The second model had the driver's position and machine-gun reversed, while the front plate was all in one piece. The skirting plates had also been redesigned, with four return rollers in place of the five girder-mounted return rollers of the previous model, while the armament remained the same.

Like most Japanese tanks, the Ot-Su fared badly against Allied armour such as the M4 Sherman because they were undergunned and underarmoured by comparison, due to the Japanese disinterest in tanks for most of the war.

Type 97 Chi-Ha Medium Tank

Probably the most successful of all Japanese tank designs, the Chi-Ha saw service throughout World War II, having been selected for mass production in 1937. However, its medium status could really only be considered in Japanese tank production, for in combat it was no match for the Sherman or other Allied medium tanks. It was essentially a scaled-up version of the Type 95 Ha-Go Light Tank fitted with a two-man turret and armed with a 57mm/2.24in short-barrelled main gun and two machine-guns, one of which was mounted at the turret rear. With a crew of four, this tank weighed nearly 15 tons, had a helical suspension system with clutch and brake steering, and was powered by a 126.8kW/170hp air-cooled diesel engine with a top speed of 39kph/24mph. As the war progressed and the Japanese came to realize just how underdeveloped their AFVs were when compared with the opposition, the demand grew for more powerful equipment. A later development (1942) was the Shinhoto Chi-Ha ("New Turret" Chi-Ha), an interim model Type 97 Chi-Ha fitted with a modified turret which mounted a long-barrelled, high-velocity 47mm/1.85in main gun.

LEFT: **This Chi-Ha was photographed at the Aberdeen Proving Ground in the USA. Unfortunately, most of their exhibits are outdoors, so they inevitably deteriorate.**

Type 97 Chi-Ha Medium Tank

Entered service: 1937
Crew: 4
Weight: 15,000kg/14.8 tons
Dimensions: Length – 5.5m/18ft 0.5in
    Height (over turret hatch) – 2.23m/7ft 4in
    Width – 2.33m/7ft 7.5in
Armament: Main – 57mm/2.24in gun
    Secondary – 2 x 7.7mm/0.303 machine-guns
Armour: Maximum – 25mm/0.98in
Powerplant: Mitsubishi 97 V12 diesel,
    126.8kW/170hp
Performance: Speed – 39kph/24.2mph
    Range – 200km/124.3 miles

Vickers Commercial Dutchman Light Tank

ABOVE: **A modern photograph of the Bovington Tank Museum's "Dutchman" in its striking pre-war camouflage. Mechanically similar to the Vickers Mark IV Light Tank, it was powered by a Meadows 65.6kW/88bhp engine.**

Between the wars, Vickers Armstrong, having absorbed Carden-Loyd, became a major player in the international arms industry, building prototypes and exporting AFVs all over the world. The Commercial Dutchman was one such venture, sold to the Dutch East Indies and China. Some were still in the UK when war broke out and were pressed into service, although used only for training. This vehicle was to all intents and purposes mechanically the same as the Vickers Light Mark IV, the only major difference being its hexagonally shaped turret.

Vickers Commercial Dutchman Light Tank

Entered service: 1936
Crew: 2
Weight: 3,860kg/3.8 tons
Dimensions: Length – 3.63m/11ft 11in
 Height (over turret hatch) – 2m/6ft 7in
 Width – 1.8m/5ft 11in
Armament: Main – Vickers 7.7mm/0.303in MG
Armour: Maximum – 10mm/0.39in
Powerplant: Meadows 6-cylinder, 65.6kW/88bhp
Performance: Speed – 65kph/40mph
 Range – 209.2km/130 miles

BELOW: **Sharing this colourful stand with the Vickers 6 Ton at the Bovington Tank Museum is the other Vickers export model, the Light Tank, Model 1936, also known as the "Dutchman" (it was sold to China and to the Dutch East Indies).**

Vickers 6 Ton Tank

Although the British Army was not interested in purchasing the Vickers 6 Ton Tank, it became one of the bestsellers of its day – being exported to many countries, including the USSR, Poland, Bulgaria, Greece, Finland, Portugal, Bolivia, Thailand and China. The first versions had twin turrets with Vickers 7.7mm/0.303in machine-guns, and the later ones a 3pdr (47mm/1.85in) main gun and coaxial machine-gun in a single turret. The Vickers 6 Ton had a crew of three and featured some new features, including a "Laryngophone" system for internal communication, new improved suspension and had a fitted fireproof partition separating the engine from the fighting compartment. For some countries it was an influential design that

was copied (such as the Polish 7TP and Russian T-26), being mechanically straightforward and, for its size, well-armoured with good firepower.

Although rejected by the British, they established a formidable combat record in foreign service. For example, they saw action for the first time in the Gran Chaco War, when Bolivian 6 Tonners fought in the battle for Nanawa in August 1933. Later, in both the Spanish Civil War and the Winter War between Russia and Finland, 6 Tonners fought each other. It was also one of the principal tanks of the Polish armoured corps, so fought against the German invasion in 1939. The Chinese used theirs against the Japanese in Manchuria, and the Thais did the same in the 1940–41 war against Indo-China.

ABOVE: **Although it was called the Vickers 6 Ton Tank, it actually weighed 7,115kg/7 tons! It was sold (and copied) all over the world, but was not initially purchased by the British Army. They did eventually take over some of the undelivered overseas orders and used them for training purposes when World War II began in 1939.**

Vickers 6 Ton Tank	

Entered service: 1928
Crew: 3
Weight: 7,115kg/7 tons
Dimensions: Length – 4.57m/15ft
    Height (over turret hatch) – 2.08m/6ft 10in
    Width – 2.42m/7ft 11in
Armament: Main – 2 x 7.7mm/0.303in
    machine-guns (later, 1 x 3pdr and 1 machine-gun)
Armour: Maximum – 13mm/0.51in
Powerplant: Armstrong-Siddeley 4-cylinder petrol,
    64.8kW/87hp
Performance: Speed 32kph/20mph
    Range – 200km/124 miles

A–Z of Modern Tanks

1945 to the Present Day

The Cold War and the limited wars in such places as the Far and Middle East have ensured the continuing need for tanks. In particular, there has been a requirement for Main Battle Tanks (MBTs) with improved, more powerful weapons, sophisticated gun control and viewing equipment, more effective protection, and better engines and running gear. MBTs have grown larger and heavier, yet are faster and more manoeuvrable, with tanks like the Abrams and Challenger being far superior to their World War II equivalents. Major changes have also occurred among tank builders. In the last war it was really only the USA, USSR, Germany and the UK that produced tanks. Now there are some 30 nations either building their own MBT, a "cloned" replica of a major producer's tank, or an upgraded version of an older model. China is now a major producer, as are, once again, Germany and France. Even smaller nations like Israel and Japan build excellent MBTs. With the advent of global terrorism, there has also been a shift in requirement away from MBTs towards more strategically mobile AFVs, but mounting larger weapon systems than in the past.

LEFT: **Vastly superior to Leopard 1, the Leopard 2 is currently one of the best Main Battle Tanks in service in the world.**

A41 Centurion Medium Tank

The A41 Centurion is undoubtedly one of the major British successes in tank design and production. The mock-up was ready in May 1944, but troop trials did not begin until May 1945 (due to a Government ruling banning development work on all projects that could not be in service by 1944), so it never saw action during World War II. Twenty pilot models were ordered mounting a 17pdr gun as their main weapon and with a mixture of Polsten cannon (in a ball-mount) or Besa machine-gun as secondary armament, the first ten only having Polstens. The Mark II (A41A) incorporated numerous improvements including a cast turret, commander's vision cupola and a combined gunner's periscope and coaxial Besa machine-gun. This became the first production model, known thereafter as the Centurion 2.

Over 4,400 Centurions in 12 different models were produced, the most plentiful being over 2,800 Centurion 3s. This version incorporated numerous major improvements, including the more efficient 484.7kW/650bhp Rolls-Royce Meteor engine, the Ordnance Quick-Firing 20pdr main gun together and new gun control equipment. It was the first British tank that could fire accurately on the move thanks to its gyroscopic gun control system, while the policy of not storing ammunition above the turret ring greatly increased its chances of survival by limiting ammunition fires. Many other modifications and improvements were constantly being added as the years went by, the most important being the fitting of the 105mm/4.13in rifled gun. Centurions saw action in Korea,

TOP: **An early Centurion Mark 3 on the test track at the Fighting Vehicle Research and Development Establishment, Chertsey. Originally armed with a 17pdr, then 20pdr and finally 105mm/4.13in gun, the Centurion was one of Britain's most successful post-war main battle tanks and sold in large numbers worldwide.** ABOVE: **Sweden made an initial order for 88 Mark 3s (known as the Stridsvagn 81). Later they would purchase more, including Centurion Mark 10s (known as Stridsvagn 102), as seen here.**

Vietnam and numerous other wars, having been purchased by many nations, perhaps most notably by the Israelis who had over 1,000 Centurions in service at one time. At the beginning of the 21st century this excellent AFV is still to be found in use with some countries.

RIGHT: **Sweden purchased two Marks of Centurion in the late 1950s, renaming them Stridsvagn 101 and 102. This is an up-armoured version of the Stridsvagn 102.** BELOW RIGHT: **The Israeli Army was at one time the largest user of the Centurion, with over 1,000 in service. This one is on show at the IDF Tank Museum at Latrun. Initially the Centurion had a poor reputation until General Israel Tal, a man of wide technical expertise and character, took a hand and instilled the essential gunnery discipline into his crews which swiftly showed the gun's inherent accuracy.** BOTTOM: **A Centurion Beach Armoured Recovery Vehicle, whose primary role was to rescue drowned vehicles to the shoreline and to keep exits from landing craft clear during beach landings. They went on serving in the British Army long after other Centurions, one each being manned by the Royal Marines on HMS *Fearless* and HMS *Intrepid* (Landing Platform Dock Ships).**

In addition to gun tanks, there are Centurion Armoured Recovery Vehicles (ARVs), specialized Beach ARVs, Assault Engineer – Armoured Vehicle Royal Engineers (AVRE) and armoured bridgelayers – Armoured Vehicle Launched Bridge (AVLB).

In 2004 there were four major countries with significant numbers of Centurion gun tanks/variants in service, although Israel has converted most of its 1,000 to other roles. Jordan had 293 (called *Tariq*), which are now being replaced by Challenger 1 Main Battle Tanks. Singapore had between 12 and 63, based in Brunei and Taiwan. South Africa had 224, which are known as *Olifant*.

A41 Centurion Medium Tank

Entered service: 1945
Crew: 4
Weight: 43,182kg/42.5 tons
Dimensions: Length – 7.47m/24ft 6in
  Height (over turret hatch) – 3.02m/9ft 11in
  Width – 3.40m/11ft 2in
Armament: Main – 17pdr (76mm/2.99in) gun
  Secondary – 7.92mm/0.312in Besa machine-gun
Armour: Maximum – 101.6mm/4in
Powerplant: Meteor V12 petrol, 484.7kW/650hp
Performance: Speed – 35.4kph/22mph
  Range – 193.1km/120 miles

M1A1/M1A2 Abrams Main Battle Tank

The M1A1/2 Abrams Main Battle Tank is the prime weapon of the US armoured forces, and is manufactured by General Dynamics Land Systems. The first M1 tank came into service in 1978, the M1A1 in 1985, and the M1A2 in 1986. Since then, system enhancement packages have kept this AFV as a state-of-the-art weapons system, and undoubtedly one of the most formidable tanks in the world.

Built using steel-encased depleted uranium armour to protect against modern HEAT (High-Explosive Anti-Tank) weapons, the M1A1's main weapon is the 120mm/4.72in M256 smoothbore gun (the original M1 had a 105mm/4.13in gun), developed by Rheinmetall GmbH of Germany, with a 7.62mm/0.3in M240 machine-gun mounted coaxially on its right. The commander also has a 12.7mm/0.5in Browning M2 machine-gun and the loader a 7.62mm/0.3in M240 machine-gun.

Needless to say, the tank is crammed full of the most advanced electronic equipment. The commander's station is equipped with an independent stabilized day and night vision

TOP: **The XM1 tank programme was begun in 1971, and five years later Chrysler was awarded a three-year contract to produce 11 pilot vehicles and spares at the Detroit Arsenal Tank Plant. In 1982, Chrysler sold its tank building subsidiary to General Motors. First-production MBT was completed in February 1980. It is anticipated that in total (up to and including the M1A2 MBT upgrades), the US Army will order over 1,000 such M1 upgrades, while sales to other countries (e.g. 555 to Egypt) were agreed and delivered in 1998. This photograph of a basic M1 gives a good impression of its power, speed and protection.** RIGHT: **A column of Abrams returning from training. With a combat weight of 57,154kg/56.3 tons and a maximum road speed of 67.6kph/42mph, the Abrams is a formidable sight to meet anywhere.**

LEFT: **Three of the four-man crew are visible in this photograph of an M1A1, two of the turret crew manning secondary armament (both 7.62mm/0.3in machine-guns), while the driver's excellent central position is evident.** BELOW: **Excellent internal view of the M1A1 turret, looking at the gunner's station and the rear of the breech.**

device with a 360-degree view, automatic sector scanning, automatic target cueing of the gunner's sight and back-up fire control. The gunner's specially modified seat also locks him in position so that even on the move his eyes are unwaveringly locked in his sight.

The powerplant was originally diesel for the M1/M1A1 models, but the M1A2 is fitted with a new gas turbine engine which is more powerful but uses more fuel. However, like all of the most modern tanks, the Abrams is built in a modular fashion, whereby new feature "suites" or packages can replace any previous one. In this way, any of the main features of the tank – turret, armament, and power pack – can be constantly refined and upgraded.

The Abrams combat effectiveness has been proved in the recent conflicts in the Gulf, where it dominated the battlefield completely. It has also been sold to Egypt, Saudi Arabia, Kuwait and Australia. Those M1A1s in service with the USMC are fitted with a Deep Water Fording Kit (DWFK).

BELOW: **Three Abrams use the concrete test slopes at the factory to show off their paces. The MBT can deal with a 60 per cent gradient, a side slope of 30 per cent and a 0.914m/3ft vertical obstacle.** BOTTOM: **Operation "Desert Storm". Abrams manoeuvre in the Iraqi desert during Operation "Desert Storm", when the US Army had 1,956 M1A1 Abrams MBTs deployed with units in Saudi Arabia.**

M1A1 Abrams MBT

Entered service: 1985
Crew: 4
Weight: 57,154kg/56.3 tons
Dimensions: Length – 9.77m/32ft 0.5in
  Height (over turret hatch) – 2.44m/8ft
  Width – 3.66m/12ft
Armament: Main – 120mm/4.72in M256
  smoothbore gun
  Secondary – 1 x 7.62mm/0.3in coaxial machine-gun,
  plus 1 x 12.7mm/0.5in machine-gun (commander)
  and 1 x 7.62mm/0.3in machine-gun (loader)
Armour: Thickness unknown, depleted uranium,
  steel
Powerplant: AGT 1500 gas turbine,
  1,118.6kW/1,500hp
Performance: Speed – 67.6kph/42mph
  Range – 465.1km/289 miles

AAI Rapid Deployment Force Light Tank

Manufactured by the AAI Corporation in conjunction with the US Army's Tank-Automotive Research and Development Command Armored Combat Vehicle Technology (ACVT), the AAI AFV was an air-portable light tank designed to boost the firepower of Rapid Deployment Forces (RDFs). This tank was a development of the HSTV(L) project and was part of the continuing attempt to perfect air-transportable firepower

that began during World War II and is especially relevant to the war scenarios of today. The vehicle shares its main armament with the earlier AAI HSTV(L) – the ARES 75mm/2.95in hypervelocity automatic gun, with a range of over 12.1km/7.5 miles at maximum elevation. This weapon was so advanced that the ARES Corporation was forbidden by the US Government to sell it to anyone other than NATO member countries. The

prohibition effectively killed off the AAI RDF, although the company did try to rescue the vehicle by bringing out a heavier model mounting a 76mm/2.99in main gun in a newly designed turret. However, there was no sales interest generated and in 1985 the project was shelved.

AAI RDF Light Tank

Entered service: 1983 (prototypes only)

Crew: 3

Weight: 13,200kg/13 tons

Dimensions: Length – 7.34m/24ft
Height (over turret hatch) – 2.24m/7ft 4in
Width – 2.54m/8ft 4in

Armament: Main – 75mm/2.95in ARES
or 76mm/2.99in M32 gun
Secondary – 7.62mm/0.3in machine-gun

Armour: Maximum – Unrevealed

Powerplant: General Motors 6V53T 6-cylinder
diesel, 224kW/300hp

Performance: Speed – 64kph/39.9mph
Range – 500km/310.6 miles

ABOVE AND LEFT: **Two views of the AAI Corporation's Rapid Deployment Force Light Tank (RDF/LT) which mounted the ARES Corporation 75mm/2.95in hypervelocity automatic gun with a range of some 12.1km/7.5 miles! Based upon an experimental AFV, it had export problems due to its experimental main armament. This meant it could not be exported outside NATO, so a 76mm/2.99in gun was offered as an alternative.**

Alan Degman Main Battle Tank

First revealed in the late 1990s, the Croatian Degman MBT traces its origins back to the Yugoslavian M-84A, itself a Russian T-72 derivative manufactured in Yugoslavia since the previous decade. Specifications for this vehicle are sketchy, but it is based closely upon its predecessor and weighs approximately 40,600kg/40 tons, and is powered by a new diesel engine with automatic transmission delivering a top speed of around 60kph/37mph with a range of about 600km/370 miles. The turret is of a new Croatian design and manufacture, and includes the fitting of ERA (Explosive Reactive Armour) modules that are formed in distinctive long bands and are also positioned on the glacis plate and sides skirts. (Most Eastern European and ex-Soviet satellite states have been influenced by the Russian predilection for ERA.)

It mounts the up-rated D-81 125mm/ 4.92in smoothbore main gun, served by an automatic loader, thereby allowing a crew of just three, along with two machine-guns – one coaxial 7.62mm/ 0.3in and the other of 12.7mm/0.5in for anti-aircraft and close-quarter defence.

The vehicle's fire control is based on the Omega system designed and manufactured in Slovenia, and its communications systems have been sourced from the UK.

Other enhancements include NBC (Nuclear, Biological and Chemical) protection, navigation and safety systems. The Degman is currently in service with the Croatian Army and has also been sold to Kuwait. There are also command, ARV (Armoured Recovery Vehicle) and engineering variants.

Alan Degman MBT

Entered service: 1999
Crew: 3
Weight: Approximately 40,600kg/40 tons
Dimensions: Close to T-72 specifications
Armament: Main – 125mm/4.92in D-81 gun
Secondary – 1 x 7.62mm/0.3in and
1 x 12.7mm/0.5in machine-guns
Armour: Unspecified
Powerplant: Unspecified diesel generating around
745.7kW/1,000hp
Performance: Speed – Approximately 60kph/37mph
Range – Approximately 600km/370 miles

LEFT AND BELOW: **The RH Alan Degman Croatian MBT that was first seen in 1999 is an enhanced version of the Yugoslavian T-84A MBT, which in turn was based on the Russian T-72 MBT. Although sometimes called the M95, it is very similar to the M-84/M-84A and is armed with a 125mm/4.92in smoothbore gun with an automatic loader.**

Alvis Scimitar Combat Vehicle Reconnaissance (Tracked)

LEFT: The latest version of the original Alvis Combat Vehicle Reconnaissance Scimitar is the Alvis Sabre Reconnaissance Vehicle, which has the same original chassis as the Scimitar, but with the two-man operated Fox turret, mounting the L94 Hughes 7.62mm/0.3in chain gun and extra bins.
BELOW: A CVR(T) Scimitar on training. 165 rounds were carried (in clips of three) for the 30mm/1.18in Rarden cannon. Basically a single-shot weapon, it could fire short bursts of up to six rounds.
BOTTOM LEFT: A trio of Scimitars on training/ operations in the north of the NATO area.

The Scimitar is the light reconnaissance version of the Combat Vehicle Reconnaissance (Tracked) – CVR(T) – series produced by Alvis of Coventry. It was primarily designed to deal with hostile Armoured Personnel Carriers (APCs) and other lightly armoured vehicles at ranges of about 1,000m/1,087yds or more, and also for close reconnaissance and internal security roles.

Like the Scorpion, its outstanding cross-country performance and low silhouette, combined with its small size, enabled the Scimitar to perform these tasks very well indeed. It was also ideal for the "shoot and scoot" tactics of

fighting a delaying battle. The vehicle's hull and turret was built out of a newly developed aluminium-zinc-magnesium alloy and mounts a 30mm/ 1.18in Rarden gun as its main armament, along with a coaxial 7.62mm/0.3in machine-gun. Powered by a Jaguar XK J60, 4.2-litre 6-cylinder engine giving a top speed of 80.5kph/50mph, the Scimitar has a crew of three, with the driver in the hull and the other two in the turret side by side – each with a cupola.

A later 1993 upgrade of the Scimitar was the Sabre, equipped with a new turret, mounting the L49 Hughes 7.62mm/0.3in high velocity chain gun along with a Rarden 30mm/1.18in cannon. As with all the vehicles in this successful series, the Scimitar was sold abroad to various countries.

Alvis Scimitar CVR(T)

Entered service: 1973
Crew: 3
Weight: 7,900kg/7.8 tons
Dimensions: Length – 4.39m/14ft 4.5in
　　　　Height (over turret hatch) – 2.09m/6ft 10.5in
　　　　Width – 2.18m/7ft 2in
Armament: Main – 30mm/1.18in Rarden cannon
　　　　Secondary – 7.62mm/0.03in machine-gun
Armour: Unspecified
Powerplant: Jaguar 4.2 litre petrol, 141.7kW/190hp
Performance: Speed – 80.5kph/50mph
　　　　Range – 644km/400 miles

LEFT: **One of the latest versions of this replacement for the ubiquitous Saladin armoured car was this Scorpion 90, which Alvis fitted with a 90mm/3.54in Cockerill Mark 3 gun, reducing its ammunition load from 40 rounds with the 76mm/2.99in to 34 with the 90mm/3.54in. Malaysia bought some 26 Scorpion 90s in the late 1980s and early 90s, as did Nigeria (33), and it is also believed that Venezuela bought an undisclosed number in the 1980s (possibly over 80).**

BELOW: **The first prototype appeared in 1969 (production three years later) and has been in service in various forms ever since as the lead AFV of the Combat Vehicle Reconnaissance (Tracked) family. Used in both low and high intensity warfare, Scorpion mounts a 76mm/2.99in gun and has a crew of three.**

Alvis Scorpion Combat Vehicle Reconnaissance (Tracked)

Produced by Alvis of Coventry as a replacement for the ageing Saladin and Saracen wheeled vehicles, the Combat Vehicle Reconnaissance (Tracked) – CVR(T) – family comprised: Scorpion – Fire Support; Scimitar – Anti-APC (Armoured Personnel Carrier); Spartan – APC; Samson – ARV; Striker – Anti-Tank Guided Weapon (ATGW); Sultan – ACV (Armoured Combat Vehicle); and Samaritan – Ambulance.

All were deliberately compact enough to be air-transportable. The Scorpion, with its light but strong aluminium alloy armour weighed 7,800kg/7.67 tons and was fast, with a top speed of 80.5kph/

50mph. It had the same basic design, layout and crew numbers as the Scimitar, but was fitted with a more powerful main gun – the L23A1 76mm/2.99in – along with a coaxial 7.62mm/0.3in machine-gun.

The L23A1 fires four types of ammunition: HESH (High-Explosive Squash-Head) – capable of defeating medium armour at a range of up to 3,500m/11,500ft and also very effective against the tracks and side armour of most MBTs; HE (High-Explosive); Smoke – base ejection type; and Canister – a short-range anti-infantry round which produces 800 steel pellets to devastating

effect. The gun has a maximum range of 5,000m/16,400ft and a relatively low muzzle velocity which contributes to the accuracy by producing a light recoil and low barrel wear (each barrel can fire 3,000 HESH rounds). One of the latest versions is Scorpion 90, which is equipped with the 90mm/3.54in Cockerill Mark 3 main gun.

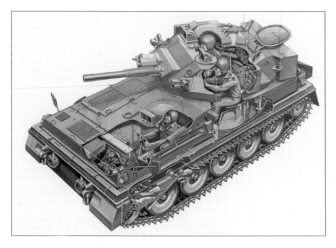

LEFT: **Cutaway drawing of a Scorpion CVR(T), fitted with its flotation screen. It was built of aluminium alloy armour, which did produce some problems; however, it was certainly both light and fast. The original version is no longer in British Army service. However, as the other photographs show, a variety of other models are still available.**

Alvis Scorpion CVR(T)

Entered service: 1973
Crew: 3
Weight: 7,800kg/7.67 tons
Dimensions: Length – 4.39m/14ft 5in
    Height (over turret hatch) – 2.08m/6ft 10in
    Width – 2.18m/7ft 2in
Armament: Main – 76mm/2.99in or 90mm/3.54in gun
    Secondary – 7.62mm/0.03in machine-gun
Armour: Maximum – Unspecified thickness, aluminium
Powerplant: Jaguar 4.2 petrol, 141.7kW/190hp
Performance: Speed – 80.5kph/50mph
    Range – 644km/400 miles

AMX-13 Light Tank

Designed just after World War II, the AMX-13 (the "13" in its name is its original designated weight in tonnes) was initially manufactured in 1950 by Atelier de Construction Roanne, then from the early 1960s by Mecanique Creusot-Loire, and finally by GIAT into the late 1980s, a lengthy period that saw it grow into a large family of successful variants.

The AMX-13 was manned by a crew of three and powered by a SOFAM 8-cylinder petrol engine, giving it a top speed of 60kph/37.3mph and a range of 400km/248.5 miles. Its most distinctive feature was the extraordinary rear-mounted, low-profile, oscillating turret.

Initially mounting a long-barrelled 75mm/2.95in self-loading main gun based on a pre-1945 German design, it was then upgraded to a 90mm/3.54in weapon and then in 1987 Creusot-Loire introduced a 105mm/4.13in low-recoil gun option. When the AMX-13 was sold abroad, some other countries also mounted their own weapons of choice.

All these main gun upgrades continued to be based on the original oscillating turret, which proved to be troublesome. The excellent tough chassis remained essentially the same, though there were changes of engine from petrol to diesel. Variants included an

ABOVE: **The highly successful AMX-13, designed soon after the end of World War II by Atelier de Construction d'Issy les Moulineaux, the significance of the "13" being its original weight in tonnes. Production was subsequently moved to the Creusot-Loire factory at Chalon sur Saone, and over 7,700 AFVs were eventually built, including variants such as self-propelled artillery guns, anti-aircraft guns and infantry fighting vehicles. One feature of the original model was its oscillating FL-10 turret, containing a 75mm/2.95in gun and coaxial machine-gun.**

armoured personnel carrier, a light recovery vehicle, an armoured bridgelayer, different calibres of self-propelled gun and an artillery rocket-system launch platform. Regular upgrade packages extended the AMX-13's service life, and almost 8,000 vehicles were manufactured.

ABOVE: **Now on show at the Israeli Tank Museum at Latrun, Israel purchased a number of AMX-13s from France in 1956 and used them in the Six Day War. However, the gun, with its two revolver-type magazines (each 6 rounds), was ineffective against the front armour of Soviet-sourced tanks such as T-54/T-55, so it was phased out and sold elsewhere.**

AMX-13 Light Tank

Entered service: 1950
Crew: 3
Weight: 15,000kg/14.8 tons
Dimensions: Length – 4.88m/16ft
    Height (over turret hatch) – 2.3m/7ft 6.5in
    Width – 2.51m/8ft 3in
Armament: Main – 75mm/2.95in or 90mm/3.54in
    or 105mm/4.13in
    Secondary – 2 x 7.5mm/0.295in or 7.62mm/0.3in
    machine-guns
Armour: Maximum – 25mm/0.98in
Powerplant: SOFAM 8Gxb petrol, 186.4kW/250hp
Performance: Speed – 60kph/37.3mph
    Range – 400km/248.5 miles

AMX-30 Main Battle Tank

Manufactured by Giat Industries, the AMX-30 Main Battle Tank was first produced in the mid-1960s as a lighter yet more powerfully armed replacement for the American-supplied M47. It had a crew of four and mounted one 105mm/4.13in main gun with a coaxial 20mm/0.79in cannon and a 7.62mm/0.3in machine-gun. It was powered by a Hispano-Suiza 12-cylinder multi-fuel engine that gave it a top speed of 65kph/40.4mph and a range of 450km/280 miles.

The AMX-30 B2 was an improved version of the AMX-30, some of them newly made and some with the B2

upgrade packages retrofitted to earlier models. The upgrade included an automatic fire-control system and NBC (Nuclear, Biological and Chemical warfare) proofing, enabling the AMX-30 to fight in a contaminated atmosphere. Over 3,500 of this vehicle were built, including variants such as self-propelled howitzers, anti-aircraft missile or gun systems and armoured recovery vehicles.

TOP: **Good photograph of an AMX-30 in a Paris street. Like AMX-13 and others, the AMX-30 was designed post-war to replace the American M47s which had been supplied by the USA via the Mutual Defence Aid Programme.** ABOVE: **The AMX-30 D armoured recovery vehicle has a dozer blade mounted at the front of the hull, plus two winches and a hydraulic crane.** LEFT: **Most advanced of the AMX-30 models is the AMX-30 B2, which was the one in main French Army service. It incorporated many of the improvements, such as laser rangefinder, low-light TV and an integrated fire-control system. There is even an AMX-30 "Stealth" MBT fitted with radar-absorbing material and carefully shaped to reduce the radar signature.**

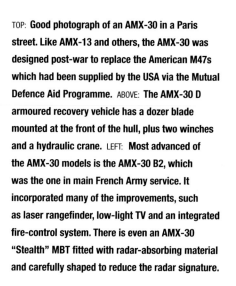

AMX-30 MBT

Entered service: 1967
Crew: 4
Weight: 36,000kg/35.43 tons
Dimensions: Length – 9.48m/31ft 1in
    Height (over turret hatch) – 2.29m/7ft 6in
    Width – 3.1m/10ft 2in
Armament: Main – 105mm/4.13in smoothbore gun
    Secondary – 1 x 20mm/0.79in cannon and
    1 x 7.62mm/0.3in machine-gun
Armour: Maximum – 80mm/3.15in
Powerplant: Hispano-Suiza HS 110 multi-fuel,
    522kW/700hp (for AMX-30 B2)
Performance: Speed – 65kph/40.4mph
    Range – 450km/280 miles

AMX-32 Main Battle Tank

The AMX-32 was developed in 1975 as an export model of the AMX-30 and was available with either a 105mm/4.12in rifled main gun or a 120mm/4.72in smoothbore alternative, along with a coaxial 20mm/0.79in cannon and a 7.62mm/0.3in anti-aircraft machine-gun. The layout, weight, armour and crew numbers remained the same as its predecessor, but the engine was upgraded to the more recent Hispano-Suiza 110-S2R supercharged model developing 800hp, coupled with the ENC gearbox, with lock-up torque converter and hydrostatic steering. However, when no sales interest was generated, the project was dropped in favour of the AMX-40.

TOP: **The AMX-32 was the export model of the AMX-30, having a redesigned turret and thicker front hull armour to give better armoured protection. Weighing just over 38 tons and mounting a 120mm/4.72in smoothbore (second prototype) gun, it was much more powerful than the AMX-30, but had a marginally worse performance.** ABOVE: **Good side view of the AMX-32 export model.** BELOW LEFT: **Despite the improvements, including an all-welded turret in the second prototype, no purchasers materialized, and the AMX-32 was withdrawn.**

AMX-32 MBT

Entered service: 1979
Crew: 4
Weight: 39,000kg/38.38 tons
Dimensions: Length – 9.48m/31ft 1in
   Height (over turret hatch) – 2.29m/7ft 6in
   Width – 3.24m/10ft 7in
Armament: Main – 120mm/4.74in gun
   Secondary – 1 x 20mm/0.79in cannon and
   1 x 7.62mm/0.3in machine-gun
Armour: Maximum – 80mm/3.15in
Powerplant: Hispano-Suiza HS 110-S2R,
   596.6kW/800hp
Performance: Speed – 65kph/40.4mph
   Range – 530km/329 miles

AMX-40 Main Battle Tank

In the early 1980s came the next in the Giat manufactured, export-driven AMX series. As the AMX-32 had failed to attract any sales, the company decided to produce yet another upgrade, the AMX-40. This vehicle was based on the earlier AMX-32, with its essential design and layout remaining much the same, including the main 120mm/4.72in smoothbore main gun and the COTAC fire-control system.

The main improvements came in armour and mobility, the armour thickness being increased, especially on the frontal arc. A new engine was also installed, the Poyaud 12-cylinder diesel, with a top speed of 70kph/43.5mph and a range of 530km/329 miles. In order for the vehicle to make use of this additional power, an extra road wheel was added to each side, and wider tracks were fitted to reduce ground pressure and increase traction, all of which improved the overall performance of the vehicle.

Brought out in 1983, and despite three prototypes completed by late 1984, there was insufficient sales interest in the AMX-40, so it was withdrawn.

ABOVE, BELOW AND BOTTOM LEFT: **Another "hopeful"** French export tank, the AMX-40 was designed by Giat Industries, using the AMX-32 as its model. It first appeared in 1983, and had a better overall performance and agility than its predecessor, although many of its basic characteristics remained unchanged. Sadly, it did not produce any buyers and was therefore withdrawn at prototype stage.

AMX-40 MBT		
Entered service: 1983		
Crew: 4		
Weight: 43,700kg/43 tons		
Dimensions: Length – 10m/32ft 9.5in		
Height (over turret hatch) – 2.29m/7ft 6in		
Width – 3.3m/10ft 10in		
Armament: Main – 120mm/4.72in gun		
Secondary – 1 x 20mm/0.79in cannon and		
1 x 7.62mm/0.3in machine-gun		
Armour: Maximum – 100mm/4in		
Powerplant: Poyaud V12X diesel, 820.3kW/1,100hp		
Performance: Speed – 70kph/43.5mph		
Range – 530km/329 miles		

LEFT: **At 54,000kg/53.1 tons, with a 120mm/ 4.72in smoothbore gun and a speed in excess of 65kph/40.4mph, the Italian Ariete is a formidable second-generation MBT and well able to hold its own on the modern battlefield. Its Oto Breda 120mm/4.72in smoothbore gun can engage targets both by day and night, while it has a laser warning system for added protection (electrically operated smoke grenades being automatically launched when the MBT is lazed by the enemy).**

Ariete Main Battle Tank

The 1995 Consorzio Iveco Fiat and Oto Melara produced C1 Ariete, which is the latest Italian main battle tank. Weighing 54,000kg/53.1 tons and with a crew of four, it is powered by a Fiat V12 MTCA turbo-charged, 12-cylinder diesel engine, giving it a top speed in excess of 65kph/40.4mph and a range of 550km/342 miles. The turret, with crew of commander, gunner and loader, mounts the Oto Breda 120mm/4.72in

smoothbore main gun and is also armed with a 7.62mm/0.3in machine-gun mounted coaxially and another 7.62mm/ 0.3in machine-gun fitted on the roof for air defence. The vehicle carries the latest optical and digital-imaging and fire-control systems, enabling it to fight day and night and to fire on the move. The tank is built in a modular fashion so that elements such as the power pack can be replaced swiftly and easily.

Ariete MBT	
Entered service: 1988	
Crew: 4	
Weight: 54,000kg/53.1 tons	
Dimensions: Length – 7.59m/24ft 11in	
Height (over turret hatch) – 2.5m/8ft 2in	
Width – 3.60m/11ft 9.5in	
Armament: Main – 120mm/4.72in gun	
Secondary – 2 x 7.62mm/0.3in machine-guns	
Armour: Unspecified	
Powerplant: IVECO V12 MTCA diesel, 970kW/1,300hp	
Performance: Speed – 65kph/40.4mph	
Range – 550km/341.8 miles	

Arjun Main Battle Tank

The Arjun Mark 1 is India's first indigenous main battle tank, designed to replace the Vickers Vijayanta. This project began in 1974 as an attempt at armour autonomy but production was delayed by various problems, and the Arjun was held up for many years before finally entering service

at prototype stage in 1987. Built using composite armour, the vehicle is manned by a crew of four (commander, loader and gunner in the turret, and driver in the hull) and mounts a 120mm/4.72in stabilized main gun and also a 7.62mm/ 0.3in machine-gun in its turret, along with all the necessary modern additions

of stabilization, digital fire control, optical and laser sighting and fire suppression. Powered by a MTU MB 838 Ka 501 water-cooled diesel engine delivering a top speed of 72kph/44.7mph and equipped with hydro-pneumatic suspension, the Arjun has a range of approximately 400km/248.5 miles.

LEFT: **In 1974, the Indian Combat Research and Development Establishment began work on a successor to the ageing Vijayanta. However, it was not until April 1987 that its successor, the Arjun, was unveiled. The new MBT has a crew of four and mounts a 120mm/4.72in rifled gun. It is anticipated that some 125 MBTs will be produced in "slow time" for "home" consumption.**

Arjun MBT	
Entered service: 1987 (prototype)	
Crew: 4	
Weight: 58,000kg/57.1 tons	
Dimensions: Length – 9.8m/32ft 2in	
Height (over turret hatch) – 2.43m/8ft	
Width – 3.17m/10ft 5in	
Armament: Main – 120mm/4.72in gun	
Secondary – 1 x 12.7mm/0.5in and	
1 x 7.62mm/0.3in machine-guns	
Armour: Unspecified	
Powerplant: MTU MB 838 Ka 501 diesel, 1,045kW/1,400hp	
Performance: Speed – 72kph/44.7mph	
Range – 400km/248.5 miles	

LEFT: Designed and developed as a private venture by Santa Barbara Sistemas of Spain and Steyr-Daimler-Puch of Austria, this is a combination of the ASCOD IFV chassis which is already in production in Austria, with a South African 105mm/4.13in Rooikat turret. To date, an order for 15 plus a command vehicle has been placed by the Royal Thai Army. The ASCOD 105 in this first colour photograph has an Oto Melara 105LRF turret fitted for trials.
BELOW AND BOTTOM LEFT: The chassis and hull are of all-welded steel armour which provides protection against small-arms fire and shell splinters, its total weight being 28,500kg/28 tons, with a four-man crew. The light tank is now ready for production, but to date the Thais are the only customers.

ASCOD 105 Light Tank

The ASCOD 105 Light Tank emerged in 1996, built as a private commercial venture by a consortium of Spanish and Austrian companies, Santa Barbara Sistemas of Spain and Styr-Daimler-Puch of Austria, who manufactured the vehicle between them and also purchased some of its parts internationally.

Known as the "Ulan" in Austria and in Spain as the "Pizarro", the ASCOD 105 is a light tank variant of the APC ASCOD already being built by the Austrian part of the consortium, Styr-Daimler-Puch. The tank uses the chassis of its sister vehicle, which can carry up to eight infantrymen in addition to the crew of three. The main difference between the two is in the turret and its main armament – the ASCOD 105 being fitted with South

African Denel turret, mounting a 105mm/4.13in GT7 main gun. Weighing 28,500kg/28 tons and fitted with torsion bar suspension, the ASCOD 105 is powered by a German MTU 8VTE22 V90 diesel engine, giving it a top speed of 70kph/43mph and a range of 500km/310 miles.

Alternative main armament mounts include a two-man South African Rooikat turret with a 20mm/0.79in Mauser cannon, an Italian turret fitted with a 25mm/0.98in cannon and two TOW ATGW (Tube-launched, Optically-tracked, Wire-guided Anti-Tank Guided Weapon) launchers and a lower, flatter American turret with just an externally mounted 105mm/4.13in main weapon that reduced the vehicle's profile considerably.

All turret configurations feature digital fire control, gun stabilization, as well as the latest night-vision, navigation and safety systems. As well as being deployed by both Austrian and Spanish armoured forces, the vehicle has also been sold to Thailand.

ASCOD 105 Light Tank

Entered service: 1996
Crew: 4
Weight: 28,500kg/28 tons
Dimensions: Length – 6.61m/21ft 8in
   Height (over turret hatch) – 2.76m/9ft 0.5in
   Width – 3.15m/10ft 4in
Armament: Main – 105mm/4.13in GT7 gun
   Secondary – 2 x 7.62mm/0.3in machine-guns
Armour: Unspecified
Powerplant: MTU 8V183TE22 V90 diesel,
   447.4kW/600hp
Performance: Speed – 70kph/43.5mph
   Range – 500km/310.7 miles

ASU-57 Tank Destroyer

The ASU-57 was part of the USSR's attempt to develop air-portable firepower for use by airborne forces in the years of the Cold War, entering service in 1957. Weighing 7,400kg/ 7.3 tons and manned by a crew of three, it mounted a 57mm/2.24in CH-51M gun around which the superstructure was built, which was set back and sloped to the front where the gun protruded. It also mounted a 7.62mm/0.3in machine-gun for anti-aircraft and close-quarter defence. Powered by a ZIL-123 6-cylinder petrol engine, the ASU-57 had a top speed of 65kph/40.4mph and a range of 320km/198.8 miles. The ASU-57 was used by Soviet forces and their satellite client states well into the 1980s, at which time it would have been beyond the capability of its gun to knock out the then current NATO MBTs, so it was used for other purposes such as LAA (light anti-aircraft).

ASU-57 TD	
Entered service: 1957	
Crew: 3	
Weight: 7,400kg/7.3 tons	
Dimensions: Length – 3.73/12ft 3in	
Height (over turret hatch) – 1.42m/4ft 8in	
Width – 2.2m/7ft 2.5in	
Armament: Main – 57mm/2.24in gun	
Secondary – 1 x 7.62mm/0.3in machine-gun	
Armour: Maximum – 15mm/0.59in	
Powerplant: ZIL-123 6-cylinder petrol, delivering 82kW/110hp	
Performance: Speed – 65kph/40.4mph	
Range – 320km/198.8 miles	

ASU-85 Tank Destroyer

The ASU-85 was a continuation of the ASU series, emerging in 1962 and based upon a PT-76 chassis, though not required to be amphibious but rather air-portable. The main changes from the ASU-57 approach were to the superstructure, which was now completely enclosed, and in its armament, which was upgraded to an 85mm/3.35in D-70 gun in a fixed mount along with a coaxial 7.62mm/0.3in SGMT machine-gun and cupola-mounted 12.7mm/0.5in anti-aircraft machine-gun. At more than double the weight of its predecessor, the ASU-85 now required a new engine, and was fitted with a V6 diesel engine, giving it a speed of 45kph/28mph and a range of 260km/ 161 miles.

ASU-85 TD	
Entered service: 1962	
Crew: 4	
Weight: 15,500kg/15.26 tons	
Dimensions: Length – 6m/19ft 8in	
Height (over turret hatch) – 2.1m/6ft 10.5in	
Width – 2.8m/9ft 2in	
Armament: Main – 85mm/3.35in D-70 gun	
Secondary – 1 x 12.7mm/0.5in and 1 x 7.62mm/0.3in machine-guns	
Armour: Maximum – 40mm/1.58in	
Powerplant: V6 diesel, 179kW/240hp	
Performance: Speed – 45kph/28mph	
Range – 260km/161.5 miles	

LEFT: The US Army provided Brazil with a number of their M41 Light Tanks, which the Brazilians took into service and improved. For example, their M41B had its old petrol engine replaced by a 302kW/ 450hp diesel, while the M41C (seen here) had better vision equipment, additional armour plate and a new 90mm/3.54in gun.

Bernardini M41 Light Tank

Bernardini M41C Light Tank

Entered service: 1983
Crew: 4
Weight: 25,000kg/24.6 tons
Dimensions: Length – 8.21m/26ft 11in
  Height (over turret hatch) – 2.76m/9ft 0.5in
  Width – 3.2m/10ft 6in
Armament: Main – 90mm/3.54in gun
  Secondary – 1 x 12.7mm/0.5in and
  1 x 7.62mm/0.3in machine-guns
Armour: Unspecified
Powerplant: Scania DS14 diesel, 302kW/450hp
Performance: Speed – 70kph/43.5mph
  Range – 600km/372.8 miles

A clever choice or sales pitch determined a useful future for the US-made M41 Walker Bulldog. After an upgrade package which combined items shopped for on the open market and indigenously produced parts which were then assembled locally, the Brazilian Government equipped their armoured forces with an AFV well suited for their

requirements. The first drawback was the short operational range of the original M41 petrol engine. This was soon identified and quickly dealt with by replacement using a locally built Scania DS14 diesel engine, along with new cooling and electrical systems. The original 76mm/2.99in gun was also upgraded by being re-bored locally to

90mm/3.54in, and the final upgrade, the M41C, had additional armour and improved vision equipment. By March 1985, 386 M41s had been upgraded.

Bernardini X1A1 and X1A2 Light Tanks

The Bernardini X1A1 was another example of tank recycling for the US, who was able to call on "obsolete" tanks, and helped Brazil in the development of their own armaments industry. It was based on the M3A1 Stuart Light Tank, combined with another indigenously put together upgrade package consisting of

a new locally designed and built turret which mounted a French-bought 90mm/ 3.54in main gun.

This model, however, did not progress beyond the prototype stage and was followed by the X1A2, which had a completely redesigned chassis fitted with a new two-man turret in which to

mount the 90mm/3.54in main gun. The X1A2 model that was accepted by the Brazilian Army weighed almost 19 tons, with its Saab-Scania 6-cylinder 224kW/300hp diesel engine giving it a top speed of 55kph/34mph and a range of 600km/372.8 miles.

LEFT: The Bernardini X1A2 Light Tank. Essentially its predecessor had been an upgraded US M3A1 Stuart Light Tank fitted with a locally produced 90mm/3.54in French gun. In due course it was replaced by the 100 per cent Brazilian-made X1A2 seen here, which had a brand-new two-man turret and 90mm/3.54in gun. This came into service in the Brazilian Army, but its successor, the X1A3, did not.

Bernardini X1A2 Light Tank

Entered service: 1978
Crew: 3
Weight: 19,000kg/18.7 tons
Dimensions: Length – 6.5m/21ft 4in
  Height (over turret hatch) – 2.45m/8ft 0.5in
  Width – 2.6m/8ft 6.5in
Armament: Main – 90mm/3.54in gun
  Secondary – 1 x 12.7mm/0.5in and
  1 x 7.62mm/0.3in machine-guns
Armour: Unspecified
Powerplant: Saab-Scania DS11 diesel,
  224kW/300hp
Performance: Speed – 55kph/34.2mph
  Range – 600km/372.8 miles

Challenger 1 Main Battle Tank

Manufactured by Vickers Defence Systems (VDS), the Challenger 1 is the last in the progression of British MBTs tracing their origin back to the Centurion through Chieftain. It is based on the Shir 2 – originally an updated Chieftain variant, designed as an export project for the Shah of Iran's armed forces, but accepted by the British Army under the re-designation "Challenger". Built using advanced Chobam composite armour and cast and rolled steel, the emphasis is on protection and firepower rather than mobility. The CR1 mounts a Royal Ordnance 120mm/4.72in L11A5 rifled main gun, fitted with

ABOVE: **Operation "Desert Storm". A CR1 moves up into position. Note the additional armour plates on its sides and fuel drums on its rear.** BELOW LEFT: **The "Chinese Eye" on the side of the turret denotes that this CR1 belongs to 1 RTR.**

a thermal sleeve, fume extractor and muzzle brake, and has two 7.62mm/0.3in machine-guns, one coaxial with the main gun. These weapons are operated by a three-man turret crew – commander, gunner and loader, with the aid of the latest digital and optical range-finding and fire-control equipment. It is powered by a Rolls-Royce CV12 engine, giving it a top speed of 57kph/35mph and a range of 450km/280 miles. Three different models of the CR1 have been developed, with upgrade suites fitted to ensure pre-eminence as one of the world's most formidable tanks.

In September 1978, the MOD had placed an order with the ROF Leeds to supply 243 Challenger 1s. Four years later, in December 1982, the MBT was accepted by the General Staff, by which time production was well under way. The first order was sufficient to equip four armoured regiments, and in July 1984 there was a further order for 64 more to equip a fifth regiment. In 1986, ROF Leeds was bought by Vickers Defence Systems and a new factory was built at Leeds, identical to the VDS Newcastle works. The new factory was operational by late 1987, when a further order for another 76 CR1s was placed by MOD. The last of the CR1s was delivered in mid-1990. Ten years later the last CR1 was phased out of British Army service (late 2000), being replaced by Challenger 2 MBT. Then in March

1999 it was agreed that 288 CR1s would be supplied to Jordan (renamed Al Hussein in Jordanian service).

In addition to the MBTs, the following variants were built: 17 Challenger Training Tanks and 30 Challenger Armoured Repair and Recovery Vehicles (CR ARRV).

The CR1 demonstrated its battle-winning capabilities with a highly successful combat record in the first Gulf War. It was heavily involved in Operation "Desert Storm", destroying some 300 Iraqi MBTs for the loss of no Challengers.

ABOVE AND BELOW: **Factory fresh. These remarkably crisp photographs were taken on "Roll-out" Day at ROF Leeds before it closed. They give excellent all-round views of CR1 No. 33KA 95.** BOTTOM LEFT: **This CR1 is part of IFOR on operational service in the Balkans.**

Challenger 1 MBT	
Entered service: 1982	
Crew: 4	
Weight: 62,000kg/61.02 tons	
Dimensions: Length – 8.33m/26ft 4in	
Height (over turret hatch) – 2.5m/8ft 2.5in	
Width – 3.52m/11ft 6.5in	
Armament: Main – 120mm/4.72in L11A5 gun	
Secondary – 2 x 7.62mm/0.3in machine-guns	
Armour: Unspecified	
Powerplant: Rolls-Royce CV12 diesel, 894.8kW/1,200bhp	
Performance: Speed – 57kph/35.4mph	
Range – 450km/279.6 miles	

Challenger 2 Main Battle Tank

A logical development of the Vickers-built Challenger 1, the Challenger 2 shares its predecessor's hull and automotive parts but has many new and improved features, making it a vastly improved MBT. These include Chobham second-generation composite armour, an NBC (Nuclear, Biological and Chemical) protection suite, and, for the first time in any British tank, both a heating and a cooling system in the crew compartment.

The vehicle's armament consists of a gyrostabilized Royal Ordnance 120mm/4.72in rifled main gun designated the L30, along with a coaxial McDonnell Douglas Helicopter Systems 7.62mm/0.3in chain gun and a 7.62mm/0.3in anti-aircraft machine-gun. Its fire-control system is the latest generation in digital computer technology, as are its range-finding, sighting and fire-suppression systems.

The CR2 carries a crew of four. Power is supplied by a Rolls-Royce Perkins Condor CV12 894.8kW/1,200bhp engine and it is equipped with a Hydrogas variable spring suspension system.

The initial order placed by the MOD in June 1991 was for 127 CR2 MBTs, plus 13 Driver Training Tanks. First to be completed were the Driver Training Tanks (in 1993), so that training could commence before the gun tanks began to arrive.

Interestingly, CR2 was the first post-World War II British tank to be designed, developed and produced by a single manufacturer, VDS (now Alvis Vickers – part of BAe Systems). The first CR2 MBTs were formally accepted into service on May 16, 1994.

TOP AND ABOVE: **The British Army's latest MBT, Challenger 2 (CR2) is now battle-proven, having seen active service both in the Balkans and the Gulf War. As can be seen from these two photographs taken on training, the turret incorporates second-generation Chobham armour – known as "Dorchester", which gives significantly improved protection against both Kinetic and Chemical Energy attacks.**

Two months later, VDS were awarded a second contract to supply a further 259 CR2 MBTs and nine Training Tanks, together with the necessary training and logistic support. This was sufficient to maintain a total of six CR2 MBT-equipped armoured regiments each of 36 CR2s, of which the Royal Scots Dragoon Guards were the first to be so equipped in June 2000. Of course, events have moved on since then, and

RIGHT, BELOW RIGHT AND BOTTOM: **Three views of Britain's Challenger 2 Main Battle Tank on training and operations. This was originally a private venture begun in the 1980s by Vickers Defence Systems and eventually led to a firm production proposal in 1988. The MOD approved the building of nine prototypes (seven at Leeds and two at Newcastle), which led to a contract being awarded for 127 CR2s, plus 13 Driver Training Tanks. CR2 was the very first British Army tank to be completely developed by a single contractor, VDS (now Alvis Vickers – part of BAe Systems). The tank did exceptionally well in Operation "Telic" (the war in Iraq), being rated as one of the best MBTs in the world, along with Abrams, Merkava and Leopard 2.**

the CR2-equipped 7th Armoured Brigade has taken part in war fighting in Iraq, proving the excellence of both the MBT and its crewmen to the world. Sadly, its reward appears to have been a "restructuring" that will reduce the number of CR2s in front-line service. Presumably the rest will be "mothballed". It was at the end of February 2002 that the British Army took delivery of the last of its CR2s, the total being 386.

To date, there has been only one export success, namely to Oman. Their first order, placed in July 1993, was for 18 CR2s, four CR ARRVs and two Driver Training Tanks. This was followed in November 1997 by a further order for 20 CR2 MBTs, again for Oman.

Challenger 2E Main Battle Tank

In the early 1990s, VDS (now Alvis Vickers) embarked on the development of an enhanced export model of the CR2 MBT. It ran for the first time in 1994 and since that date has completed many trials in temperate and desert conditions. The aim has been to take it as the manufacturers have stated: "a generation ahead of current in service MBTs". Undoubtedly CR2 has proved itself to be a "Top Gun" among the world's leading MBTs.

Challenger 2 MBT	

Entered service: 1994
Crew: 4
Weight: 62,500kg/61.51 tons
Dimensions: Length – 8.33m/27ft 4in
   Height (over turret hatch) – 2.49m/8ft 2in
   Width – 3.52m/11ft 6.5in
Armament: Main – 120mm/4.72in L30A1 gun
   Secondary – 1 x 7.62mm/0.3in L94A1 chain gun
   and 1 x 7.62/0.3in L37A2 machine-gun
Armour: Unspecified
Powerplant: Perkins CV12 TCA Condor diesel,
   894.8kW/1,200hp
Performance: Speed – 60kph/37.3mph
   Range – 450km/279.6 miles

Chieftain Main Battle Tank (FV 4202)

Britain's successor to their world-beating Centurion was originally designed in 1956 by Leyland Motors, Centurion's "design parents", who built three prototypes. Then in 1961–62, six more were completed and trials took place. The following year the tank was taken into British Army service and production continued at ROF Leeds and Vickers Defence Systems, Newcastle.

The first true British Main Battle Tank (Centurion was strictly a medium gun tank), the Chieftain had a somewhat chequered early career due to problems with its engine (cracking of cylinder liners, failure of lip seals and piston ring breakages), which meant that it had to be continually up-rated from 436.3kW/585bhp (Mark 4A), to 484.7kW/650bhp (Mark 5A), then to 536.9kW/720bhp (Mark 7A) and finally to 559.3kW/

TOP: **Chieftain on training. There were a total of 12 different Marks of Chieftain, the last (Mark 12) being a Mark 5 with IFCS, Stillbrew armour, TOGS and the No. 11 NBC system.** ABOVE: **A Chieftain MBT moves across the RAC Centre training area during the yearly "Open Day" that used to be held at Gallows Hill, north of Bovington – but sadly no longer.**

750bhp (Mark 8A). Designed as a multi-fuel engine, it was normally run on diesel and as such was extremely dirty. It also showed a tell-tale smoke plume when starting up, which could give away its position. Nevertheless, despite these early problems the Chieftain settled down to become a reliable and well-liked tank.

It was of conventional design with a forward driving compartment, central fighting compartment and a rear compartment for the engine, gearbox and transmission. The driver was centrally positioned in the hull and when closed down adopted a reclining position, which meant that the hull height could be reduced, thus lowering the overall height of the tank's silhouette. In the fighting compartment the loader/radio operator was on the left of the main armament, with the gunner and commander seated on the right. All had the necessary inter-communication equipment and all-round vision devices, both for day and night viewing.

The main armament was the highly effective 120mm/4.72in L11A5 rifled tank gun, which used the bagged charge system for the first time in a British tank, the projectile and charge being separately loaded, the latter being ignited by means of an electrically fired vent tube. This reduced loader fatigue and gave a maximum rate of fire of some eight to ten rounds in the first minute, then six rpm thereafter. Initially the system employed a Ranging machine-gun – a 12.7mm/0.50cal Browning Heavy machine-gun which fired flashing tipped trace ammunition, but this was later replaced by a Tank Laser Sight.

Apart from the Mark 1s, all Chieftains in British Army service were retro-fitted with the fully integrated Improved Fire-Control System (IFCS), which ensured a considerable degree of accurate, first round hits on static targets at up to 3,000m/9.843ft and on moving targets at up to 2,000m/6,562ft.

The Marconi Fighting Vehicle Control System gave four modes of control (stabilizer, power traverse, hand and emergency) and allowed targets to be engaged with reasonable accuracy while on the move. Other gunnery equipment included night IR/WL sights (used in conjunction with the IR/WL searchlight mounted on the left-hand side of the turret) and TOGS (Thermal Observation and Gunnery Sight).

The L60 engine was coupled to a TN 12 epicyclic gearbox, incorporating a Merrit-Wilson differential steering system and electrohydraulic gear selection, with six forward and two reverse gears, plus an emergency low reverse. In all, there were 12 Marks of Chieftain, with various armour configurations, including a passive armour package known as Stillbrew. Some 1,350 Chieftains were built, of which 450 were exported.

The Chieftain was phased out of British Army service in 1996, but may still be found in Iran, Iraq, Jordan, Oman and Kuwait (their Chieftains saw combat during the Iraqi invasion in 1990). The Chieftain was also used as a test bed for the Marconi Marksman twin anti-aircraft gun turret and the "Jagd Chieftain" which mounted a 120mm/4.72in gun in its hull, and was also used to develop the Shir 1 (Chieftain 800), Shir 2 (Chieftain 900) and Khalid (FV 4211). Additionally, there were three variants which are still serving in various parts of the world;

• Chieftain ARRV (Armoured Repair and Recovery Vehicle), which is basically a Chieftain ARV fitted with a powerful crane that can lift a complete CR1 power pack.

• Chieftain AVRE (Armoured Vehicle, Royal Engineers) which, unlike the Centurion AVRE, does not mount a 165mm/6.49in demolition gun but can carry out a variety of engineer tasks with its bulldozer blade (removing obstacles), plastic pipe fascines (filling ditches), plus mine-clearing (either with a mine plough fitted or by using its Giant Viper rocket-propelled system) and laying Class 60 trackway.

• Chieftain AVLB (Armoured Vehicle Launched Bridge), that can be fitted with a variety of single span, folding or "scissors-type" bridges.

TOP: **A Chieftain fitted with the Pearson Engineering track width mine plough system (as fitted to some Chieftain AVLBs during Operation "Desert Storm").** ABOVE: **Chieftain 900, the Royal Ordnance Factory's private venture main battle tank completed in 1982. Its layout was basically the same as the Chieftain, but with the British-developed Chobham armour.** BELOW: **A Chieftain AVRE, carrying pipe fascines and towing a Giant Viper mine clearing rocket device.**

Chieftain Mark 5 MBT (FV 4201)

Entered service: 1963 (Mark 1)

Crew: 4

Weight: 55,000kg/54.13 tons (combat-loaded)

Dimensions: Length (gun forward) – 10.87m/ 35ft 8in
Width (including searchlight) – 3.66m/12ft
Height (overall) – 2.89m/12ft

Armament: Main – 120mm/4.72in L11A7 rifled gun
Secondary – 2 x 7.62mm/0.3in machine-guns, one coaxial and one on the commander's cupola

Armour: Not given

Powerplant: Leyland L60 petrol engine (Mark 7A), 536.9kW/720bhp

Performance: Speed – 48kph/30mph
Range – 400–500km/250–300 miles

Charioteer Tank Destroyer

The Charioteer was a post-World War II development that gave the Royal Armoured Corps a tank destroyer armed with a 20pdr main gun and replaced the aging A30 Avenger and Archer anti-tank weapons that had been manned by the Royal Artillery. This was achieved without any new vehicle having to be designed and was built using existing resources to fill the gap in requirements until something better could be sourced. A recycled Cromwell chassis was modified to take a new, larger turret mounting the same 20pdr main gun as that of the new Centurion tank. This created a powerful tank destroyer at a low unit cost. With a weight of 28,960kg/28.5 tons and powered by a Rolls-Royce Meteor V12 petrol engine, the Charioteer had a top speed of 50kph/31mph and a range of 266km/165 miles. When compared with the Centurion Main Battle Tank, however, its performance was poor, and after 1958, when the Centurion's main armament was upgraded with the 105mm/41.3in L7 gun, the Charioteer became obsolete.

ABOVE AND LEFT: **The FV 4101 Charioteer Tank Destroyer was a refurbished Cromwell on which was mounted a new, larger turret containing the 20pdr gun that was also fitted to the Centurion. These two photographs are of the Charioteer at the Bovington Tank Museum.**

Charioteer TD	

Entered service: 1954
Crew: 4
Weight: 28,960kg/28.5 tons
Dimensions: Length – 6.43m/21ft 1in
    Height (over turret hatch) – 2.44m/8ft
    Width – 3.05m/10ft
Armament: Main – 20pdr (83.88mm/3.3in) QF
    (quick-firing) gun
Armour: Maximum – 60mm/2.36in
Powerplant: Rolls-Royce Meteor V12 petrol,
    447.4kW/600hp
Performance: Speed – 50kph/31mph
    Range – 266km/165 miles

Conqueror Heavy Tank

The appearance of the Russian JS-3 Heavy Tank, with its powerful 122mm/4.8in main gun and thick armour, established the need for heavier British main battle tanks. In 1946 it was therefore decided to produce a completely new range of tanks based on the FV200 Universal Tank, of which the FV201 was the basic gun tank.

Conqueror was developed from the original FV201 prototype, powered by a Rolls-Royce Meteor M120 V12 petrol engine with Merritt-Brown transmission with a modified Horstman suspension. Its main armament, the 120mm/4.72in rifled L1 gun, mounted in a well-shaped turret, was derived from an American tank gun, which in turn was derived from an anti-aircraft gun.

The Conqueror was the first British tank in which the shell case and projectile were separate – and with the Conqueror this was not an advantage because a large brass shell case was used to hold the propellant rather than a bag charge, and this made it very heavy and

ABOVE: **The massive Conqueror Heavy Tank weighed 66,043kg/65 tons. While they were capable of dealing with the heavy Soviet tanks (like JS-3), Conqueror was sadly too large and too heavy, being withdrawn in the mid-1960s when the Centurion 105mm/4.13in gun came into service.**
BELOW LEFT: **The Conqueror Heavy Tank on training.**

cumbersome to load, while the stowage was limited to 35 rounds in the turret. Throughout its career the Conqueror was plagued by various electrical and mechanical malfunctions, and while necessary to combat the threat of the Soviet heavy tanks, it proved difficult and cumbersome to use and was generally unpopular with the crews.

Conqueror Heavy Tank	

Entered service: 1956
Crew: 4
Weight: 66,043kg/65 tons
Dimensions: Length – 11.58m/38ft
    Height (over turret hatch) – 3.35m/11ft
    Width – 3.96m/13ft
Armament: Main – 120mm/4.72in L1 gun
    Secondary – 2 x 7.7mm/0.303in machine-guns
Armour: Maximum – 178mm/7.01in
Powerplant: Rover Meteor M120 petrol, 604kW/810hp
Performance: Speed – 34kph/21.1mph
    Range – 153km/95.1 miles

CV90-120-T Light Tank

The CV90-120-T is a light tank based on the latest CV90 infantry vehicle chassis fitted with a Hagglunds twin-hatch turret. Weighing almost 25 tons, the CV90-120 is powered by a Scania 4-cylinder 447.4kW/600hp diesel engine, giving it a top speed of 70kph/43.5mph and a range of 670km/416.3 miles. The main armament is a Swiss-manufactured, fully stabilized 120mm/4.72in high-pressure smoothbore CTG 120/L50 gun with a vertical sliding breech and a rate of fire of up to 14 rounds per minute. There is also a state-of-the-art fire-control system and a crew video network with displays at each crew station. Its Defensive Aids Suite (DAS) contains a laser, radar and missile approach warning system and a Multi-Spectral Aerosols (MSA) active countermeasure system equipped with top attack radar that can identify smart indirect munitions. The turret incorporates stealth characteristics.

Betraying its CV90 roots, it has a rear door entry in the hull and room inside for up to four extra men in addition to the crew of four.

CV90-120-T Light Tank	
Entered service: 1998	
Crew: 4	
Weight: 25,000kg/24.6 tons	
Dimensions: Length – 6.47m/21ft 2.5in	
Height (over turret hatch) – 2.90m/9ft 6in	
Width – 3.10m/10ft 2in	
Armament: Main – 120mm/4.72in gun	
Secondary – 7.62mm/0.3in machine-gun	
Armour: Unspecified	
Powerplant: Scania diesel, generating 447.4kW/600hp	
Performance: Speed – 70kph/43.5mph	
Range – 670km/416.3 miles	

LEFT: **Here is the CV90-120 on the Alvis Vickers stand at DSEi 1999.** BELOW: **The Swedish CV90-120 Light Tank is armed with the Swiss Ordnance Enterprise Corporation 120mm/4.72in Compact Tank Gun, weighs some 25,000kg/24.6 tons and has a crew of four. It was built by Hagglunds, now part of Alvis Vickers.**

EE T1 Osorio Main Battle Tank

The Osorio was the first indigenous MBT design of the growing Brazilian armaments industry, developed mainly for export by Engesa in the late 1980s, with help in the turret design and manufacture from Vickers. Weighing 43,690kg/43 tons and powered by a MWM TBD 234 12-cylinder diesel engine with automatic suspension, the Osorio had a top speed of 70kph/43.5mph and a range of 550km/341.8 miles.

It was armed at first with a Royal Ordnance 105mm/4.13in main gun, but later a French Giat 120mm/4.72in gun was mounted in a modified turret, along with a 7.62mm/0.3in machine-gun and a 12.7mm/0.5in anti-aircraft gun.

Despite initial interest and successful tests in Saudi Arabia, the Gulf War intervened and Saudi interest in the Osorio transferred rapidly to the now battle-proven Abrams.

TOP AND BELOW LEFT: **The Brazilians began to design and build their own MBT in the 1980s, in co-operation with Vickers Defence Systems. The EE T1 Osorio was the result, Engesa concentrating on the chassis and running gear, while VDS designed the three-man turret. In fact two turrets were eventually built – one mounting the ROF 105mm/4.13in gun, the other a French 120mm/4.72in built by Giat Industries.** ABOVE: **Loading the main armament on the Osorio. The makers stressed that the tank was designed for use by crews with a wide range of skill levels, simplicity of operation being the key.**

EE T1 Osorio MBT

Entered service: 1985

Crew: 4

Weight: 43,690kg/43 tons

Dimensions: Length – 7.13m/23ft 4.5in
　　Height (over turret hatch) – 2.89m/9ft 6in
　　Width – 3.26m/10ft 8.5in

Armament: Main – 120mm/4.72in gun
　　Secondary – 1 x 12.7mm/0.5in and
　　1 x 7.62mm/0.3in machine-guns

Armour: Unspecified

Powerplant: MWM TBD 234 12-cylinder diesel,
　　775.5kW/1,040hp

Performance: Speed – 70kph/43.5mph
　　Range – 550km/341.8 miles

Hetzer G13 Tank Destroyer

Over 2,500 of the successful low-profile tank destroyers – the Hetzer (Hunter) – were produced by the Germans in World War II, using the basic components of the excellent Czech-built PzKpfw 38(t) and making use of the extensive Skoda works at Pilsen. The 38(t)'s hull was enlarged and the main 75mm/2.95in PaK39 L/48 gun mounted in a *Saukopf* (boarshead) mantlet on the right-hand side of the hull front.

Following the end of World War II, the Swiss Army purchased a number of Hetzers from Czechoslovakia, who continued to make this vehicle after the end of the hostilities, and modified them to suit their own needs.

This consisted primarily of relocating the machine-gun to the rear plate and fitting a commander's periscope in its place. It was renamed the Hetzer G13, and about 160 vehicles remained in

service with the Swiss Army until the early 1970s. With a weight of just over 15 tons, the Hetzer had a speed of 42kph/26.1mph and a range of 180km/111.8 miles, and was manned by a crew of four.

ABOVE AND BELOW LEFT: **This wartime German tank destroyer was originally based upon the highly successful Skoda LT-38 Medium Tank. Over 1,500 were built and they were highly prized because they were small enough to hide with ease, yet could knock out most Allied tanks. Hetzer continued in service post-war with the Swiss Army, also becoming a firm favourite with AFV restorers.**

Hetzer G13 TD	

Entered service: 1947
Crew: 4
Weight: 15,750kg/15.5 tons
Dimensions: Length – 6.38m/21ft
    Height (over turret hatch) – 2.17m/7ft 2in
    Width – 2.63m/8ft 8in
Armament: Main – 75mm/2.95in L48 gun
    Secondary – 7.62mm/0.3in machine-gun
Armour: Maximum – 60mm/2.36in
Powerplant: Praga AC2 6-cylinder petrol,
    197.6kW/265hp
Performance: Speed – 42kph/26.1mph
    Range – 180km/111.8 miles

LEFT: **Photographed at Yuma Proving Ground, Arizona, in 1979, the High Mobility Agility (HIMAG) Test Vehicle was part of the US Army's Tank Research and Development Command's attempt to combat the major increase in weight of MBTs. It was simply a test vehicle with a hydro-pneumatic suspension, which was armed with a 75mm/2.95in ARES gun on an exposed mounting. It was only ever built as a prototype.**

High Mobility Agility Test Vehicle

Designed by the US Army's Tank-Automotive Research and Development Command, the HIMAG (High Mobility Agility) Test Vehicle was part of an ongoing attempt to design an air-portable tank to add firepower to its airborne forces that must deploy rapidly far afield.

The HIMAG used a conventional tank hull and running gear and was powered by a Continental AVCR 1360 12-cylinder supercharged diesel engine with hydro-pneumatic suspension, delivering a top speed 96.6kpm/60mph and a range of 160km/100 miles. To keep its silhouette low, the vehicle did not have a turret – instead, the main armament was mounted on its own barbette with nothing else around it. This was the state-of-the-art ARES 75mm/2.95in hypervelocity automatic anti-armour cannon, linked to infrared search and computer fire-control systems.

In the end, although the HIMAG remained only a prototype, a great deal of useful information was accrued.

HIMAG

Entered service: 1978 (prototypes only)
Crew: 3
Weight: 40,824kg/40.2 tons
Dimensions: Length – 8.94m/29ft 4in
  Height (over turret hatch) – 3.67m/12ft 0.5in
  Width – 3.81m/12ft 6in
Armament: Main – 75mm/2.95in ARES gun
Armour: Unspecified
Powerplant: Continental AVCR 1360 12-cylinder diesel, 1,118.6kg/1,500hp
Performance: Speed – 96.6kph/60mph
  Range –160km/100 miles

High Survivability Test Vehicle (Lightweight)

LEFT: **The HSTV(L) – the High Survivability Test Vehicle (Lightweight) – resembled in some ways the Swedish "S" tank, with a flat, very low profile turret in which was also mounted a 75mm/2.95in ARES gun. Trials took place in the early 1980s, some of the components being used in further development, so the work on HSTV(L) was most useful (compared to HIMAG).**

The second vehicle designed under the aegis of the US Army's ACVT (Armored Combat Vehicle Technology) programme was the High Survivability Test Vehicle (Lightweight) or HSTV(L). Looking more like a conventional tank, albeit with a very low-silhouette turret, the HSTV(L) had a crew of three, two seated semi-reclined in the hull, both equipped with driving controls and the commander, also semi-reclined, in a turret which mounted the same gun as the HIMAG – the ARES 75mm/2.95in hypervelocity cannon. All three crew members were equipped with sights and digital fire-control systems in order for anyone to be able to fire the gun. A camera mounted on the engine deck gave a rear view.

Elements of the HSTV(L) would also occur on the next vehicle – the AAI RDF Light Tank – as the research moved on, so much useful information was accrued.

HSTV(L)

Entered service: 1980 (prototypes only)
Crew: 3
Weight: 20,450kg/20.13 tons
Dimensions: Length – 8.53m/28ft
  Height (over turret hatch) – 2.41m/7ft 11in
  Width – 2.79m/9ft 2in
Armament: Main – 75mm/2.95in ARES gun
Armour: Maximum – 75mm/2.95in
Powerplant: Avco Lycoming 650 gas turbine, 484.7kW/650hp
Performance: Speed – 83kph/51.5mph
  Range – 160km/99.4 miles

IKV-91 TD

Entered service: 1975
Crew: 4
Weight: Unknown
Dimensions: Length – 6.41m/21ft 0.5in
Height (over turret hatch) – 2.32m/7ft 7.5in
Width – 3m/9ft 10in
Armament: Main – 90mm/3.54in gun
Secondary – 2 x 7.62mm/0.3in machine-guns
Armour: Unspecified
Powerplant: Volvo-Penta 6-cylinder diesel,
268.4kW/360hp
Performance: Speed – 65kph/40.4mph
Range – 550km/341.8 miles

IKV-91 Tank Destroyer

The IKV-91 was developed in the 1960s as a replacement for the Strv 74 and entered service with the Swedish Army in 1975. Moving away from the turretless fixed gun concept that emerged at the end of World War II, the IKV-91 managed to have a turret but still keep its profile fairly low through cunning design – the turret tapering down at the front. Powered by a Volvo-Penta 6-cylinder turbocharged diesel engine, the vehicle had a top speed of 65kph/40.4mph, a range of 550km/341.8 miles and mounted a 90mm/3.54in main gun with 60 rounds of ammunition.

Of the four crew, three – commander, gunner and loader – are positioned in the turret with the driver in the hull front left.

The IKV-91 is also fully amphibious, being propelled in the water by its tracks. There was also a trial version which had the three-man 90mm/3.54in armed turret

replaced by a Rheinmetall turret armed with the Rh 105-11 super-low recoil gun. This version was tested by both Sweden and India and proved effective over an arc of 90 degrees left and right. The IKV-91 served with the Swedish Army but was not sold abroad.

TOP, LEFT AND BELOW: **This Swedish tank destroyer was developed in the late 1960s/early 70s to replace earlier Swedish tank destroyers. Its powerful 90mm/3.54in main gun carried 60 rounds of ammunition (with one up the spout!) and it had a streamlined, all-welded hull and a crew of four, with three men in the turret.**

JS-3 Heavy Tank

Towards the end of 1944, Kotin designed the JS-3 Heavy Tank in conjunction with two other designers, Shashmurin and Rybin. Coming into service with Red Army tank troops in January 1945, it did not make its mark until after the end of World War II. The JS-3 retained all the advantages of its predecessors but had better armour, including a new front glacis plate and a new mushroom carapace-shaped turret, giving it an overall lower silhouette.

One immediately distinctive feature was its bow shape, which came to a point in the middle, earning it the nickname of the "Pike". The JS-3 weighed 46,250kg/45.52 tons, had a crew of four, was powered by a V2 IS diesel engine and was equipped with a torsion bar suspension system, giving it a top speed of 37kph/23mph and a range of around 209km/129.9 miles.

The main armament was the D-25 L/43 122mm/4.8in gun, a weapon that made this vehicle the most formidable tank in the world at that time, and far bigger than anything the opposing NATO forces could field (hence the decision to build Conqueror).

Secondary armament consisted of two 7.62mm/0.3in DT machine-guns and a single 12.7mm/0.5in anti-aircraft machine-gun fitted to the commander's cupola. Although the limitations of its main armament ammunition stowage remained a critical factor (it could only hold 28 rounds), it continued in service long after the end of World War II, serving in many Eastern Bloc armies and other armies all over the world.

Following the Korean War, the Red Army asked for the JS-3 to be modernized and this resulted in a new model, designated as the JS-4, which weighed slightly more, had a more powerful 514.5kW/690hp engine and thicker armour on its hull sides.

JS-3 Heavy Tank

Entered service: 1945
Crew: 4
Weight: 46,250kg/45.52 tons
Dimensions: Length – 6.81m/22ft 4in
　　Height (over turret hatch) – 2.93m/9ft 7.5in
　　Width – 3.44m/11ft 3.5in
Armament: Main – 122mm/4.8in D-25 gun
　　Secondary – 1 x 12.7mm/0.5in and
　　2 x 7.62mm/0.3in machine-guns
Armour: Maximum – 230mm/9.06in
Powerplant: V2 IS 12-cylinder diesel,
　　387.8kW/520hp
Performance: Speed – 37kph/23mph
　　Range – 209km/129.9 miles

LEFT: **JS-3 Red Army Heavy Tank, also known as the Pike. This new configuration was completed in November 1944, with thick, heavily rounded turret armour. The 46,250kg/45.52-ton tank, with its powerful 122mm/4.8in gun, became the standard Soviet heavy tank of the post-war period.**

Jagdpanzer Kanone TD

Entered service: 1965
Crew: 4
Weight: 25,700kg/25.3 tons
Dimensions: Length – 8.75m/28ft 6in
   Height (over turret hatch) – 2.05m/6ft 8.5in
   Width – 2.98m/9ft 9.5in
Armament: Main – 90mm/3.54in gun
   Secondary – 2 x 7.62mm/0.3in machine-guns
Armour: Maximum – 50mm/1.97in
Powerplant: Daimler-Benz MB837 8-cylinder diesel,
   372.9kW/500hp
Performance: Speed – 70kph/43.5mph
   Range – 400km/248.5 miles

LEFT AND BELOW: **Armed with a powerful 90mm/3.54in limited traverse gun, the Jagdpanzer Kanone was something of a hangover from the highly successful German wartime tank destroyers. One major advantage was that it could fire standard US Army 90mm/3.54in tank gun ammunition. It continued in service for many years, some being modified so as to carry and launch the TOW anti-tank guided missile.**

Jagdpanzer Kanone Tank Destroyer

The Jagdpanzer Kanone was a Cold War tank destroyer based on the Hetzer of World War II. The idea behind these vehicles was to use the defensive capacity of a low-silhouette chassis to mount larger fixed guns with limited traverse and elevation. This concept originated from German tank designers reacting to the desperate events at the end of the World War II when various chassis were used to develop tank destroyers.

Hidden away in barns or buildings, or in prepared hull-down positions, they were very effective in the last-ditch defence of the Nazi regime. The thinking remained essentially the same when faced with the massive forces of the Soviet Eastern Bloc, and so the Jagdpanzer Kanone was built.

It mounted a powerful Rheinmetall 90mm/3.54in limited traverse main gun and two 7.62mm/0.3in machine-guns. Power was provided by a Daimler-Benz 8-cylinder diesel engine, giving it a top speed of 70kph/43.5mph and a range of 400km/248.5 miles. However, no sooner had production been completed than the whole concept of a fixed gun tank

destroyer was brought into question and quickly fell out of fashion. Fortunately for the Jagdpanzer Kanone, its excellent chassis could be easily modified and converted to other uses.

With their guns removed and plated over, they morphed to become the Jagdpanzer Rakete Jaguar 2, mounting TOW (Tube-launched, Optically-tracked, Wire-guided) anti-tank guided missiles. A total of 750 Jagdpanzer Kanones were

built for the Germany Army between 1965 and 1967. Then, in late 1972 the Belgians ordered some 80 improved versions of the tank destroyer, which had the complete Renk transmission, final drives, suspension and tracks of the German Marder Mechanised Infantry Combat Vehicle, and gave it the Belgian Army designation of "JPK-90". None of these tank destroyers are now in front-line service with either army.

Jagdpanzer Rakete Jaguar Tank Destroyer

The Jagdpanzer Rakete Jaguar was developed from the Jagdpanzer Kanone, which it replaced. The first prototype was completed by Hanomag and was followed by a further six, three of which were built by Hanomag and three by Henschel from 1963 onwards.

Four years later the Jagdpanzer Rakete Jaguar had succeeded the Jagdpanzer Kanone in production, 370 being built by the following year, half by each of the manufacturers. The main difference between the two is in the main weapon system mounted, although there were also other modifications to the Jagdpanzer Kanone's chassis, hull and front superstructure in order to mount the new weapon system. This was the European manufactured long-range HOT (*Haute subsonique Optiquement Téléguidée*) anti-tank missile, fired from a single roof-mounted launcher equipped with a thermal sight for nightfighting.

Powered by the same Daimler-Benz 8-cylinder diesel engine, the Rakete Jaguar had the same speed and range as its predecessor. The second version of the Jagdpanzer Rakete was a retrofit to the Jagdpanzer Kanone itself, with its main gun removed and the hole plated over in order to mount the TOW (Tube-launched, Optically-tracked, Wire-guided) missile system.

ABOVE AND BELOW: **The Jaguar replaced the Jagdpanzer Kanone, and is based on its modified chassis, coming into production in the late 1960s. It mounted a long-range anti-tank guided missile, there being two models – Jaguar with the HOT missile and Jaguar 2 with TOW.**

A total of 162 Jagdpanzer Kanones were converted into TOW ATGW (Anti-Tank Guided Weapon) carriers from 1983–85. The system already had its Texas Instruments night sight, while the TOW missile flies faster than HOT but has an almost identical range (3,750m/12,303ft as compared with 4,000m/13,123ft).

Jagdpanzer Rakete Jaguar TD

Entered service: 1967
Crew: 4
Weight: 25,500kg/25.1 tons
Dimensions: Length – 6.77m/22ft 2.5in
　　Height (over turret hatch) – 2.16m/7ft 1in
　　Width – 2.95m/9ft 8in
Armament: Main – HOT missile launcher
　　Secondary – 2 x 7.62mm/0.3in machine-guns
Armour: Maximum – 50mm/1.97in
Powerplant: Daimler-Benz MB837 8-cylinder diesel, 372.9kW/500hp
Performance: Speed – 70kph/43.5mph
　　Range – 400km/248.5 miles

ABOVE: **Jagdpanzer Rakete Jaguar, mounting the HOT missile, which has both semi-automatic IR guidance and optical manual guidance, where the commands are transmitted via a wire which is immune to jamming. Missiles largely took over from guns in the post-war anti-tank role.**

183

LEFT: **Shir 1.** Originally built to fill an order from the Shah of Iran, the Shir 1 (Lion) was a combat-improved Chieftain (FV 4030) which incorporated all the new features, such as IFCS (Improved Fire-Control System), CV12 Rolls-Royce 894.8kW/1,200hp engine, automatic gearbox and new hydro-pneumatic suspension. The Shah was deposed and the Shir 1 was subsequently sold to Jordan, and is now known as the Khalid.
BELOW AND BOTTOM: **The Shir 2 was essentially the same as the British Army Challenger 1, and so had the same basic layout as Chieftain.**

Khalid Shir Main Battle Tank

The Khalid Shir traces its development through the Chieftain series of vehicles. A late-production, combat-improved Chieftain called the Shir was designed by the UK's Royal Ordnance for the Shah of Iran, but the project was cancelled after the Iranian Revolution of 1979 toppled the Peacock Throne. It had been a massive order – 125 Shir I (FV 4030/2) and 1,225 Shir 2 (FV 4030/3), so its cancellation by the new Iranian Government in February 1979 was a considerable blow to the British Royal Ordnance, who had already begun production of Shir I, with the first production tanks being scheduled for delivery in 1980.

Fortunately, however, they were able to switch to another Middle Eastern customer, namely Jordan, who in November 1979, placed an order with the UK for 270 "Khalid Shirs" (their name for the Shir I) for delivery from 1981. The two tanks were not completely identical, there having been some modifications, such as upgrading the fire-control systems. The Khalid Shir is therefore in essence a combat-improved Chieftain.

Powered by a Perkins Condor V12 diesel engine, the vehicle has a top speed of 48kph/29.9mph and a range of 400km/248.5 miles. With a crew of four (three in the turret and a driver in the hull), the Khalid Shir mounts the 120mm/4.72in L11A5 rifled bore main gun (the same as the Chieftain) with a digital fire-control system, along with two 7.62mm/0.3in machine-guns – one coaxial in its ergonomically shaped turret.

Khalid Shir MBT	

Entered service: 1981
Crew: 4
Weight: 58,000kg/57.08 tons
Dimensions: Length – 8.39m/27ft 6.5in
    Height (over turret hatch) – 2.98m/9ft 9in
    Width – 3.52m/11ft 6.5in
Armament: Main – 120mm/4.72in L11A5 gun
    Secondary – 2 x 7.62mm/0.3in machine-guns
Armour: Unspecified
Powerplant: Perkins Condor V12 diesel,
    894.8kW/1,200hp
Performance: Speed – 48kph/29.9mph
    Range – 400km/248.5 miles

M8 Ridgeway Armoured Gun System

The M8 Ridgeway Armoured Gun System (AGS) was another US attempt in the never-ending quest to boost the firepower of RDF (Rapid Deployment Force) troops with an air-portable tank – and it reflects the size of that superpower that there is much more than one strand in their development programme.

Developed and manufactured by United Defense (formerly FMC), the M8 AGS comprises the XM35 105mm/4.13in rifled gun with an automatic loader, giving the gun a rate of fire of 12 rounds

per minute. The vehicle's weight was kept down by employing variable suites of armour, including appliqué and ERA (Explosive Reactive Armour), so it was fully transportable in a C-130 Hercules transport aircraft.

Perhaps because the US Army's Tank-Automotive Research and Development Command Armored Combat Vehicle Technology (ACVT) was busy co-developing the HIMAG and HSTV airborne AFVs (also destined to be discontinued), the M8 was not pursued,

which left the company to try to sell it elsewhere. Despite initial interest from Japan and Turkey, no orders materialized and the project was terminated.

ABOVE AND BELOW LEFT: **Developed in the early 1990s as a light tank to replace the M551 Sheridan, the M8 AGS reached production status in the mid-1990s, but the US Army then cancelled the programme. They have since tried to interest Turkey and Japan in the project, but without success. The light tank mounts a respectable 105mm/4.13in gun and weighs 23,590kg/23.2 tons.**

M8 Ridgeway AGS	
Entered service: 1995	
Crew: 3	
Weight: 23,590kg/23.2 tons	
Dimensions: Length – 8.97m/29ft 5in	
Height (over turret hatch) – 2.55m/8ft 4.5in	
Width – 2.69m/8ft 10in	
Armament: Main – 105mm/4.13in M35 gun	
Secondary – 1 x 7.62mm/0.3in machine-gun and either 1 x 12.7mm/0.5in or 1 x 7.62mm/0.3in machine-gun or 1 x 40mm/1.58in grenade launcher	
Armour: Unspecified	
Powerplant: Unspecified	
Performance: Speed – 72kph/44.7mph	
Range – 451km/280 miles	

Leclerc Main Battle Tank

Stemming from an abandoned Franco-German MBT design project of the 1980s, the Leclerc (named after the World War II Free French liberator of Paris) entered service in 1992 and is the prime weapon of the French armoured forces. Built using welded rolled steel and composite armour, weighing 56,000kg/55.1 tons and fitted with a hydro-pneumatic suspension system, it is powered by a SACM V8X-1500 12-cylinder diesel engine, giving a top speed of 72kph/ 44.7mph and a range of 450km/279.6 miles.

The main armament is a 120mm/4.72in smoothbore gun served by an automatic loader capable of delivering 12 rounds per minute. There is also a 12.7mm/0.5in heavy machine-gun mounted coaxially and a 7.62mm/0.3in machine-gun for anti-aircraft and close quarter defence.

The Leclerc also carries all the latest digital optical, fire-control and battlefield management systems. Giat Industries have designed a new turret for the Leclerc which can accommodate a 140mm/5.51in smoothbore gun together with an automatic loader in the turret bustle, but currently there are no plans to replace the existing gun. There are plans for future improvements that include enhanced command and control systems, battlefield identification friend-or-foe, automatic target-tracking, a defensive aids suite, a new thermal imager and enhanced armour.

Leclerc variants include an ARV (Armoured Recovery Vehicle), an ARV with K2D mine-clearing equipment and an armoured engineer vehicle which is similar to the ARV but can be fitted with specialist engineering equipment (now in prototype stage).

In 2002 the French revealed that they were studying further upgrades to the Leclerc MBT in service with the French Army, aiming for 2015. These are likely to include mobility, lethality, survivability, command and control, communications and intelligence, and support. As far as survivability is concerned, Giat Industries are looking to incorporate several layers of protection, the first line of defence being stealth and the second a soft kill kit. They have built an AMX-30 Stealth demonstrator and are evaluating a version of the stealth kit for the Leclerc. The soft kill kit will probably be based upon

ABOVE: **The Giat Industries MBT – called the Leclerc from 1986 onwards – was first mooted in 1985 and made its first appearance just five years later in 1990 at the Satory defence exhibition. This photograph shows it in the ring at the French Armour School's annual demonstration at Saumur. So far, over 400 have been built and used to equip French tank regiments, while the United Arab Emirates have also purchased 436 tropicalized Leclercs.** LEFT: **A French Army Leclerc on operations in Kosovo.**

ABOVE: **A Close-up of the FINDERS Battle Management System as installed in a Leclerc MBT.**
RIGHT: **A pair of Leclercs on training. The 120mm/ 4.72in smoothbore gun is the same calibre as that fitted to Leopard 2 and has an automatic loader containing 22 ready-rounds.**

a basic countermeasures kit, to which will be added a system to detect and foil guided missiles and tank rounds. There will also be a third layer, namely a hard kill system capable of destroying incoming munitions.

Finally, it is worth noting that while the Leclerc has an impressive specification, it has yet to be tried in combat. As such, it has not achieved the "Top Gun" status of other MBTs such as the Abrams, Challenger 2 and Merkava. The vehicle has been purchased by the United Arab Emirates.

RIGHT: **This impressive gathering of tanks and men is probably part of a French armoured regiment while on training. Each French Army regiment equipped with the Leclerc MBT has a total of 40 tanks – one at RHQ and three squadrons of 13 each.** BELOW: **A Leclerc ARV pulls a Leclerc MBT during a training exercise in Qatar. The first of these ARVs was completed in Spring 1994. As well as recovering disabled tanks and towing them to safety, the ARV has the necessary equipment to carry out repairs in forward areas, such as power pack changes.**

Leclerc MBT

Entered service: 1992
Crew: 3
Weight: 56,000kg/55.1 tons
Dimensions: Length – 9.87m/32ft 4.5in
  Height (over turret hatch) – 2.53m/8ft 3.5in
  Width – 3.71m/12ft 2in
Armament: Main – 120mm/4.72in gun
  Secondary – 1 x 12.7mm/0.5in and
  1 x 7.62mm/0.3in machine-guns
Armour: Unspecified
Powerplant: SACM V8X-1500 12-cylinder diesel,
  1,118.6kW/1,500hp
Performance: Speed – 72kph/44.7mph
  Range – 450km/279.6 miles

Leopard 1 Main Battle Tank

Originating from an earlier development project shared by Germany, France and Italy, the Leopard 1 was the German vehicle that resulted when that programme failed. First manufactured in 1963 by Krauss-Maffei of Munich, the initial design was influenced by the French AMX-30, where the armour was kept relatively light when compared with other contemporary MBTs in order to gain on mobility (although it was increased in later Marks).

With a weight of almost 40 tons and powered by a MTU MB 10-cylinder 618.9kW/830hp multi-fuel engine, it has a top speed of 65kph/40.4mph and a range of 600km/373 miles. The main armament is the British-made 105mm/4.13in rifled gun fitted with a gyroscopic stabilizer for accurate firing on the move. There are also two 7.62mm/0.3in machine-guns, one mounted coaxially. The vehicle has a crew of four and is fitted with automatic fire control, NBC (Nuclear, Biological and Chemical) protection and night-vision equipment.

With its good design and all-round reliability, the Leopard 1 has had a successful commercial history, over 6,000 vehicles being exported to nine NATO countries and also Australia, as well as being made under licence in Italy. Over its long lifespan the Leopard 1 has seen various extra armour upgrades and variants appear, including a mine-clearer and bulldozer. Though now replaced by Leopard 2 in the German Armed Forces, it is still in service with many other armies.

ABOVE: **This Leopard 1 is on training in the south of Holland.** BELOW: **Following rehabilitation, post-war German main battle tank development was initially a tripartite programme between Germany, Italy and France. For the Germans this resulted in Leopard 1, with Krauss-Maffei as prime contractor. Although it was a satisfactory tank, Leopard 1 was really too light and it lacked armoured protection. Nevertheless, it stayed in service up to the Leopard 1 A5 model at the end of the century. It is still in service worldwide although some, in places like Brazil and Chile, originate from other NATO countries rather than Germany.**

LEFT: **Excellent view of an Italian Leopard 1. They were not ordered until 1970, 720 being ordered and delivered. In addition MaK delivered a further 120 gun tanks, 69 ARVs and 12 AEVs.** ABOVE: **Leopard 1 could be fitted with a snorkel mast for deep wading.** BELOW: **As with Challenger, Leopard 1 had a driver training model where the turret was replaced by an observation cabin. German models still had the 105mm/4.13in gun barrel (Dutch and Belgian models did not).** BOTTOM LEFT: **Good internal view of a Leopard 1 turret.**

The first NATO country to place an order for Leopard 1 was Belgium (in 1967), and in all they have 334 gun tanks, plus a further 100 or more variants, of which 55 are the Gepard AA vehicle with twin 35mm/1.38in Oerlikon cannon. Next came the Netherlands, who ordered 468 Leopard 1s between 1968–70. Now, as well as the countries mentioned already, Canada, Denmark, Greece, Norway and Turkey have all purchased Leopard 1s from Germany, while Brazil has 87 from Belgium, and Chile has 200 from the Netherlands.

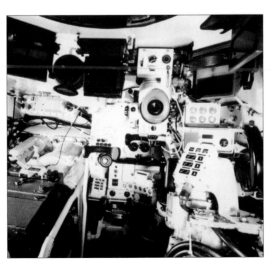

Kraus-Maffei Wegmann, who have factories in Munich and Kassel, still offer a wide range of modification kits for the Leopard 1 MBT which include: extra armour for the turret and mantlet; armoured skirts (side plates); automatic transmission; integral thermal imaging; snow grousers (plus stowage brackets on the glacis plate); a dozer blade (already adopted by Australia); additional external stowage boxes; tracks with replaceable track pads; and a fire-suppression system.

Leopard 1 MBT

Entered service: 1963
Crew: 4
Weight: 40,400kg/39.76 tons
Dimensions: Length – 9.54m/31ft 3.5in
　　Height (over turret hatch) – 2.76m/9ft 0.5in
　　Width – 3.41m/11ft 2.5in
Armament: Main – 105mm/4.13in gun
　　Secondary – 2 x 7.62mm/0.3in machine-guns
Armour: Maximum – 70mm/2.76in
Powerplant: MTU MB 828 M500 multi-fuel,
　　618.9kW/830hp
Performance: Speed – 65kph/40.4mph
　　Range – 600km/373 miles

Leopard 2 Main Battle Tank

TOP AND ABOVE: **Excellent views of the Leopard 2 Main Battle Tank. It was in 1970 that Germany decided to proceed with a new MBT – the Leopard 2. Numerous production lots have since been built and taken into service with the German, Greek, Spanish, Dutch, Austrian, Danish, Finnish, Norwegian, Polish, Swiss and Swedish armies. In total, well over 1,000 have been produced, all built by Krauss-Maffei Wegmann GmbH. Leopard 2 is one of the finest MBTs currently in world service, and in addition to the gun tank, there are AVLBs, ARVs and driver training vehicles, while the latest developments involve the fitting of a new gun.**

The Leopard 2 is produced by Krauss-Maffei of Munich – and like the Leopard 1, originated in another failed, shared AFV project, this time between Germany and the USA, and known as the MBT 70. Using many components designed for that project, Leopard 2 emerged in 1979, after a spate of prototypes and intensive trials. The all-round quality of the Leopard 2's performance is indicative of the meticulous development cycle this vehicle has undergone. With upgrade packages including improved spaced armour, main gun, stabilization, suspension, navigation and fire control, it is still very much a contemporary "Top Gun" MBT.

Leopard 2 weighs almost 59 tons and is powered by an MTU MB 873 12-cylinder diesel engine, giving it a top speed of 72kph/44.7mph and a range of 550km/310.7 miles. The main armament was initially the L4, a Rheinmetall 120mm/4.72in smoothbore gun, but this has more recently been upgraded to the longer-barrelled L55. There are also two 7.62mm/0.3in machine-guns, one mounted coaxially to the main armament.

Used and manufactured under licence by many NATO member countries, the Leopard 2 has spawned many indigenous variants, mounting different extra armour, weapons and fire-control systems, or otherwise modified for a specific purpose such as the ARV (Armoured Recovery Vehicle) and mine-clearer versions. The Swiss Army now has about 400 Leopard 2 (Pz 87 Leo) MBTs, 60–70 per cent of which were built in Switzerland.

The latest model is the Leopard 2A5/2A6 MBT, which is virtually identical to its predecessor but has the following improvements: commander's roof-mounted periscope now has a thermal sight whose image is transmitted to a monitor inside the turret; all-new electrical gun control equipment has replaced the earlier hydraulic system, now quieter, easier to maintain and uses less electrical energy; improved armour protection for the frontal arc of the turret, giving it a distinctive arrowhead shape; new driver's hatch that slides to the right; TV camera installed at the rear of the hull to allow for safer reversing (it has a 65-degree field of view both in horizontal and vertical planes); a hybrid navigation system enabling the commander to navigate in any operational environment; and modifications to the laser range data processor.

There have also been a number of improvements to the Swedish Leopard 2 (known as Strv 122), which include: more protection to the front and sides of the chassis similar to that for the turret; improved roof protection against bomblets; and an eye-safe laser range finder.

TOP: **This Leopard 2 Main Battle Tank is one of about 400 ordered by the Swiss Army, the first being operational by early 1988.** ABOVE: Leopard 2 deep-wading at the factory. BELOW: **The Leopard 2 moving cross-country.**

Leopard 2 MBT

Entered service: 1979
Crew: 4
Weight: 59,700kg/58.76tons
Dimensions: Length – 9.97m/32ft 8.5in
 Height (over turret hatch) – 2.64m/8ft 8in
 Width – 3.74m/12ft 3in
Armament: Main – 120mm/4.72in gun
 Secondary – 2 x 7.62mm/0.3in machine-guns
Armour: Unspecified
Powerplant: MTU MB 873 Ka501 12-cylinder diesel, 1,118.5kW/1,500hp
Performance: Speed – 72kph/44.7mph
 Range – 500km/310.7 miles

M41 Walker Bulldog Light Tank

Designed after the end of World War II to replace the M24 Chaffee, the M41 Walker Bulldog eventually surfaced in 1951 after an extensive period of prototype testing. With a weight of 23,495kg/23.1 tons, it was powered by a Continental AOS 95-3 6-cylinder supercharged petrol engine, delivering a top speed of 72.4kph/45mph, and had a range of 161km/ 100 miles. The main armament was a 76mm/2.99in main gun supplemented by two machine-guns, one of 12.7mm/ 0.5in and the other 7.62mm/0.3in.

The Walker Bulldog was fast and packed a powerful punch for its size. It saw action in Vietnam and served in many NATO member armies, as well as being exported to various countries in South America and Asia.

Some of these countries have carried out extensive modifications, as well as building "lookalikes" such as the Bernardini M41 manufactured in Brazil, while other extensive work was done in the 1980s by Spain to convert the M41 to an anti-tank role,

The Belgian company Cockerill successfully replaced the existing 76mm/2.99in main gun with a 90mm/3.54in, and that particular model was adopted by Uruguay.

Production of the Bulldog has long ceased, but the M41 is still to be found in service all over the world. Perhaps the strangest use for it was as a remote-controlled tank for testing air-to-ground missiles by the US Navy in the 1980s. It was also widely used for trial purposes by the USA, especially for work on the M551 Sheridan project. Modifications included a variety of weapons systems, including an Anti-Aircraft (AA) variant armed with twin 40mm/1.58in M2A1 Bofors AA guns.

ABOVE: **American-built and widely sold overseas, more than 5,500 of these excellent little light tanks were built and exported, many fighting both in Korea and Vietnam, being one of the most effective weapons of the South Vietnamese. It mounted a 76mm/2.99in gun which had a good anti-armour performance. This M41 belonged to the New Zealand Armoured Corps.** BELOW: **The 23,495kg/ 23.1 ton M41 was a relatively easy transporter load, as is seen here. First production models appeared in 1951, there being three Marks (A1, A2 and A3), as well as the chassis being used for both AA and SP gun conversions.**

ABOVE: **The M41 was exported worldwide. In Brazil it was upgraded to the Bernardini M41 and serves both with the Brazil and Uruguay armies, mounting a 90mm/3.54in Cockerill gun.** RIGHT: **A breech-end view inside the turret of an M41 Walker Bulldog.** BELOW: **Realistic training in the USA included anti-gas exercises with both the infantry and tank crews wearing respirators.**

Fifty years after it was rushed into service, the Walker Bulldog still remains "on the books" of eight countries, five of which are in South America. Largest holdings, however, are currently in Taiwan – estimated to be between 400 and 675. With a new engine, performance of the tank has been greatly increased; for example, a maximum road speed of 72kph/45mph and a range of 450km/280 miles. The Walker Bulldog lives on!

M41 Walker Bulldog Light Tank

Entered service: 1951
Crew: 4
Weight: 23,495kg/23.1 tons
Dimensions: Length – 8.21m/26ft 11in
  Height (over turret hatch) – 2.72m/8ft 11in
  Width – 3.2m/10ft 6in
Armament: Main – 76mm/2.99in gun
  Secondary – 1 x 12.7mm/0.5in and
  1 x 7.62mm/0.3in machine-guns
Armour: Maximum – 32mm/1.26in
Powerplant: Continental AOS 95-3 petrol,
  372.9kW/500hp
Performance: Speed – 72.4kph/45mph
  Range – 161km/100 miles

M47 Medium (Patton) Tank

Named after the famous US World War II General, George S. Patton, the M47 was the first truly post-war American tank to be produced, being rushed into production during the Korean crisis in 1952. Its interim predecessor, the M46, which was to all intents and purposes an improved M26 Pershing, did fight in Korea and was also known as the Patton.

The M47 was based on the M46 hull with a newly designed turret, and weighed 46,165kg/45.4 tons. Using a torsion bar suspension system and powered by a Continental AVDS

1790 5B 12-cylinder supercharged petrol engine, it had a top speed of 48kph/29.8mph and a range of 129km/80.1 miles. The new cast turret made the M47 easily identifiable, as it bulged out to the rear and tapered sharply to the front to a small mantlet mounting the M36 90mm/3.54in main gun. For the secondary armament there were two Browning machine-guns, one of 12.7mm/0.5in and the other 7.62mm/0.3in.

The M47 was the last American tank with a five-man crew and it did not have NBC (Nuclear, Biological and Chemical) protection, night-fighting or computerized fire-control systems, so it could not fire accurately while on the move. It proved to be a stopgap development soon invalidated by the advent of the M48.

Although it did not serve for long with US forces, it was exported extensively to her allies, including Taiwan, Greece, Iran, Italy, Japan, Jordan, Netherlands, Pakistan, Portugal, Saudi Arabia, South Korea, Spain, Turkey and Yugoslavia. A final upgrade programme began in the late 1960s, resulting in the M47M, using the engine and fire-control system from the M60A1 to further extend this vehicle's operational life.

There were some faults with the M47 that were recognized even before production began. Indeed, work had already

ABOVE AND LEFT: **First of the truly post-war American tanks was the 90mm/3.54in gun tank, designated as the M47, but popularly known as the Patton after the famous General George S. Patton, Jnr, who had been killed in a road accident in 1945. It would soon be replaced by the M48, also called the Patton.**

ABOVE: **Trials took place to fit the British 105mm/4.13in L7A1 tank gun into the M47s in service with the Italian Army, which proved to be very successful because the up-gunned result was much more stable. The M47s in Spanish service were fitted with the Rheinmetall 105mm/4.13in smoothbore gun (known as the M47-E2).** RIGHT: **This highly painted M46 is located at the Tank Museum, Bovington. The M47 used the same hull.** BELOW: **Part of a tank company of M47s on the firing line at the Armor School, Fort Knox, Kentucky, 1953.**

begun on its successor while it was being accepted by the US Army Equipment Review Board. For example, it was clear that turret protection was generally lower than that of the hull and that the fuel carried was insufficient to last through a normal battlefield day. It would never see action with the regular US Army and would soon be relegated to the National Guard (November 1953). In fact, it was a better training vehicle because its five-man crew (the M48 had only four) meant that 20 per cent more men could be trained in each training cycle.

M47 Medium (Patton) Tank

Entered service: 1952
Crew: 5
Weight: 46,165kg/45.4 tons
Dimensions: Length – 8.56m/28ft 1in
   Height (over turret hatch) – 3.35m/11ft
   Width – 3.2m/10ft 6in
Armament: Main – 90mm/3.54in M36 gun
   Secondary – 1 x 12.7mm/0.5in and 1 x
   7.62mm/0.3in machine-guns
Armour: Maximum – 115mm/4.53in
Powerplant: Continental AVDS 1790 5B V12 petrol,
   604kW/810hp
Performance: Speed – 48kph/29.8mph
   Range – 129km/80.1 miles

M48 Patton Main Battle Tank

The M48 Patton Main Battle Tank was another American tank to be rushed into production during the Korean crisis, and it initially suffered from teething problems as a consequence. However, it went on to have a long and distinguished service life, including combat with US forces in Vietnam.

It had a lower wider hull than the previous M47, along with a new, less bulging turret, with a visually distinctive and powerful searchlight just above the main gun. Weighing 48,987kg/48.2 tons, the M48 was powered by a Continental AVDS 1790 2 12-cylinder engine, giving it a top speed of 48kph/29.8mph and a range of 499km/310.1 miles.

The main armament of the M48 was a 90mm/3.54in gun, supplemented by a 7.62mm/0.3in coaxial machine-gun and a 12.7mm/0.5in anti-aircraft machine-gun mounted on the commander's cupola.

It was one of the first tanks to have an analogue mechanical fire-control system and saw various upgrades. These included different engines, suspension, fire-control and weapons systems, and main armament, which was upgraded to a 105mm/4.13in gun almost immediately. The M48 was very popular on the US export market, being supplied to many countries worldwide. Some of these customers modified it extensively for their own use, including Spain, Israel and Taiwan.

ABOVE AND BELOW: The M48 Patton tank was originally armed with a 90mm/3.54in gun, later to be replaced by a 105mm/4.13in gun. Despite being rushed into service in 1952 and having some faults, the Patton was a popular tank, with large numbers being built (over 11,000). It was produced in five Marks (up to A5) and sold to Greece, Germany, South Korea, Spain, Taiwan, Turkey, Iran and Israel.

Starting in 1958, the West German army was supplied with a total of 1,400 M48 series AFVs, including armoured recovery vehicles (M88), M55 SP howitzers and M48 AVLB as well as gun tanks. It is also most interesting to note that subsequently, after fruitless negotiations direct with the USA, Israel was able to obtain their first M48s from the Germans, a party of selected Israeli tank officers being trained on a crash course in great secrecy in Germany!

The Taiwanese M48H, also known as Brave Tiger, was produced in 1990 by combining M60 hulls with M48 turrets, mounting an indigenously built version of the 105mm/4.13in rifled main gun, along with other elements including digital fire control and sight stabilization from the Abrams M1.

TOP LEFT: **The Tank Museum's M48 in a display of NATO tanks.** ABOVE LEFT: **The M67 flamethrower version of the M48 is seen here in Vietnam in 1968 in the act of using its flamethrower. None of this model are still in service.** ABOVE: **The M48H, also known as Brave Tiger, was a modified M48 with a home-produced version of the British 105mm/4.13in gun. The tank actually uses the hulls of the US M60, M60A1, M60A3, as well as the M48A5 and South Korean K1. In addition, it is said that some Merkava Marks 1 and 2 are also employed, so it really is a hybrid!** LEFT: **An M48 moving into action in Vietnam. M48A1, A2 and A3 all saw active service there, as did the M48 AVLB and M88 recovery vehicle.**

M48 Patton MBT

Entered service: 1953
Crew: 4
Weight: 48,987kg/48.2 tons
Dimensions: Length – 9.31m/30ft 6.5in
   Height (over turret hatch) – 3.01m/9ft 10.5in
   Width – 3.63m/11ft 11in
Armament: Main – 105mm/4.13in L7 gun
   Secondary – 1 x 12.7mm/0.5in and 1 x 7.62mm/0.3in machine-guns
Armour: Maximum – 180mm/7.07in
Powerplant: Continental AVDS 1790 2 12-cylinder diesel, 559.3kW/750hp
Performance: Speed – 48kph/29.8mph
   Range – 499km/310.1 miles

M50 Ontos Tank Destroyer

In the mid-1950s the USA developed the M50 Ontos (*Ontos* is Greek for "thing") as an early attempt to provide rapidly deployable air-portable firepower for airborne troops. It was based on the chassis of the T55/T56 series of experimental vehicles, combined with a new a distinctive pyramidal mini-turret which mounted six 106mm/4.17in M40A1 recoilless (RCR) rifles, three to a side, firing mainly HEAT (High-Explosive Anti-Tank) but also anti-personnel munitions. These weapons were aimed by using a Spotting Rifle fitted to the top tubes which was fired first to determine the range and bearing of the target, the six recoilless rifles then being discharged singly or en masse.

The Ontos weighed 8,641kg/8.5 tons, had a crew of three and was powered by a Chrysler V8 engine, giving it a speed of 48kph/30mph and a range of 241km/ 150 miles. This vehicle suffered from a number of serious disadvantages: the loader was vulnerable to enemy fire when reloading the weapons system because he had to get out of the vehicle; the recoilless rifles lacked any real accuracy; and there was a massive and dangerous back-blast from the rifle tubes when discharged.

The Ontos was really only a stopgap measure, with as few as 300 being made before it was discontinued. It saw action only briefly in Vietnam, where it was used by troops on the ground primarily in an artillery mode from prepared firebases. In 1966 the engine was upgraded to the Chrysler V8, generating 134.2kW/180hp, but the vehicle was soon superseded and withdrawn from service in 1970 to be replaced by other air-portable alternatives offering more firepower and protection.

ABOVE AND BELOW LEFT: **Designed in the mid-1950s as a small air-portable tank destroyer, Ontos (Greek for "thing") comprised six 106mm/4.17in recoilless rifles mounted on a modified APC chassis. While the US Army dropped the idea in preference for Jeep-mounted recoilless rifles, the USMC avidly seized on the proposal, and it went into production in 1955, some 300 being built. It saw action in Dominica and Vietnam and knocked out various light tanks (e.g. AMX-13). It was retired in the late 1960s. It was also used for experiments with titanium armour as the T55 Ontos APC, while another version proposed was a light assault vehicle, armed with four or eight machine-guns. Finally, there were three more proposals, all with various anti-tank guns. None were ever built.**

M50 Ontos TD	🇺🇸

Entered service: 1955
Crew: 3
Weight: 8,641kg/8.5 tons
Dimensions: Length – 3.83m/12ft 7in
   Height (over turret hatch) – 2.13m/7ft
   Width – 2.60m/8ft 6.5in
Armament: Main – 6 x 106mm/4.17in recoilless rifles
   Secondary – 7.62mm/0.3in machine-gun
Armour: Maximum – 13mm/0.51in
Powerplant: General Motors 302 V6 petrol, 108.1kW/145hp
Performance: Speed – 48kph/29.8mph
   Range – 241km/149.8 miles

LEFT AND BELOW LEFT:

Another light airborne support weapon was the Scorpion 90mm/ 3.54in anti-tank gun mounted on an all aluminium hull and weighing a total of just 7,144kg/7 tons. Its major drawbacks were the lack of crew protection and a vulnerable petrol engine. It was soon replaced by the M551 Sheridan.

M56 Scorpion Tank Destroyer

Known officially as the M56 Self-Propelled Anti-Tank (SPAT), the M56 was another US attempt at developing air-portable firepower during the 1950s for use with rapidly deployable troops.

To save on weight, the vehicle had an aluminium hull and no turret, with only a small gun-shield for protection – an approach that didn't endear it to the troops that had to operate it. It was actually based on the unarmoured chassis of the M76 amphibious cargo carrier, the gun being on a low pedestal mount on top of the hull, which carried four road-wheels on either side suspended by torsion bars.

The engine, driver and his controls took up all of the remaining space in the hull, leaving the gun-layer to ride on top of the vehicle. Where the remaining two crewmen travelled is not clear, although logically they must have gone with any ammunition vehicle attached to the detachment. Presumably when the Scorpion went into action and they had to change position, they would simply hang on to the outside as best they could! At 7,144kg/7 tons, the M56 was powered by a Continental AOI-4025 6-cylinder petrol engine, giving it a top speed of 45kph/28mph and a range of 225km/139.8 miles. It mounted a 90mm/3.54in M54 main gun and saw action in Vietnam, where it tended to be used as a support weapon in a prepared position.

Under-armoured, under-powered and unpopular, it was soon replaced by the M551 Sheridan.

M56 Scorpion TD

Entered service: 1953
Crew: 4
Weight: 7,144kg/7 tons
Dimensions: Length – 5.84m/19ft 2in
    Height (over turret hatch) – 2.05m/6ft 8.5in
    Width – 2.57m/8ft 5in
Armament: Main – 90mm/3.54in M54 gun
Armour: None
Powerplant: Continental AOI-4025 6-cylinder petrol,
    149.kW/200hp
Performance: Speed – 45kph/28mph
    Range – 225km/139.8 miles

M60 Main Battle Tank

Manufactured by General Dynamics, the M60 is one of the world's most successful MBTs, with over 15,000 built. First entering service with the US Army in 1960, it went on to serve in the armies of at least 22 countries. The tank has provided excellent battlefield performance over four decades and has been continuously advanced and upgraded with appliqué armour, increasingly powerful engines, new guns and fire-control systems, ammunition and other features.

Weighing almost 52 tons and with a crew of four, the M60 is powered by a Continental AVDS 1790 2A V12 turbo-charged diesel engine, giving it a top speed of 48kph/29.8mph and a range of 500km/310.7 miles. The main armament is the 105mm/4.13in M68 rifled gun derived from the L7A1 105mm/4.13in gun of the British Centurion, along with two machine-guns – a coaxial 7.62mm/0.3in M240 and a 12.7mm/0.5in.

The M60A1, with a new turret and thicker armour, was manufactured from 1962 to 1980. The M60A2, with a new turret mounting a 152mm/5.98in gun and missile launcher, was produced in 1972. From 1978 to 1987 the M60A3, with improvements to its fire control, was the most successful and numerously produced of the series.

ABOVE AND LEFT: **Two views of the Tank Museum's M60 Main Battle Tank, including one of it going through a "wall of fire". The M60 was approved in the late 1950s and the contract awarded to Chrysler in 1959. Since then, over 5,400 have been built for the US forces and many thousands sold worldwide, the Israelis being the next largest user. The tank has a 105mm/4.13in gun and a very prominent searchlight.**

ABOVE: **An IDF (Israeli Defence Force) M60 moves into battle with some extra passengers.** LEFT: **Hard at work building M60 turrets in the Chrysler factory.**
BELOW: **The M60A1 fitted with ERA (Explosive Reactive Armour). A small number of USMC M60A1s were used during Operation "Desert Storm" in 1991. The Israeli-invented ERA gives added protection to vulnerable areas such as the turret.**

Having such a long front-line life in so many countries, the M60 has seen many variants, modifications and enhancements, with Israel in particular upgrading M60s into their own types, including the Magach and the Sabra. With so many countries still fielding M60s, General Dynamics Land Systems (GDLS) has recently brought out the M60-2000 upgrade package, using the turret and 120mm/4.72in M256 smoothbore main gun of the M1 Abrams, along with a new up-rated engine, fire-control and safety systems. In this way the service life of this excellent MBT has been prolonged still further.

M60A1 MBT

Entered service: 1960
Crew: 4
Weight: 52,617kg/51.8 tons
Dimensions: Length – 9.44m/31ft
    Height (over turret hatch) – 3.27m/10ft 8.5in
    Width – 3.63m/11ft 11in
Armament: Main – 105mm/4.13in M68 gun
    Secondary – 1 x 12.7mm/0.5in and
    1 x 7.62mm/0.3in machine-guns
Armour: Maximum – 143mm/5.63in
Powerplant: Continental AVDS 1790 2A V12 diesel,
    559.3kW/750hp
Performance: Speed – 48kph/29.8mph
    Range – 500km/310.7 miles

LEFT: **A US Army M60 takes cover in a corn field during a NATO exercise in the 1960–70s, being totally ignored by the farmer and his wife!**

201

LEFT: **The Sheridan Light Tank. Worried by the ever increasing size and weight of modern main battle tanks, the Sheridan was a US attempt to combine a gun and missile system in one 152mm/5.98in launcher. The 15,830kg/15.6-ton light tank had a crew of four and was developed in 1959.**

BELOW: **Good photograph of an anti-armour Shillelagh missile being launched. The Sheridan continued to serve until the 1990s.**

M551 Sheridan Light Tank

The M551 Sheridan is yet another air-portable American light tank developed for its airborne divisions to replace the unsatisfactory M56 Scorpion. Entering service in 1968 with a weight of 15,830kg/15.6 tons and a crew of four, the Sheridan was powered by a Detroit Diesel 6V-53T 6-cylinder turbocharged engine, giving it a top speed of 72kph/44.7mph and a range of 600km/372.9 miles.

The main armament was the MGM-51 Shillelagh tube-launched, wire-guided missile system, which could also fire 152mm/5.98in shells, along with a

7.62mm/0.3in machine-gun for close-quarter protection. However, there were lots of problems with this weapons system, which held up the vehicle's entry into service and plagued it thereafter.

It was also lightly armoured with aluminium to save on weight, and as a consequence very vulnerable to a whole range of weapons. During combat in Vietnam the missile system was soon rejected in favour of more conventional munitions, but the Sheridan still did not perform well, being adversely affected by the moist conditions and, with little

protection on its hull bottom, it was very vulnerable to mines. Nevertheless, the Sheridan continued in service until the 1990s; for example, 82 Airborne Division's Sheridans were among the first AFVs to arrive in the Persian Gulf in 1990.

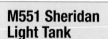

M551 Sheridan Light Tank	
Entered service: 1968	
Crew: 4	
Weight: 15,830kg/15.6 tons	
Dimensions: Length – 6.30m/20ft 8in	
Height (over turret hatch) – 2.95m/9ft 8in	
Width – 2.82m/9ft 3in	
Armament: Main – 152mm/5.98in gun/ missile system	
Secondary – 7.62mm/0.3in machine-gun	
Armour: Unspecified	
Powerplant: Detroit Diesel 6V-53T 6-cylinder diesel, 223.7kW/300hp	
Performance: Speed – 72kph/44.7mph	
Range – 600km/372.9 miles	

LEFT: **The missile system was the 152mm/5.98in Shillelagh missile system, whose HEAT warhead could knock out any known tank. Sheridan was swiftly deployed in Vietnam. The missile guidance system was withdrawn and replaced by the "beehive" anti-personnel round, but this also led to many problems.**

LEFT: The Israeli name for their upgrade of the American M60 MBT was Magach, a Hebrew acronym for the Jewish letters: Mem and Chaf plus the middle letter "Gimel" which stands for "Germany", the first source of Israeli M48s. Latest of the continuing upgrades is Magach 7, which is fitted with passive armour to its hull and turret. BELOW LEFT: Another view of the M60 Magach. This was the first version specifically up-armoured for urban combat.

Magach Main Battle Tank

The Magach is the Israeli Defence Force (IDF) name for what was the Patton M48/M60 MBT series of US tanks which have been in active service with the Israeli armoured forces for over 30 years. In that time they have undergone sustained indigenous modification and enhancement to keep the Magach as a state-of-the-art weapons system, continuously tried and tested in combat.

Armed with the original 90mm/3.54in main gun, they first saw action during the 1967 Six Day War and were then upgraded (Magach 3 and 5) with a new 105mm/4.13in M68 L7 gun (as carried by the Centurion) and used in the 1968 War of Attrition. Deployed in time for the 1973 Yom Kippur War, the M60 (Magach 6 and 7) models went on to become the mainstay of the IDF's armoured corps

for many years. These Magachs were upgraded with Explosive Reactive Armour (ERA), new engines, tracks and improved fire control and then used in the 1982 Israeli invasion of Lebanon.

The Magach 7 had further new upgrade suites, some of which could be retrofitted to earlier versions, including engine and transmission packs, passive armour, optical systems, ranging and new fire-control systems, NBC (Nuclear, Biological and Chemical) protection, fire suppression, navigation and weapons systems.

Magach MBT	✡

Entered service: 1970
Crew: 4
Weight: 54,857kg/54 tons
Dimensions: Length – 8.56m/28ft 1in
   Height (over turret hatch) – 3.35m/11ft
   Width – 3.2m/10ft 6in
Armament: Main – 90mm/3.54in and
   then 105mm/4.13in gun
   Secondary – 3 x 7.62mm/0.3in machine-guns, 1 x
   12.7mm/0.5in coaxial machine-gun above main gun
Armour: Maximum – 115mm/4.53in
Powerplant: General Dynamics AVDS 1790 A
   V12 diesel, 677.1kW/908hp
Performance: Speed – 48kph/29.8mph
   Range – 129km/80.6 miles

Merkava Main Battle Tank

The Merkava (Chariot) is an unusual MBT of innovative design, attributed to the Major General Israel Tal of the IDF's (Israeli Defence Force) Armoured Corps, which places special emphasis on crew protection. To further this aim, the engine is located in the front of the vehicle and special attention has been paid to the siting of extra-spaced armour on the frontal arc, the side skirts and track protectors, and the bulkheads between the crew and the fuel and ammunition. There is even a special protective umbrella for the tank

commander when his hatch is open. Another unusual feature is that the tank has rear doors in the hull, enabling it either to carry extra ammunition or a small squad of infantry.

The Merkava Mark 1 came into service in 1979, when 40 tanks were delivered to 7th Armoured Brigade. Weighing 60,963kg/60 tons and powered by a TCM diesel AVDS 1790 9AR engine delivering a top speed of 46kph/28.6mph and a range of 400km/248.5 miles, the Mark 1 mounted a 105mm/4.13in main gun along with a coaxial 7.62mm/0.3in machine-gun and a 12.7mm/0.5in commander's machine-gun. The Merkava Mark 2 had increased engine performance, which gave it a top speed of 55kph/34mph and a range 500km/310 miles. Merkava first saw action in Lebanon, between April and June 1982.

ABOVE: **No nation has more post-war armoured battle experience than the Israelis, who have been fighting almost non-stop since 1948. It was in 1967 after the Six Day War that they decided to design and build their own main battle tank, the revolutionary Merkava, test rigs being based on both the M48 and Centurion, under the expert eye of General Israel Tal. First production models appeared in 1978, but the MBT did not see action until 1982 in Lebanon. This photograph is of a Merkava Mark 2.** LEFT: **An impressive line-up of Merkava Mark 2s, which weighed over 60 tons and mounted a 105mm/4.13in rifled gun.**

ABOVE: **This Merkava Mark 2 was photographed in Lebanon during Operation "Peace for Galilee".** RIGHT: **An early Mark 1 on show at the IDF Tank Museum at Latrun.** BELOW: **A Mark 3, known as Baz (Hawk), which mounts a 120mm/4.72in smoothbore gun, a modular armour suite and an improved suspension.**

New suites covering the various elements of the tank are constantly being updated in the light of combat experience. For Merkava Mark 3 these included a new suspension system, a 894.8kW/1,200hp engine and new transmission, an upgraded 120mm/4.72in main gun developed by Israel Military Industries with a thermal sleeve to increase accuracy by preventing heat distortion, and ballistic protection provided by further special add-on armour modules. The Merkava Mark 4 has further improved night and remote vision devices, a new MTU 1,118.5kW/ 1,500hp diesel engine, an enhanced main gun package and increased modular passive armour.

Merkava Mark 3 MBT	✡

Entered service: 1977 (Mark 1)
Crew: 4
Weight: 62,000kg/61.02 tons
Dimensions: Length – 7.6m/24ft 11in
    Height (over turret hatch) – 2.64m/8ft 8in
    Width – 3.7m/12ft 1.5in
Armament: Main – 120mm/4.72in gun
    Secondary – 3 x 7.62mm/0.3in machine-guns
Armour: Unspecified
Powerplant: Teledyne AVDS 1790 9AR V12 diesel,
    894.8kW/1,200hp
Performance: Speed – 55kph/34.2mph
    Range – 500km/310.7 miles

Main Battle Tank 70

The MBT-70 was a joint US–German heavy tank project that was launched in the 1960s and formed the source vehicle for both the Abrams M1 and Leopard 2 main battle tanks. The MBT-70 incorporated some radical new design elements, including a main

gun that could fire wire-guided missile munitions as well as conventional rounds, and a bustle-mounted automatic loading system for the main gun, thereby doing away with the need for a loader and reducing the crew to three.

Weighing 46,000kg/45.3 tons, equipped with hydro-pneumatic suspension and powered by a Continental AVCR 12-cylinder multi-fuel engine, the MBT-70 had a top speed of 70kph/43.5mph and a range of 650km/403.9 miles. The American model mounted the 152mm/ 5.98in gun/missile system – as later fitted to the Sheridan M551 – while the German version had a 120mm/4.72in smoothbore main armament – both with

ABOVE: **In 1963, West Germany and the USA signed an agreement to build a main battle tank which they called MBT-70. While it had many innovative modern features, agreement on a standardized vehicle could not be reached, and the project was eventually cancelled in 1970. Nevertheless, numerous features were brought forward into the two nations' tank-building programmes for the Abrams and the Leopard 2.**
LEFT AND BELOW LEFT: **Two photographs of MBT-70 pilot number two which shows the tank with the fire-control equipment installed.**

a state-of-the-art digital fire-control and gun-stabilization system. However, in the end the two countries could not agree on a standardized vehicle, so in 1970 the project was cancelled and each partner went their own way to develop individual main battle tanks.

MBT-70

Entered service: 1967 (prototypes only)
Crew: 3
Weight: 46,000kg/45.3 tons
Dimensions: Length – 6.99m/22ft 11in
   Height (over turret hatch) – 2.59m/8ft 6in
   Width – 3.51m/11ft 6in
Armament: Main – 152mm/5.98in gun/missile
   system or 120mm/4.72in smoothbore gun
   Secondary – 7.62mm/0.3in machine-gun
Armour: Unspecified
Powerplant: Continental AVCR 12-cylinder multi-fuel,
   1,099.9kW/1,475hp
Performance: Speed – 70kph/43.5mph
   Range – 650km/403.9 miles

Olifant Medium Tank

The South African Olifant is a Centurion-derived medium tank which became the mainstay of the South African armoured forces for a long period of time. The Olifant was made in South Africa by Vickers OMC Company in conjunction with the larger British parent Vickers. Since its introduction in the 1980s it has undergone various upgrades and enhancements to maintain it as a viable battlefield weapons system.

Weighing over 55 tons and powered by a V12 diesel engine with a top speed of 45kph/28mph and a range of 500km/310.6 miles, the Olifant has a crew of four and mounts as its main armament either the LIW GT-7 105mm/4.13in, or a LIW proprietary 120mm/4.72in smoothbore tank gun. Either of these is fitted into a newly designed turret incorporating a bustle-mounted ammunition carousel and all the latest fire-control and safety features, including blow-off panels on the turret deck.

The latest model (Mark 1B) also boasts a new power pack, new torsion bar suspension, new electronic systems and modular add-on-armour packages.

In addition to the gun tank, there are ARV (Armoured Recovery Vehicle), AVLB (Armoured Vehicle Launched Bridge) and mine-clearing variants.

ABOVE AND RIGHT: **Designed in 1976 and based on the British Centurion, the South African Olifant (Elephant), weighs 56,000kg/55.1 tons, has a crew of four and mounts a 105mm/4.13in gun. The latest version (the Mark 1B) has numerous modern features. South Africa has a total of 224 Olifant Mark 1A and 1Bs in service.**

LEFT: **In addition to the gun tank, there are ARVs, AVLBs and mine-clearing vehicles. The ARV seen here is based upon an Olifant Mark 1A.**

Olifant Medium Tank

Entered service: 1980
Crew: 4
Weight: 56,000kg/55.1 tons
Dimensions: Length – 8.29m/27ft 2.5in
  Height (over turret hatch) – 2.94m/9ft 7.5in
  Width – 3.39m/11ft 1.5in
Armament: Main – 105mm/4.13in LIW GT-7
  or 120mm/4.72in LIW gun
  Secondary – 2 x 7.62mm/0.3in machine-guns
Armour: Unspecified
Powerplant: V12 diesel, delivering 708.4kW/950hp
Performance: Speed – 45kph/28mph
  Range – 500km/310.6 miles

OF-40 Main Battle Tank

First emerging in 1977, the Italian Oto Melara OF-40 was designed and manufactured by Oto Melara and Fiat, who provided the power pack. It was based on the German Leopard 1 A4 which it strongly resembled and was designed exclusively for export.

Weighing 45,000kg/44.3 tons and powered by a Fiat MTU 90 diesel engine, it had a speed of 60kph/37.3mph and a range of 600km/372.8 miles. The OF-40 had a crew of four and mounted an Oto Melara-designed 105mm/4.13in rifled main armament, along with secondary 7.62mm/0.3in and 12.7mm/0.5in machine-guns in its turret. It was also fitted with

a fire-control system combining a computer and a laser range finder. United Arab Emirates bought 18 OF-40 Mark 1s, the first being delivered in 1981. Since then they have taken delivery of a further 18 OF-40 Mark 2s and three ARVs (Armoured Recovery Vehicles), while the Mark 1s have been retrofitted up to Mark 2 standard, which essentially involves the fitting of a new fire-control and stabilization system. No other sales have materialized.

A later model was planned, along with an ARV and a self-propelled gun (Palmaria 155 howitzer), but following the dismal sales of the gun tank, this was not put into production and the OF-40 MBT is no longer being marketed.

The all-welded steel hull of the OF-40 is divided conventionally, the driver being at the front on the right, with three periscopes, the centre one of which can be replaced by an Image Intensification (II) periscope for night driving. To his left is the NBC pack and 42 rounds of ammunition, the other 15 being in the turret for immediate use.

Turret layout is normal: commander and gunner on the right; loader on the left. The commander has a circular hatch cover with eight periscopes, one of which can be replaced by an II periscope. He does not have a cupola, but mounted in the

ABOVE AND LEFT: **Designed in 1977 by Oto Melara and Fiat (power pack), this 45,000kg/44.3-ton Italian MBT has a crew of four and mounts a 105mm/4.13in rifled gun. Offered (but not accepted) for local production in Spain and Greece, demonstrated in Thailand and Egypt, the OF-40 is also in service in Dubai.**

OF-40 MBT

Entered service: 1977
Crew: 4
Weight: 45,000kg/44.3 tons
Dimensions: Length – 6.89m/22ft 7in
    Height (over turret hatch) – 2.76/9ft 0.5in
    Width – 3.35m/11ft
Armament: Main – 105mm/4.13in gun
    Secondary – 1 x 7.62mm/0.3in and
    1 x 12.7mm/0.5in machine-guns
Armour: Unspecified
Powerplant: MTU 90 diesel, 620.4kW/832hp
Performance: Speed – 60kph/37.3mph
    Range – 600km/372.8 miles

ABOVE: **No longer being marketed, the OF-40 hull has been used to mount other weapon systems such as the Gepard anti-aircraft turret and as the basis of the Oto Melara Palmaria 105mm/4.13in SP howitzer.** LEFT: **The OF-40 MBT was designed by Oto Melara and Fiat for the export market, however despite being tested in Thailand, demonstrated in Egypt and offered for local production in Spain and Greece, the only purchasers have been UAE (Dubai).** BELOW: **Firing now! A well-trained crew can achieve a rate of fire of nine rounds per minute with their Oto Melara-designed 105mm/4.13in rifled gun.**

roof of his hatch is the Officine Galileo day/night sight, which is stabilized and fitted with II night-vision equipment. The gunner (seated in front of the commander) has a forward-facing roof-mounted periscope and an optical sight.

The Alenia C215 articulated x 8 magnification telescope is mounted coaxially with the 105mm/4.13in gun. The loader also has a circular hatch cover in front of which are two roof-mounted periscopes that give observation to the front and left side.

The 105mm/4.13in main armament has a falling wedge breechblock, concentric buffer and recuperator. It is fired electrically, but there is also a manually actuated impulse generator. There is a thermal sleeve on the barrel and a bore evacuator.

A well-trained crew can achieve a rate of fire of nine rounds per minute, the gun firing standard NATO ammunition, including APDS, canister, HEAT, HESH and smoke. The gun can be stabilized in both elevation and traverse. One machine-gun is coaxially mounted; the other on the turret roof for AA use.

Mounted on either side of the turret are banks of four electrically operated smoke grenade dischargers. The engine, transmission and cooling system are assembled to form the power pack, which can be removed by four men with a crane in under 45 minutes.

PT-76 Amphibious Light Tank

Having suspended light tank production, believing them to be of limited use, the USSR returned to the idea of a fast, lightly armoured all-terrain reconnaissance vehicle with the PT-76 in 1952. This 14,000kg/13.8-ton light tank had an extremely useful additional feature – it was amphibious. Water-borne propulsion was provided by a double hydro-jet system, which used water taken in at the front of the vehicle and pumped to the rear, where it was expelled at high pressure. Based on an arctic tractor chassis with a torsion bar suspension system and powered by a V6 6-cylinder diesel engine, the vehicle had

a top speed of 45kph/28mph and a range of 280km/174 miles. The PT-76 was a robust little tank with a good all-round performance which made it popular with crews despite its light armour. The D056T 76.2mm/3in rifled main gun was mounted in an archetypal Soviet low silhouette turret with a slightly cylindrical top and a wide two-man elliptical cupola. Secondary armament was provided by two machine-guns, one 7.62mm/0.3in and one 12.7mm/0.5in in calibre.

The PT-76 was a successful light tank, with over 7,000 being built and exported widely to Soviet satellite and client states in the Cold War era, as well as being built under licence in China. It saw combat in the Vietnamese and Indo-Pakistan wars and various African conflicts. Production ceased in 1967.

ABOVE: **Inevitably the PT-76 saw action in the Arab-Israeli wars, and this model is on show at the IDF Tank Museum at Latrun.** LEFT: **Light tanks went out of favour in the Red Army towards the end of World War II due to their vulnerability. However, post-war in the early 1950s the PT-76 Amphibious Light Tank came back into vogue. While its 76.2mm/3in gun is small, it is adequate for the job, and its light weight (14,000kg/13.8 tons) and reliability have made it a winner worldwide.**

Upgraded PT-76

The Israeli company NIMDA offers a complete upgrade package which includes fitting a new power pack, a Detroit Diesel 6V-92T developing 223.7kW/300hp at 2,100rpm, coupled to the original transmission with a new clutch assembly. There is also a new alternator, new cooling and electrical systems and numerous other modifications to the exhaust, air inlet, hull and top deck.

The 76.2mm/3in gun is replaced by the new 90mm/3.54in Cockerill Mark III gun that fires a wide range of ammunition, including fin-stabilized APDS. The Russian coaxial machine-gun has been replaced by a Western one and another added on the turret roof for AA protection. There is a new solid state stabilization and power control system, together with a new fire-control system incorporating a new day/night sight and laser rangefinder. It is understood that part of the Indonesian PT-76 fleet have already been upgraded with this package.

ABOVE LEFT, ABOVE AND LEFT: **This adaptable tank is at home in water and on land. It has seen service in China and Vietnam, and also in the Indo-Pakistan wars.**

PT-76 Amphibious Light Tank

Entered service: 1952
Crew: 3
Weight: 14,000kg/13.8 tons
Dimensions: Length – 6.91m/22ft 8in
  Height (over turret hatch) – 2.26m/7ft 5in
  Width – 3.14m/10ft 3.5in
Armament: Main – 76.2mm/3in gun
  Secondary – 1 x 7.62mm/0.3in and
  1 x 12.7mm/0.5in machine-guns
Armour: Maximum – 17mm/0.67in
Powerplant: V6 6-cylinder diesel, 179kW/240hp
Performance: Speed – 45km/28mph
  Range – 280km/174 miles

PT-91 Main Battle Tank

The Polish PT-91 was brought out in 1993 to replace the locally built version of that country's ageing Russian T-72 series of main battle tanks. Manufactured by Bumar-Labedy and weighing almost 45 tons, the PT-91 has a crew of three and is powered by a S12U V12 supercharged diesel engine delivering a top speed of 60kph/ 37.3mph and a range of 650km/ 403.9 miles. The main armament is the 125mm/4.92in gun, along with two secondary machine-guns, one of 7.62mm/0.3in and one of 12.7mm/0.5in. Other modern enhancements included digital fire control, night-vision and engine management systems, as well as the Explosive Reactive Armour (ERA) in which the vehicle was sheathed.

While still in use with the Polish armoured forces, production of the PT-91 has now ceased, although the manufacturers have developed an enhanced version for export.

ABOVE AND LEFT: **Also known as** *Twardy* **(Hard), the PT-91 is a development of the Russian-designed T-72M1 which had been built in Poland for a number of years. It has numerous modifications and has even been built as an enhanced version for export. The current PT-91 has a 125mm/ 4.92in smoothbore gun with an automatic loader, while a future model may well have a 120mm/4.72in NATO smoothbore gun.**

PT-91 MBT

Entered service: 1993
Crew: 3
Weight: 45,300kg/44.6 tons
Dimensions: Length – 9.67m/31ft 6in
   Height (over turret hatch) – 2.19m/7ft 2in
   Width – 3.59m/11ft 9.5in
Armament: Main – 125mm/4.92in gun
   Secondary – 1 x 7.62mm and 1 x 12.7mm/
   0.5in machine-guns
Armour: Unspecified
Powerplant: S12U V12 diesel, 633.8kW/850hp
Performance: Speed – 60kph/37.3mph
   Range – 650km/403.9 miles

Pz 61 Medium Tank

Switzerland had no tank-building capability until the 1950s, when it decided to build the Panzer 58, armed with a Swiss-produced 90mm/3.54in gun, to replace their ageing fleet of British Centurions. In the mid-1960s this MBT was replaced by the Panzer 61, armed with a British gun. Based on the previous Pz 58, itself a development of the American M48/M60 series, the Pz 61 was designed and built by RUAG Land Systems, its appearance resembling its predecessors.

With a single-cast hull and turret and weighing over 37 tons, it was powered by a MTU MB-837 V8 diesel engine delivering a top speed of 55kph/34.2mph, and had a range of 300km/186.4 miles. The Pz 61 mounted the British-designed L7 105mm/4.13in rifled main gun built under licence in Switzerland, and had two 7.62mm/0.3in secondary machine-guns.

It was replaced by the Pz 68, which went on in service until final replacement in 1999 by the Leopard 2.

Pz 61 Medium Tank

Entered service: 1965
Crew: 4
Weight: 38,000kg/37.4 tons
Dimensions: Length – 6.78m/22ft 3in
  Height (over turret hatch) – 2.72m/8ft 11in
  Width – 3.08m/10ft 1.5in
Armament: Main – 105mm/4.13in gun
  Secondary – 2 x 7.62mm/0.3in machine-guns
Armour: Maximum – 120mm/4.72in
Powerplant: MTU MB-837 V8 diesel,
  469.8kW/630hp
Performance: Speed – 55kph/34.2mph
  Range – 300km/186.4 miles

RIGHT: **The Pz 61 Medium Tank. This and the Pz 68 certainly had a number of improvements but did not represent a major change in tank design and were very similar in outward appearance. The 105mm/4.13in gun has a fume extractor, thermal sleeve and muzzle reference system fitted, while there is the Bofors Lyran (illuminating rocket system) fitted at both the commander's and loader's stations which will launch an illuminating rocket out to 1,300m/4,265ft.**

Pz 68 Main Battle Tank

The Pz 68 was the next development in the Swiss-manufactured series derived from the US M48/M60, emerging in 1971 as the upgrade model of the Pz 61. Though still armed with the 105mm/4.13in main gun and two 7.62mm/0.3in secondary machine-guns, many of the tank's other subsystems were upgraded over a period of years. These included an up-rated MTU MB-837 diesel engine and a new gun stabilization and fire-control system, allowing it to engage targets while on the move. Wider tracks were also fitted to reduce ground pressure and improve overall vehicle performance.

Other enhancements have followed to maintain the vehicle's viability and service life, and a RUAG-designed 120mm/4.72in main gun replacement is also under development. A total of 390 Pz 68s were built and of these nearly 200 have been upgraded with the installation of a new fire-control system, the resulting upgraded tank being known as Pz 68/88. An ARV (Armoured Recovery Vehicle), Amoured Bridgelayer and Target Tank have also been produced. The Pz 68, like its predecessors, is only in service with the Swiss Army. It has now been joined by the Swiss-built Leopard 2 (Pz 87 Leo).

Pz 68 MBT

Entered service: 1971
Crew: 4
Weight: 39,700kg/39.1 tons
Dimensions: Length – 6.88m/22ft 7in
  Height (over turret hatch) – 2.75m/9ft
  Width – 3.14m/10ft 4in
Armament: Main – 105mm/4.13in gun
  Secondary – 2 x 7.62mm/0.3in machine-guns
Armour: Maximum – 120mm/4.72in
Powerplant: MTU MB-837 V8 diesel,
  492.2kW/660hp
Performance: Speed – 56kph/34.8mph
  Range – 350km/217.5 miles

LEFT: **Approved for production in 1974, some 50 Pz 68 Mark 2s were delivered to the Swiss Army in 1977.**

LEFT AND BELOW: **The Sabra (literally "a native-born Israeli") was developed from the US M60A3 series by Israeli Military Industries. It is fitted with an IMI 120mm/4.72in smoothbore gun (the same as the Merkava Mark 3) and a hybrid armour package. The Sabra Mark II (most recent model) is being offered with either an up-rated General Dynamics AVDS V12 diesel engine which develops 894.8kW/1,200hp or a German 745.7kW/1,000bhp MTU diesel engine.** BOTTOM LEFT: **This Sabra photograph was taken at the Israeli Tank Museum at Latrun.**

Sabra Main Battle Tank

The Sabra Main Battle Tank is another AFV to come out of the Israeli "cauldron" of tank development, and is based upon the US M60A3 series which was originally purchased in the 1960s. The continuous warfare in which the state of Israel has been involved since its inception has resulted in the constant upgrading of all the AFVs they possess, including captured enemy vehicles, as well as the development of their indigenous arms industry.

Weighing 55,000kg/54.1 tons, and built with an eye for the export market, the Sabra MBT is powered by a General Dynamics AVDS 1790 5A diesel engine, giving it a top speed of 48kph/29.8mph and a range of 450km/279.6. Its main armament is a new 120mm/4.72in smoothbore gun cunningly developed to fit the relatively small turret dimensions

of the older M60s with no extra machining or welding necessary. Even within the turret there has been only minimal change – to the ammunition racking and the fire-control systems.

Combined with the new main weapon, add-on armour, engine, safety, navigation and fire-control system, regular enhancement packages keep the

Sabra in the front line and will do so for some time to come. In early 2002 Turkey negotiated a contract with Israel to upgrade 170 M60A3s to Sabra Mark III standard, with the Israeli 120mm/4.72in smoothbore gun, a new power pack and automatic transmission. The upgrade programme is underway at the Israeli Ordnance Corps Workshops at Tel Aviv.

Sabra MBT   ✡

Entered service: 1999
Crew: 4
Weight: 55,000kg/54.1 tons
Dimensions: Length – 8.26m/27ft 1in
    Height (over turret hatch) – 3.05m/10ft
    Width – 3.63m/11ft 11in
Armament: Main – 120mm/4.72in gun
    Secondary – 3 x 7.62mm/0.3in machine-guns
Armour: Unspecified
Powerplant: General Dynamics AVDS 1790 5A
    V12 diesel, 677.1kW/908hp
Performance: Speed – 48kph/29.8mph
    Range – 450km/279.6 miles

LEFT AND BELOW LEFT: **Built by Steyr-Daimler-Puch in the mid-1960s, this neat little 17,700kg/17.2-ton Austrian SK 105 Light Tank is also known as the Kürassier. It was developed from the Saurer APC, mounts a 105mm/4.13in Giat gun and has a crew of three. In service with Austria (286) and six other countries, over 650 have been built. An upgrade package is also now being marketed.**

SK 105 Kürassier Light Tank

Based on the Saurer Armoured Personnel Carrier, the SK 105 Kürassier Light Tank was built by Steyr-Daimler-Puch and brought into service to improve the anti-tank capability of the Austrian armed forces. With a crew of three and weighing 17,700kg/17.2 tons, it was powered by a Steyr 7FA diesel engine and fitted with a torsion bar suspension system, providing a top speed of 65kph/40.4mph and a range of 300km/186.4 miles. In its two-man hydraulically powered turret the Kürassier mounts a French Giat

105mm/4.13in rifled gun as main armament, served by an autoloader with two rotating carousels in the turret bustle. There is also a coaxial 7.62mm/0.3in machine-gun.

Upgrades carried out over the last few years have further equipped the SK 105 with improved rangefinding, fire control, gun stabilization, communications and night-fighting systems, as well as add-on armour modules to the frontal arc, turret and vehicle sides. There is also an ARV (Armoured Recovery Vehicle) and engineer variant.

SK 105 Kürassier has been sold to Argentina, Bolivia, Brazil, Botswana, Morocco and Tunisia. The latest model is the SK 105 A2, which replaces the manual gear shift with a ZF6HP automatic transmission and features a new fully stabilized and partly oscillating turret fitted with upgraded armour and retaining the Giat 105mm/4.13in main gun and autoloader, but with improved night-vision equipment and a digital fire-control system.

SK 105 Kürassier Light Tank

Entered service: 1965
Crew: 3
Weight: 17,700kg/17.2 tons
Dimensions: Length – 5.58m/18ft 3.5in
  Height (over turret hatch) – 2.53m/8ft 3.5in
  Width – 2.5m/8ft 2.5in
Armament: Main – 105mm/4.13in gun
  Secondary – 7.62mm/0.3in machine-gun
Armour: 40mm/1.58in
Powerplant: Steyr 7FA diesel, 238.6kW/320bhp
Performance: Speed – 65kph/40.4mph
  Range – 300km/186.4 miles

LEFT: **The Stingray Light Tank was developed by Cadillac Gage in the 1980s as a private venture and was modernized with new armour and fire-control system ten years later. It mounts a 105mm/4.13in LRF gun. Layout of both models is similar. To date, the only overseas order has been for the Royal Thai Army in late 1987, who took delivery of 106 vehicles.**

Stingray I Light Tank

Cadillac Gage Textron developed the US Stingray Light Tank for the export market in 1984. It was specifically manufactured using as many existing components of other American AFVs as possible in order to keep costs down.

With a weight of 21,205kg/20.9 tons, torsion bar suspension and a crew of four, the Stingray was powered by a Detroit Diesel 8V-92TA engine, giving it a top speed of 67.6kph/42mph and a range of 482.8km/300 miles.

The Stingray mounts a British-built Royal Ordnance 105mm/4.13in Low Recoil Force (LRF) main gun in the distinctive tapered-front three-man turret, along with digital fire control, stabilization and two machine-guns – one 7.62mm/0.3in coaxial and one 12.7mm/0.5in AA. The vehicle is also fitted with night-vision and thermal imaging equipment and was sold successfully to Thailand in 1988, leading to the development of the Stingray II.

Stingray I Light Tank

Entered service: 1988
Crew: 4
Weight: 21,205kg/20.9 tons
Dimensions: Length – 9.30m/30ft 6in
   Height (over turret hatch) – 2.55m/8ft 4.5in
   Width – 2.71m/8ft 10.5in
Armament: Main – 105mm/4.13in LRF gun
   Secondary – 1 x 7.62mm/0.3in and
   1 x 12.7mm/0.5in machine-guns
Armour: Unspecified
Powerplant: Detroit Diesel 8V-92TA,
   398.9kW/535hp
Performance: Speed – 67.6kph/42mph
   Range – 482.8km/300miles

Stingray II Light Tank

Also built by Cadillac Gage Textron, the Stingray II is an evolutionary progression of its predecessor, with a cascade of improvements ranging from new add-on appliqué, laminate and titanium armour suites, a new independent trailing arm suspension system, wider tracks, and new digital fire-control,

navigation, communication and safety systems added. The Stingray II can also mount the new Textron LAV-105 turret (still distinctively tapered into a diamond lozenge at the front), armed with the M35 105mm/4.13in main gun and fed by an automatic loader, thereby reducing the crew to three.

Stingray II Light Tank

Entered service: 1996
Crew: 4
Weight: 22,600kg/22.2 tons
Dimensions: Length – 9.35m/30ft 8in
   Height (over turret hatch) – 2.55m/8ft 4.5in
   Width – 2.8m/9ft 2in
Armament: Main – 105mm/4.13in LRF gun
   Secondary – 1 x 7.62mm/0.3in and
   1 x 12.7mm/0.5in machine-guns
Armour: Unspecified
Powerplant: Detroit Diesel 8V-92TA generating
   398.9kW/535hp
Performance: Speed – 70kph/43.5mph
   Range – 525km/326.2 miles

LEFT: **The Stingray II is virtually identical to the Stingray I except for the new "2001" special high-hardness steel armour which gives added protection over the frontal arc. It will protect against small-arms fire up to 23mm/0.91in calibre. Studies have shown that it is possible to fit the Swiss RUAG 120mm/4.72in compact gun into Stingray II.**

LEFT: **This dramatic photograph shows an Strv 74 being struck by a Bofors Bill top-attack ATGW (Anti-Tank Guided Weapon).** BELOW AND BOTTOM LEFT: **During World War II the Swedes built a series of light tanks such as the M/38 and M/41, which led to the post-war development of the Strv 74. It had a four-man crew and was armed with an effective 75mm/2.95in gun.**

Strv 74 Light Tank

The Strv 74's development path stretches back through the Strv M/40 and M/42 to the original 16,257kg/16-ton Lago tank, manufactured by the Swedish firm Landswerk for the Hungarian Army. The Strv 74 was therefore in essence a modernized version of the World War II M/42 tank which was itself an attempt to bring Swedish tanks up to the standard of the rest of war-torn Europe. It was most successful.

Produced in 1958, weighing 39,700kg/22.14 tons and powered by a Scania-Vabis 239kW/320.5hp diesel engine, the Strv 74 had a top speed of 45kph/28mph and a range of 200km/124.3 miles. With a crew of four, it mounted a 75mm/2.95in main gun and had three machine-guns in its updated turret, which was later further modified with a more sophisticated fire-control system and an upgrading of the main armament to increase its velocity.

Strv 74 Light Tank

Entered service: 1958
Crew: 4
Weight: 39,700kg/22.14 tons
Dimensions: Length – 4.9m/16ft 1in
　　Height (over turret hatch) – 1.61m/5ft 3.5in
　　Width – 2.2m/7ft 2.5in
Armament: Main – 75mm/2.95in gun
　　Secondary – 2 x 7.62mm/0.3in and
　　1 x 12.7mm/0.5in machine-guns
Armour: Maximum – 80mm/3.15in
　　Minimum – 15mm/0.59in
Powerplant: Scania-Vabis diesel, 239kW/
　　320.5hp
Performance: Speed – 45kph/28mph
　　Range – 200km/124.3 miles

Strv 103 S Main Battle Tank

The Swedish Strv 103 S tank is another highly unusual MBT which was developed in response to a detailed study into the hits and injuries sustained by tanks and their crews in combat. This showed that there was a high percentage of disabled turrets and guns, but very few impacts below 1m/3ft in height. The Swedes therefore decided by to dispense with the turret entirely, mounting the main weapon directly on the chassis, which then had to be turned for the gun to be traversed. They also added a front-mounted dozer blade so that the tank could prepare its own hulldown positions and a flotation screen so that it could cope with the many waterways found in Sweden.

With a weight of almost 40 tons, hydro-pneumatic suspension and a crew of three, the S tank was powered by a Rolls-Royce K60 multi-fuel engine (sited in the front of the vehicle for added crew protection), giving a top speed of 50kph/31.1mph and a range of 390km/242.3 miles. There was also a second engine – a Boeing 553 gas turbine – to aid with cold-weather starting and to give the vehicle extra power when in combat or moving cross-country.

The main armament was the Royal Ordnance 105mm/4.13in L7 gun fitted with an automatic loader, along with two coaxial 7.62mm/0.3in machine-guns and another for anti-aircraft defence. 300 Strv 103s were built between 1967 and 1971, equipping three armoured brigades of 72 each and two independent tank battalions.

ABOVE AND LEFT: **Views of the Strv 103 S Tank from Sweden, now located at the Tank Museum, Bovington. The Stridsvagn 103 was a revolutionary Swedish main battle tank, designed in the 1960s to replace the fleet of 300 British Centurions that had been in service for many years. Weighing 39,700kg/ 39.07 tons and armed with a 105mm/4.13in gun in an external mounting, the tank had no turret to traverse so the crew had to "track" instead. However, its automatic loader allowed for a rate of fire of some 15 rounds per minute.**

Removing the traversing turret of an AFV undoubtedly reduces its offensive capability, but conversely increases its defensive ability. This AFV's design reflects the intelligent and essentially peaceful, but realistic intentions of the Swedes.

Early production models were not fitted with either the dozer blade or flotation screen, and were known as the Strv 103A, while later production models were fitted with both, and were known as the Strv 103B.

The former was carried folded under the nose of the tank and when required was swung forward and secured by two rods, then operated by adjusting the hydro-pneumatic suspension. The flotation screen was carried around the top of the hull and took about 15–20 minutes to erect. The tank was then propelled in the water by its tracks at a speed of 6kph/3.75mph. When afloat, the driver stood on top at the rear with a remote throttle control and steered by means of reins attached to the main tiller.

ABOVE, BELOW AND BOTTOM: **Three further views of the S Tank, which show exactly how low the tank can go, and some of its other technical innovations.**

Strv 103 S MBT

Entered service: 1966
Crew: 3
Weight: 39,700kg/39.07 tons
Dimensions: Length – 8.42m/27ft 7.5in
  Height (over turret hatch) – 2.50m/8ft 2.5in
  Width – 3.62m/11ft 10.5in
Armament: Main – 105mm/4.13in gun
  Secondary – 2 x 7.62mm/0.3in and
  1 x 12.7mm/0.5in
Armour: Unspecified
Powerplant: Rolls-Royce K60 multi-fuel, generating
  365.4kW/490hp
Performance: Speed – 50kph/31.1mph
  Range – 390km/242.3 miles

Israeli upgrades

Few states have seen as much continuous military action since their inception as that of Israel. As a result, any and all available armour that was bought, borrowed or captured was turned to good use, with nothing being wasted. The readily available M4A1 Sherman was soon selected by the Israeli Defence Force (IDF) for enhancement, including a new suspension system, sprockets and idlers, and a new mantlet to take the British 105mm/4.13in L7 main gun with new fire-control and later night-vision equipment.

The British Centurion was renamed Sh'ot (Scourge) by the Israelis and it proved to be just that as far as the Arabs were concerned. Israel bought many different variants over the years from a number of countries. The original Centurions were swiftly up-gunned with the British 105mm/4.13in L7, along with new fire-control and night-vision equipment. The vehicle's rear deck was raised so that a new larger diesel engine could be fitted, which more than doubled its operational range, and the armour was increased with a succession of add-on suites, including Blazer (Israeli explosive reactive armour).

The opposing forces lost hundreds of tanks and AFVs in their wars against Israel, the most common being the Soviet-made T-54 and T-55. These were swiftly re-engined, re-gunned with the standard 105mm/4.13in gun used in the Centurion, and renamed Tiran. When used in combat they could cause considerable confusion with the Arab forces.

ABOVE: **This M51 Super Sherman was pictured during the Six Day War of 1967. It had been refitted with a Cummings diesel engine and up-gunned with the 105mm/4.13in L44 gun.** BELOW: **This version of the Sherman served the IDF in many guises, but as a gun tank it was armed with the 105mm/4.13in French gun (from the later models of the AMX-13). The suspension is the more modern Horizontal Volute Spring Suspension (HVSS) rather than the original Vertical Volute type. It also had modified steering and a new turret bustle.**

With the advent of the US M48/M60 series, together with the other conversions becoming available, the Tirans were soon relegated – either to be given to allies such as the SLA (South Lebanon Army) militia, or converted into an APC (Armoured Personnel Carrier) called the Achzarit.

The Israeli Armoured Corps has come a long way since its beginnings in 1948, when their only heavy armour was just one derelict Sherman scheduled for the scrap heap and two elderly Cromwells "acquired" from the British Army in Palestine. Next to arrive was a company of French Hotchkiss light tanks that had been smuggled into Israel under the guise of "farm machinery".

These were its humble beginnings, but now, more than half a century later, Israel has one of the largest and best-equipped armoured forces in the world, with a tradition second to none. In addition, they are not only still prepared to modify constantly and enhance whatever tanks they have in service, but they have also joined the world's elite tank builders with their own revolutionary designs.

TOP: **The upgraded (captured) T-55/62, still with the original 115mm/4.53in gun and known as the T-62I.** ABOVE: **An Israeli-modified Centurion at Latrun: the Sh'ot (Scourge) version with an air-cooled diesel engine (this batch was purchased in the 1960s).** BELOW: **Another Israeli-modified Sherman photographed at the IDF Tank Museum, Latrun. Note the differing suspension and weapon system, namely the AMX-13 turret.**

M51 Sherman Medium Tank ✡

Entered service: 1960
Crew: 5
Weight: 39,625kg/39 tons
Dimensions: Length – 5.89m/19ft 4in
   Height (over turret hatch) – 2.75m/9ft
   Width – 2.62m/8ft 7in
Armament: Main – French 105mm/4.13in
   CN 105-F 1 gun
   Secondary – 2 x 7.62mm/0.3in and
   1 x 12.7mm/0.5in machine-guns
Armour: Maximum – 203mm/7.99in
Powerplant: Cummins diesel, 343kW/460hp
Performance: Speed – 45kph/28mph
   Range – 270km/167.8 miles

Upgraded Centurion MBT ✡

Entered service: 1967
Crew: 4
Weight: 53,500kg/52.7 tons
Dimensions: Length – 7.84m/25ft 8.5in
   Height (over turret hatch) – 3.01m/9ft 10.5in
   Width – 3.38m/11ft 1in
Armament: Main – 105mm/4.13in gun
   Secondary – 3 x 7.62mm/0.3in
   machine-guns
Armour: Maximum – 152mm/5.98in
Powerplant: General Dynamics AVDS 1790 2AC
   diesel, 599.3kW/750hp
Performance: Speed – 50kph/31.1mph
   Range – 500km/310.7 miles

LEFT: **It was the German company Rheinmetall who developed the TAM (*Tanque Argentino Mediano*) to meet the requirements of the Argentine Army, the first prototype being produced in 1976. The TAM had a crew of four, an all-up weight of 30,000kg/ 29.53 tons and mounted a 105mm/4.13in rifled gun. The original requirement was for 512 TAM medium tanks and tracked armoured personnel carriers, but for financial reasons only about 350 were built. Some recent reports, however, indicate that production may well have recommenced.**

TAMSE TAM Medium Tank

The TAM was initially designed and produced by the German arms company Rheinmetall and then by TAMSE in Argentina to replace Argentina's ageing fleet of M4 Shermans. A critical factor in the selection of this tank by the Argentines was meeting the weight restrictions imposed by the country's bridge and road infrastructure. Following on from prototype testing in the mid-1970s, the vehicle was accepted and production began in Argentina under licence. The TAM was first delivered to the Argentine amoured forces in the early 1980s, although none saw action in the Falklands War in 1982.

Weighing almost 30 tons and with a crew of four, the TAM is powered by a MTU 6-cylinder diesel engine, giving it a top speed of 75kph/46.6mph and a range of 940km/584.1 miles. The chassis of the vehicle was based on the Marder APC, which was also

manufactured by Rheinmetall but with a newly designed three-man turret mounting a 105mm/4.13in rifled main gun and a 7.62mm/0.3in coaxial machine-gun, with another 7.62mm/0.3in gun mounted on the turret roof for anti-aircraft and close-quarter defence. The TAM also has modern gun stabilization,

fire-control, communications and safety equipment, and variants so far produced include a self-propelled howitzer, an ARV (Armoured Recovery Vehicle) and a multiple-launch rocket system. However, it is no longer being marketed and the manufacturer TAMSE has gone out of business.

LEFT: **Other versions included the Israeli LAR 160 multiple rocket system, the original turret being replaced by two 18-round launcher pods. It is thought that a small number of these were delivered to the Argentine Army.** BELOW LEFT: **The TAM on trials in Thailand in 1978 when the potential export model was known as the TH 301.**

TAMSE TAM Medium Tank	
Entered service: 1976	
Crew: 4	
Weight: 30,000kg/29.53 tons	
Dimensions: Length – 6.77m/22ft 3in	
Height (over turret hatch) – 2.71m/8ft 10.5in	
Width – 3.92m/10ft 10.5in	
Armament: Main – 105mm/4.13in gun	
Secondary – 2 x 7.62mm/0.3in machine-guns	
Armour: Unspecified	
Powerplant: MTU MB 833 Ka500 diesel,	
536.9kW/720hp	
Performance: Speed – 75kph/46.6mph	
Range – 940km/584.1 miles	

LEFT, BELOW AND BOTTOM LEFT:
The Lenin Heavy Tank was to all intents and purposes the last in the Soviet World War II heavy tank series, being a redesign of the JS-4 but incorporating lessons learned in the early post-war years. In fact, it was heavy, large and not as easy to move around the countryside as the more modern medium tanks such as the T-62, which replaced it in the mid-1960s.

T-10 Lenin Heavy Tank

Last in the KV and JS series of heavy tanks originating in the 1930s and being developed through World War II, the T-10 (also known as the Lenin) replaced the short-lived JS-4. Entering service in 1953, weighing 52,000kg/ 51.2 tons and fitted with torsion bar suspension, it was powered by the V12 diesel engine originally developed for the JS-4, providing a top speed of 42kph/26.1mph and a range of 250km/ 155.3 miles.

The T-10 was manned by a crew of four, protected by armour up to 270mm/ 10.63in thick on the frontal arc and armed with a D74 122mm/4.8in main gun

in a classic Soviet "mushroom head" turret which was sited well forward on the hull. There were also two 14.55mm/ 0.57in machine-guns and an optional extra 12.7mm/0.5in anti-aircraft machine-gun mounted outside on the commander's cupola.

The main drawback of the Lenin was its very limited ammunition stowage capacity of fewer than 30 rounds, although this was increased later to 50. The reality

was that the T-10 Lenin belonged to a previous generation of AFV made obsolete by new types of armour and ammunition that were enabling a new type of faster, lighter tank such as the T-62 to take on the role of the older classic heavies.

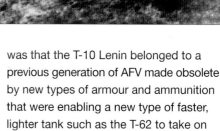

T-10 Lenin Heavy Tank

Entered service: 1953
Crew: 4
Weight: 52,000kg/51.2 tons
Dimensions: Length – 7.41m/24ft 3.5in
    Height (over turret hatch) – 2.43m/7ft 11.5in
    Width – 3.56m/11ft 8in
Armament: Main – 122mm/4.8in gun
    Secondary – 2 x 14.55mm/0.57in and
    1 x 12.7mm/0.3in machine-guns
Armour: Maximum – 270mm/10.63in
Powerplant: V2IS 12-cylinder diesel, 514.5kW/690hp
Performance: Speed – 42kph/26.1mph
    Range – 250km/155.3 miles

T-54/T-55 Medium Tank

This series of AFV ranks as one of the most prolific in terms of the sheer numbers produced, with some estimates as high as 60,000. It became the primary MBT of post-World War II Soviet tank forces and their satellite and client states all over the world for at least two decades. It was also built under licence in Czechoslovakia, Poland and China, and did not go out of production in the USSR until early in the 1990s.

The T-54 had a low-silhouette hull with a classic Soviet "mushroom dome" turret, weighed over 35 tons and was powered by a V54 V12 diesel engine, giving it a top speed of 48kph/29.8mph and a range 400km/248.5 miles. It was armed with a D10 100mm/3.94in rifled main gun, along with

ABOVE AND BELOW LEFT: **Following on from their highly successful wartime T-34/76 and T-34/85, the Soviets produced what must have been their most successful medium tanks ever – the T-54 and T-55 – with production starting in 1947. Estimates of the numbers produced since then must be in the region of 60,000, a staggering number, and even more than the wartime Sherman M4 Medium Tanks.**

a 7.62mm/0.3in coaxial machine-gun. Early versions also mounted a fixed 7.62mm/0.3in machine-gun in the bow, which was operated by the driver.

New models featured improvements as they came into service – beginning with night-vision equipment and an extra machine-gun for anti-aircraft defense, and going on to full-blown upgrade programmes with fire-control, navigation, communication and safety systems, as well as add-on armour suites. There were also the inevitably endless variants of an AFV whose use was so widespread and culturally diverse.

With the advent of the T-55 in the 1950s, the main flaw of the T54 – its automotive unreliability – was tackled with the fitting of a larger V255 V12 water-cooled diesel engine, thereby increasing the power, speed (50kph/31.1mph) and range (500km/310.7 miles) of the vehicle. There was also a new turret fitted – still a mushroom – without the loader's cupola or the prominent roof-top ventilator dome, and with two enlarged "D" roof panels. It also mounted an infrared gunner's searchlight above the main gun, but this was retrofitted to the T-54 and so is not a distinctive feature.

LEFT: **Many of these "rough and ready", highly reliable and easy-to-crew main battle tanks are still in service worldwide, with many having been sold off by European armies as they took on more sophisticated MBTs. The all-welded steel hull is divided into three compartments – driving at the front, fighting in the centre and engine at the rear.**

BELOW: **Russian tank crews working on their vehicles in their tank hangar.**

Again, improved models surfaced regularly, sporting an array of enhancements and variants, including further engine tweaks, NBC (Nuclear, Biological and Chemical) protection, add-on armour suites – especially ERA (Explosive Reactive Armour) – new main gun stabilization and fire-control systems.

Civilian conversions

Although the original production finished long ago, the T-54/T-55 is still in service with armies all over the world – a staggering 65 at last count – so it must be one of the most successful tanks ever built. Remarkably, the RFAS has also now started marketing a number of systems based on the T-54/T-55 MBT with purely civilian applications. These mainly centre around fire-fighting.

RIGHT AND BELOW: **The all-welded steel hull is divided into three compartments – driving at the front, fighting in the centre and engine at the rear. There are a wide variety of models of this 36,000kg/35.4-ton four-man tank, both T-54 and T-55 being armed with a 100mm/3.94in rifled gun.**

T-54/T-55 Medium Tank

Entered service: 1948
Crew: 4
Weight: 36,000kg/35.4 tons
Dimensions: Length – 6.45m/21ft 2in
    Height (over turret hatch) – 2.4m/7ft 10.5in
    Width – 3.27m/10ft 8.5in
Armament: Main – 100mm/3.94in gun
    Secondary – 2 x 7.62mm/0.3in and
    1 x 12.7mm/0.5in machine-guns
Armour: Maximum – 203mm/7.99in
Powerplant: V54 12-cylinder diesel, generating
    387.8kW/520hp
Performance: Speed – 48kph/29.8mph
    Range – 400km/248.5 miles

T-62 Main Battle Tank

The T-62 was the next progression in the Soviet development cycle based on the T-54/55 series, and featured an enlarged hull to fit a new turret carrying a larger bore main gun. This tank was destined to become the primary main battle tank of the Soviet amoured forces during the 1970s, with over 20,000 built.

Weighing almost 40 tons, the T-62 was powered by the same 432.5kW/580hp V12 water-cooled diesel engine as its predecessor, which provided a top speed of 50kph/31.1mph and a range of 650km/403.9 miles. Mounted centrally over the third road wheel, the new "mushroom dome" cast turret had a U-5T (2A20) Rapira 115mm/4.53in main gun with a longer, thinner barrel than the 100mm/3.94in of the T-54/55. An unusual feature of the new turret was the automatic shell ejector system, which worked from the recoil of the main gun, ejecting the spent shell casings through a port in the rear of the turret.

There was also a 7.62mm/0.3in coaxial machine-gun and a 12.7mm/0.5in anti-aircraft machine-gun mounted by the loader's hatch. A gunner's infrared searchlight was mounted on the right, above the main gun. Later models included the usual improvements – gun stabilization and fire control, NBC

(Nuclear, Biological and Chemical) protection, communication and safety systems, add-on armour suites (including ERA (Explosive Reactive Armour), appliqué and increased belly armour for mine protection). Although there were many variations on the T-54/55 chassis, there were surprisingly few on the T-62, although the gun tank was upgraded regularly.

Recent modifications to various Marks of T-62 have included the fitting of some or all of the following: the Sheksna laser beam riding missile system; the Volna fire-control system, which includes the KDT-2 laser rangefinder with a range of 4,000m/13,123ft; a 12.7mm/0.5in AA machine-gun; a thermal sleeve for the barrel of the main gun; auxiliary armour to hull,

ABOVE, LEFT AND BELOW: **Using the T-55 as the basis for its design but with a longer, wider hull and a new turret, the T-62 came into Red Army service in 1961, but was first seen in public at the Moscow May Day Parade in 1965. Production continued until 1975, by which time over 20,000 had been built, including a wide family of variants. The 40,000kg/39.4-ton MBT had a crew of four and mounted a 115mm/4.53in smoothbore gun (40 rounds carried). Numerous modifications have been incorporated since it was accepted into service, including a flamethrower version.**

LEFT: The "mushroom domed" turret is very clear on this uncluttered photograph, as are the rest of the tank's clean lines. The T-62 was first seen in public during a parade in Moscow in 1965. Over the next ten years some 20,000 T-62s would be built by the USSR. BELOW: Note the longer gun barrel of the 115mm/4.53in as compared with its predecessor. The tank carried 40 rounds of main gun ammunition, 16 in the forward part of the tank, 20 in the rear of the fighting compartment, two ready rounds in the turret and one more between the feet of both the gunner and loader! The spent shell ejection system was activated by the recoil of the gun – the empty case being ejected automatically through a trapdoor in the turret rear. The maximum rate of fire was four rounds per minute when at the halt. After firing, the gun automatically elevated to an angle of 3.5 degrees or more for reloading, and the turret could not be traversed while loading was in progress. BOTTOM: Columns of T-62 MBTs on training make a very impressive sight.

T-62 MBT

Entered service: 1961
Crew: 4
Weight: 40,000kg/39.4 tons
Dimensions: Length – 6.63m/21ft 9in
Height (over turret hatch) – 2.39m/7ft 10in
Width – 3.3m/10ft 10in
Armament: Main – 115mm/4.53in Rapira gun
Secondary – 1 x 7.62mm/0.3in and
1 x 12.7mm/0.5in machine-guns
Armour: Maximum – 242mm/9.53in
Powerplant: V55 12-cylinder diesel, delivering
432.5kW/580hp
Performance: Speed – 50kph/31.1mph
Range – 650km/403.9 miles (with additional fuel
tank), 450km/280 miles (without)

turret and belly; ERA; side skirts; Napalm protection system; local smoke launchers; modernized suspension system; R-173 radio system; and V55U engine. The Sheksna missile, which is fired from the 115mm/4.53in gun, weighs some 28kg/61.72lb and has a range of 4,000m/13,123ft. Guidance is semi-automatic beam riding, so that all the operator has to do to ensure a hit is to keep the sight crosshairs on the target.

A conservative estimate of the number of T-62s built in the USSR and still in service worldwide is in excess of 8,000, spread among some 18 countries in Asia, the Middle and Far East, with North Korea having the largest holding (1,800) after Russia. Other T-62s were produced by the Czechs for export, while they were also once built in North Korea. The Russians are, therefore, currently offering a number of upgrades that will considerably improve the T-62's battlefield survivability.

T-72 Main Battle Tank

Developed as an alternative to the highly complicated and expensive T-64 and introduced in 1972, the T-72 has a crew of three, weighs 45,500kg/44.8 tons and is powered by a V12 diesel engine, delivering a top speed of 60kph/37.3mph and a range of 550km/341.8 miles. The classic low, rounded turret is centred on the hull and has two cupolas, one each for the gunner and commander. The main armament is a stabilized 125mm/4.92in 2A46 smoothbore gun fitted with a light alloy thermal sleeve and served by an automatic carousel fitted vertically on the floor and attached to the rear wall of the turret, carrying 28 projectiles. This gun has the ability to fire both the Songster-type wire-guided missile as well as normal main gun

munitions. A 7.62mm/0.3in PKT machine-gun was also mounted coaxially to the right of the main armament and there was a 12.7mm/0.5in NSV machine-gun for anti-aircraft defence outside on the commander's cupola.

The tank also mounts a dozer blade under its nose, to clear obstacles and prepare fire positions, as well as having snorkelling equipment for deep wading. New versions had a cascade of improvements, including new engines (633.8kW/850hp, then 932.1kW/1,250hp), computerized fire-control systems, thermal and passive night-sights and fire detection and suppression systems. Variants included command, ARV, mine-clearer and bridgelayer models.

ABOVE AND LEFT: **Designed as a simpler alternative to the complicated and costly T-64, the T-72 has seen combat service in Iraq and Lebanon and is now serving with armies worldwide. Its main armament (on the T-72S) is the 125mm/4.92in smoothbore gun (45 rounds carried). The tank has recently been comprehensively upgraded and is in service with 30 different countries worldwide, the largest number (over 9,000) being in Russia. The T-72S weighs 1,000kg/2,204lb more than the T-72.**

ABOVE: **A captured Iraqi T-72 being dragged off during Operation "Desert Storm".** RIGHT: **During the 1970s the Soviets licensed the building of their T-72 to Yugoslavia, who adapted it to suit their own needs, putting in a different engine (a V12 diesel). Yugoslavia sold a number to Kuwait, and here are two of them, known as the M48A, flying Kuwaiti flags. These tanks saw combat during the first Gulf War.**

Like the T-54/55 series, the T-72 was built in massive numbers and supplied to client and satellite states, undergoing various modifications. They were also built under licence by seven other countries with their own model numbers, including the Czechoslovakian PSP T-72, the Polish PT-91 and the Yugoslavian M-84. There are even captured Arab-Israeli-modified versions.

RIGHT: **An internal view of part of the turret.**
BELOW: **A T-72 with ERA on upgrade. The ERA bricks cover much of the vulnerable frontal area.**

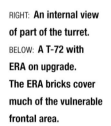

T-72 MBT
Entered service: 1972
Crew: 3
Weight: 45,500kg/44.8 tons
Dimensions: Length – 9.53m/31ft 3in
Height (over turret hatch) – 2.22m/7ft 3in
Width – 3.59m/12ft 9in
Armament: Main – 125mm/4.92in gun
Secondary – 1 x 7.62mm/0.3in and
1 x 12.7mm/0.5in machine-guns
Armour: Maximum – 250mm/9.84in
Powerplant: V46 12-cylinder diesel, generating
581.6kW/780hp
Performance: Speed – 60kph/37.3mph
Range – 550km/341.8 miles (with long-range
tanks), 480km/300 miles (without)

LEFT: **Built both in Russia and the Ukraine, the T-64 MBT was the first Russian MBT to have a three-man crew, made possible by the installation of an automatic loader. The tank is only in service within armies of the Russian Federation and has never been offered for export.** BELOW: **Two T-64s being moved by tank train, a sensible way of preserving tank mileage. They are fitted with long-range fuel drums on the rear decks.** BOTTOM LEFT: **This T-64 MBT also has long-range fuel drums fitted above the rear engine deck. Its 125mm/4.92in smoothbore gun can fire the Songster ATGW (Anti-Tank Guided Weapon), taking 9–10 seconds to reach 4,000m/13,123ft.**

T-64 Main Battle Tank

Only ever in service with the Russian Federation and associate states, the T-64 MBT was never offered for export because it incorporated too many advanced features. The main differences between the T-64 and its predecessors were in its automotive and suspension systems, which consequently gave it a superior mobility. Weighing 42,000kg/ 41.3 tons, it was powered by a 5DTF 5-cylinder opposed-piston water-cooled diesel engine delivering a top speed of 75kph/46.6mph and a range of 400km/ 248.5 miles. Centred on the hull, the classic Soviet low-profile, rounded turret had two cupolas and mounted the 125mm/ 4.92in 2A26 Rapira 3 smoothbore main gun, fitted with a vertical ammunition stowage system and automatic loader, enabling the T-64 to be the first Soviet

tank operated by a crew of three. There was also a 7.62mm/0.3in coaxial machine-gun mounted to the right of the mantlet and an infrared searchlight on the left of the main armament, as well as an optional 12.7mm/0.5in anti-aircraft machine-gun.

Other improvements included new armour to protect against HEAT (High-Explosive Anti-Tank) attack, incorporating conventional steel with ceramic inserts and called laminate, and also gill-type panels which sprung outward to detonate projectiles off the main body of the tank. As other models were introduced, the usual add-on armour suites also included

ERA (Explosive Reactive Armour), passive and appliqué, as well as updates to the vehicle's gun stabilization and fire control, NBC (Nuclear, Biological and Chemical) protection, communication and safety systems. Variants included command, ARV (Armoured Recovery Vehicle) and Kobra missile-carrier models. Only about 8,000 T-64s were ever built, of which the largest number outside the Russian Federation are some 2,200 in service with the Ukrainian Army.

T-64 MBT	

Entered service: 1972
Crew: 3
Weight: 42,000kg/41.3 tons
Dimensions: Length – 7.4m/24ft 3.5in
 Height (over turret hatch) – 2.2m/7ft 2.5in
 Width – 3.46m/11ft 4in
Armament: Main – 125mm/4.92in Rapira 3 gun
 Secondary – 1 x 7.62mm/0.3in and
 1 x 12.7mm/0.5in machine-guns
Armour: Maximum – 200mm/7.87in
Powerplant: 5DTF 5-cylinder diesel, 559.3kW/750hp
Performance: Speed – 75kph/46.6mph
 Range – 400km/248.5 miles

T-80 Main Battle Tank

The T-80 MBT was designed as an upgrade to replace the T-64, being produced at the Kirov Plant, Leningrad, and entering service in 1976. Initially only a small number were built and these were soon followed by the much improved T-80B.

Weighing 42,500kg/41.8 tons and fitted with torsion bar suspension, it was the first Soviet tank to have a gas-turbine engine – the GTD 1000 – which, coupled with a manual transmission, delivered a top speed of 70kph/43.5mph and a range of 335km/208.2 miles.

Unfortunately the engine proved a major stumbling block for the T-80, as it was very fuel-hungry and unreliable, necessitating changes to the hull shape in order to store more fuel as well as changes to the engine. The overall layout of the T-80 is similar to the T-64, but there are numerous differences in detail.

The wide flat turret is centred on the hull, with the commander's cupola on the right and the gunner's hatch on the left. It mounts a 125mm/4.92in 2A46 Rapira 3 smoothbore gun firing both ATGW (Anti-Tank Guided Weapon) missiles and normal main gun munitions, which is

served by a 28-projectile, horizontal automatic carousel loader, mounted on the floor and rear wall of the turret. A 7.62mm/0.3in coaxial machine-gun is mounted to the right of the mantlet and an infrared searchlight is mounted to the right of the main armament. The vehicle is also fitted with a dozer blade underneath the laminate armour glacis, as well as snorkelling equipment for deep wading.

The T-80B, which replaced the T-80 in 1978, had a modified up-armoured turret with an upgraded 125mm/4.92in main gun firing the new Kobra missile munition (known as Songster in US/NATO parlance) as well as a new fire-control system. Further upgrades include extensive extra frontal and ERA (Explosive, Reactive Armour) packages, a new, more powerful GTD-1250 turbine engine, a new laser-guided anti-tank main gun missile munition (Sniper), as well as an array of digital fire-control, navigation and safety systems.

Some 4,500 T-80s are in service in Russia, as well as a small number in four or five other countries, which surprisingly includes 41 in Cyprus.

TOP: **Similar to the T-64 series, the T-80 was accepted into service in 1976. It has a two-man turret and an automatic loader for its 125mm/4.92in smoothbore gun. A small number of T-80s have been purchased by Cyprus and Korea, as well as Pakistan, from the Ukraine factory. Note the large exhaust outlet at the rear.** ABOVE: **A Russian Federation T-80 firing on the ranges. It has a 125mm/4.92in 2A46M smoothbore gun, the same as that fitted to the T-72, and can fire either the Songster ATGW or 125mm/4.92in separate-loading ammunition (i.e. projectile-loaded first, then semi-combustible case, the stub base of which is the only part ejected).**

T-80 MBT

Entered service: 1976
Crew: 3
Weight: 42,500kg/41.8 tons
Dimensions: Length – 7.4m/24ft 3.5in
  Height (over turret hatch) – 2.2m/7ft 2.5in
  Width – 3.4m/11ft 2in
Armament: Main – 125mm/4.92in Rapira 3 gun
  Secondary – 1 x 7.62mm/0.3in and
  1 x 12.7mm/0.5in machine-guns
Armour: Unspecified
Powerplant: GTD 1000 12-cylinder gas-turbine, 820.3kW/1,100hp
Performance: Speed – 70kph/43.5mph
  Range – 335km/208.2 miles

T-84 Main Battle Tank

The T-84 is a recent Ukrainian upgrade of the Russian T-80, with both being manufactured at the well-established Malyshev Plant at Kharkov in the Ukraine, and using as many locally produced components as possible. The main differences from its predecessor begin with a more powerful up-rated 6TD-2 diesel engine developing 894.8kW/1,200hp, which gave the vehicle a top speed of 65kph/40.4mph and a range of 540kph/335.5 miles. To handle this extra performance, new improved tracks were fitted.

Next, the turret mounted the Ukrainian-made 125mm/4.92in KBA3 smoothbore main gun, fitted with a vertical carousel autoloader containing 28 rounds and an up-rated fire-control system including the French ALIS thermal sight. This armament fires both normal munitions and the Songster AT-11 Anti-Tank Guided Missile (ATGM).

Secondary armament consisted of two machine-guns – one of 7.62mm/0.3in and one of 12.7mm/0.5in. The T-84 also came equipped with an ARENA Active Protection System (APS) and the SHTORA-1 active IR (InfraRed) ATGM jammer – an electro-optical countermeasures system, along with Ukrainian-manufactured ERA (Explosive Reactive Armour) enhancements. Subsequent updates include improved fire-control, communication, navigation and safety systems. There is also a later model mounting the NATO standard 120mm/4.72in main gun.

In 2001 the Ukrainian Army received two new T-84s – the first new main battle tanks delivered since the country became independent from Russia. As well as being accepted by the Ukrainian Army, this vehicle has been successfully sold to Pakistan and aroused the interest of other countries, including Turkey.

ABOVE AND LEFT: **Two views of the Ukranian-built T-84, some 8,000 having been built by the Malyshev plant for the Russian Army. Based upon the T-64 and designed jointly by the Leningrad Kirov plant and Malyshev, this MBT is now almost completely built in the Ukraine. It has a crew of three, weighs 46,000kg/45.3 tons and mounts a 125mm/4.92in smoothbore gun. These photographs were taken at an arms fair.**

T-84 MBT

Entered service: 1995

Crew: 3

Weight: 46,000kg/45.3 tons

Dimensions: Length – 7.08m/23ft 2.5in
   Height (over turret hatch) – 2.22m/7ft 3.5in
   Width – 3.56m/11ft 8in

Armament: Main – 125mm/4.92in KBA3 gun
   Secondary – 1 x 7.62mm/0.3in and
   1 x 12.7mm/0.5in machine-guns

Armour: Unspecified

Powerplant: 6TD-2 6-cylinder diesel, developing 894.8kW/1,200hp

Performance: Speed – 65kph/40.4mph
   Range – 540km/335.5 miles

T-90 MBT	
Entered service: 1993	
Crew: 3	
Weight: 46,500kg/45.8 tons	
Dimensions: Length – 6.86m/22ft 6in	
Height (over turret hatch) – 2.23m/7ft 4in	
Width – 3.37m/11ft 1in	
Armament: Main – 125mm/4.92in Rapira 3 gun	
Secondary – 1 x 7.62mm/0.3in and	
1 x 12.7mm/0.5in machine-guns	
Armour: Unspecified	
Powerplant: V-84MS 12-cylinder diesel,	
626.4kW/840hp	
Performance: Speed – 60kph/37.3mph	
Range – 500km/310.7 miles	

T-90 Main Battle Tank

The T-90 traces its development back to the T-72BM MBT – the improved T-72B with built-in ERA (Explosive Reactive Armour) – and was first manufactured at the Uralvagon Plant in Nizhnyi-Tagil in the late 1980s.

Developed at the same time as the T-80, but with a less complex and therefore cheaper design ethos, the first major difference between the two was in the choice of power pack, which in the T-90 was a V84MS diesel engine, producing 626.4kW/840hp and providing a top speed of 60kph/37.3mph and a range of 500km/310.7 miles.

The classic Russian low-profile, rounded turret is centred on the hull and mounts the 125mm/4.92in 2A46 smoothbore main gun (the same as the T-72 and T-80) firing the AT-11 Sniper laser-guided ATGM (Anti-Tank Guided Missile), as well as normal main gun munitions.

There is a coaxial 7.62mm/0.3in machine-gun and a 12.7mm/0.5in heavy anti-aircraft machine-gun on the turret top by the gunner's hatch. The T-90 also mounts two infrared searchlights on either side of the main armament, which are part of the Shtora ATGM defence system, and the turret is covered with second-generation ERA on the frontal arc, making this one of the best protected of Russian main battle tanks. It is equipped with the latest fire-control, navigation and safety systems. There is also a T-90S MBT version, designed to meet the operational requirements of Asian countries – some 310 having been bought by India.

TOP AND ABOVE: **The T-90, which is yet another development of the T-72, first came to prominence in 1993 and is believed to have gone into small-scale production the following year. It has a crew of three, with a two-man turret with an automatic loader for its 125mm/4.92in gun. The photographs show a snorkel attached to the turret rear, but no long-range fuel tanks fitted on the rear. It made its first appearance outside Russia at Abu Dhabi in March 1997.** LEFT: **Standard equipment on the T-90S is the latest generation of Kontakt 5 Explosive Reactive Armour, as fitted in this photograph.**

TR-580 and TR-85 Main Battle Tanks

Both the TR-580 and TR-85 are Romanian variants of the Russian T-55 series, manufactured or modified at the Brashove factory in Romania, and the prime weapon of their armoured forces in the 1980s and 1990s.

The TR-580 was the first redesign, its alphanumeric name denoting the size of its 432.5kW/580hp engine, which necessitated a hull redesign. It was armed with the same weapons as the T-55 and its sister vehicle the TR-85, and weighed over 37 tons. It was fitted with a new torsion bar suspension system, the main visual difference between both of the Romanian vehicles and their T-55 predecessor being the sixth road wheel (the T-55 only had five).

The TR-85 also has a new German 641.3kW/860hp 8-cylinder diesel engine, providing a top speed of 60kph/38mph and a range of 310km/192.6 miles,

which required substantial modification of the rear hull and decking. In the turret the main armament mounted was the same 100mm/3.94in gun with a new fire-control system and two machine-guns – one of 7.62mm/0.3in and one of 12.7mm/0.5in.

One visual difference between the two tanks is the spoked road wheels of the TR-580. An upgrade currently under development ports additional passive armour, a new fire-control and gun-stabilization system, as well as night-vision and safety equipment updates.

LEFT: **The Romanian TR-85 MBT is a local Romanian design which is very similar to the Russian T-55. In the early 1990s the Romanians said that they had over 600 of these MBTs in service, but that figure has now dropped. The TR-85 is basically a T-55 with a fume extractor fitted to the end of the 100mm/3.94in rifled main armament and a thermal sleeve. There is also an upgrade mooted which has a new power pack (596.6kW/800hp diesel) and a fully automatic transmission. The TR-85M1 is the upgraded version of the TR-85, built in the 1970s with German help in chassis technology, the prime Romanian contractor being Arsenalul Armetel. Various foreign companies were also involved.**

TR-85 MBT

Entered service: 1987
Crew: 4
Weight: 50,000kg/49.2 tons
Dimensions: Length – 9.96m/32ft 8in
  Height (over turret hatch) – 3.10m/10ft 2in
  Width – 3.44m/11ft 3.5in
Armament: Main – 100mm/3.94in gun
  Secondary – 1 x 7.62mm/0.3in and
  1 x 12.7mm/0.5in machine-guns
Armour: Unspecified
Powerplant: MTU 8-cylinder diesel,
  641.3kW/860hp
Performance: Speed – 60kph/37.3mph
  Range – 310km/192.6 miles

RIGHT: **The other Romanian MBT is the TR-580, which is very similar to the TR-85 that it preceded in production. The main differences are that the gun does not have a thermal sleeve or laser rangefinder installed.**

TR-580 MBT

Entered service: 1982
Crew: 4
Weight: 38,200kg/37.6 tons
Dimensions: Length – 6.45m/21ft 2in
  Height (over turret hatch) – 2.4m/7ft 10.5in
  Width – 3.27m/10ft 8.5in
Armament: Main – 100mm/3.94in gun
  Secondary – 1 x 7.62mm/0.3in and
  1 x 12.7mm/0.5in machine-guns
Armour: Unspecified
Powerplant: Thought to be 12-cylinder diesel,
  432.5kW/580hp
Performance: Speed – 60kph/37.3mph
  Range – 300km/186.4 miles

LEFT: **Based upon the T-72, the TR-125 MBT is heavier (48,000kg/47.2 tons), with thicker armour and a larger engine. It can be recognized externally from the additional seventh roadwheel on either side. Armament is identical to the T-72.**

TR-125 MBT

Entered service: 1989
Crew: 4
Weight: 48,000kg/47.2 tons
Dimensions: Length – 6.9m/22ft 7.5in
  Height (over turret hatch) – 2.37m/7ft 9.5in
  Width – 3.60m/11ft 9.5in
Armament: Main – 125mm/4.92in gun
  Secondary – 1 x 7.62mm/0.3in and
  1 x 12.7mm/0.5in machine-guns
Armour: Unspecified
Powerplant: V12 diesel, 656.2kW/880hp
Performance: Speed – 60kph/37.3mph
  Range – 540km/335.5 miles

TR-125 Main Battle Tank

The TR-125 is a Romanian-built version of the Soviet T-72, manufactured at the end of the 1980s until the collapse of the USSR led to the cessation of production in favour of other vehicles. With considerably thicker armour, it was heavier than its predecessor, weighing 48,000kg/ 47.2 tons, with a crew of four. The TR-125 was powered by a V12 diesel engine, providing a top speed of 60kph/ 37.3mph and a range of 540km/335.5 miles. It was armed with a 125mm/4.92in main gun, with a coaxial 7.62mm/0.3in machine-gun and one of 12.7mm/ 0.5in for anti-aircraft defence. The main visual difference between it and other T-72 variants is in it having a seventh road wheel. It is still in service with the Romanian Army today.

TM-800 Main Battle Tank

The most recent of the Romanian-manufactured MBTs, the TM-800 first emerged in the mid-1990s as an upgraded version of the TR-580 – itself a T-55 derivative. With new laminate armour increasing its weight to 45,000kg/44.3 tons but giving it improved survivability on the battlefield, and powered by its 618.9kW/830hp diesel engine, the TM-800 has a top speed of 60kph/37.3mph and a range of 500km/310.7 miles. In its "mushroom head" two-hatched turret it mounts a 100mm/3.94in D10 series main gun with a computerized fire-control system and laser rangefinder, along with two machine-guns – one an internal coaxial of 7.62mm/0.3in and the other a heavier calibre 12.7mm/0.5in mounted on the outside of the turret for anti-aircraft (AA) defence.

LEFT: **The TM-800 is an up-rated TR-580 MBT, currently the most modern Romanian MBT. It appeared in service in 1994 and has not yet gone into full production.**

TM-800 MBT

Entered service: 1994
Crew: 4
Weight: 45,000kg/44.3 tons
Dimensions: Length – 6.74m/22ft 1.5in
  Height (over turret hatch) – 2.35m/7ft 8.5in
  Width – 3.30m/10ft 10in
Armament: Main – 100mm/3.94in gun
  Secondary – 1 x 7.62mm/0.3in and
  1 x 12.7mm/0.5in machine-guns
Armour: Unspecified
Powerplant: Diesel, 618.9kW/830hp
Performance: Speed – 60kph/37.3mph
  Range – 500km/310.7 miles

LEFT: **In the early 1950s the Soviet Union supplied China with a number of their T-54 Main Battle Tanks and afterwards, production of such MBTs was taken on by NORINCO (China North Industries Corporation) under the designation of Type 59. Later Type 59As were fitted with an IR searchlight above the 100mm/3.94in gun, while other retrofits have included a more powerful diesel and even an RO Defence 105mm/4.13in L7A3 rifled gun to improve the resulting package.** BELOW: **This Type 59 has been fitted with the British 105mm/4.13in L7A3 rifled gun, a private venture by UK Royal Ordnance (now BAe Systems). Note also the British pattern smoke dischargers.** BOTTOM: **A column of parked Chinese Type 59-IIs. They were a further development of the Type 59, and also had a number of improvements, such as stabilization for the main gun, a 432.5kW/580hp diesel engine and new radios.**

Type 59 Main Battle Tank

The Chinese Type 59 and its successor the Type 69 were both based upon the Soviet T-54 and it was the first Chinese tank built under licence at the inception of its own permanent armoured formations. With an identical layout to its Soviet predecessor, manned by the same number of crew and weighing 36,000kg/35.4 tons, its V12 diesel engine gave it a top speed of 50kph/31.1mph and a range of 420km/261 miles. Within its classic Russian "mushroom head" turret, it mounted a 100mm/3.94in rifled gun, together with two coaxial machine-guns, plus a 12.7mm/0.5in on top for anti-aircraft

defence. At first the Type 59 had only the bare essentials, but later models have mounted infrared searchlights, laser rangefinders, night-vision equipment and armour enhancements.

Both Type 59s and Type 69s have been built in large numbers for the People's Liberation Army and for export, an estimate being that some 6,000 are still in service in China, while it has been sold to over a dozen countries,

one of the largest numbers being about 1,200 in Pakistan, which now produces them locally and has exported to other countries in Asia and Africa.

Type 59 MBT	

Entered service: 1959
Crew: 4
Weight: 36,000kg/35.4 tons
Dimensions: Length – 7.9m/25ft 11in
　Height (over turret hatch) – 2.59m/8ft 6in
　Width – 3.27m/10ft 8.5in
Armament: Main – 100mm/3.94in gun
　Secondary – 2 x 7.62mm/0.3in and
　1 x 12.7mm/0.5in machine-guns
Armour: Maximum – 203mm/7.99in
Powerplant: 12150L V12 diesel, generating
　320.7kW/430hp
Performance: Speed – 50kph/31.1mph
　Range – 420km/262.5 miles

Type 61 Main Battle Tank

Japan's first post-World War II attempt at MBT construction, The Type 61 emerged in 1962 after a development phase of almost a decade, looking very like the M48 Patton that it was so obviously based on.

Built using welded rolled steel and with a cast turret, the vehicle weighed 35,000kg/34.4 tons and was fitted with torsion bar suspension. It had a crew of four, and was powered by a Mitsubishi Type 12 HM 21 WT diesel engine delivering a top speed of 45kph/28mph and a range of 200km/124.3 miles. Mounted in the dome-shaped turret with its bulging rear was a newly designed

Type 61 90mm/3.54in main gun which was not fitted with stabilization and therefore could not fire accurately on the move. There were two machine-guns – one 7.62mm/0.3in internal coaxial and the other of 12.7mm/0.5in for anti-aircraft defence.

There were also an ARV (Armoured Recovery Vehicle), AVLB (Armoured Vehicle Launched Bridge), Armoured Engineer and a Type 61 training tank.

Although it never saw action anywhere and was only in service with the Japanese Defence Force, it proved an important step in the return to indigenous tank production for the Japanese.

TOP AND ABOVE: **The first Japanese-built tank after World War II, the Type 61 was heavily influenced by the Americans. Over 500 were built of this 35,000kg/34.4-ton four-man MBT, which was armed with a 90mm/3.54in gun.**

LEFT: **Japan did not take much interest in tanks during World War II, so the Type 61 gave them a great deal of useful experience. Although it resembled the M48, it had no stabilization on its main armament. A small number are still in service.**

Type 61 MBT

Entered service: 1962
Crew: 4
Weight: 35,000kg/34.4 tons
Dimensions: Length – 8.19m/26ft 10.5in
    Height (over turret hatch) – 2.49m/8ft 2in
    Width – 2.95m/9ft 8in
Armament: Main – 90mm/3.54in Type 61 gun
    Secondary – 1 x 7.62mm/0.3in and
    1 x 12.7mm/0.5in machine-guns
Armour: Maximum – 64mm/2.52in
Powerplant: Mitsubishi HM21WT diesel,
    447.4kW/600hp
Performance: Speed – 45kph/28mph
    Range – 200km/124.3 miles

LEFT: **The Type 62 Light Tank was a reduced-size version of their Type 59 MBT, which was a licensed copy of the Red Army T-59. It was the first "home-grown" light tank in Chinese service. Some 800 were built, and many still serve in training units.**

Type 62 Light Tank

Entered service: China
Crew: 4
Weight: 21,000kg/20.7 tons
Dimensions: Length – 7.9m/25ft 11in (gun forward)
 Height (over turret hatch) – 2.25m/7ft 4.5in
 Width – 2.68m/8ft 9.5in
Armament: Main – 85mm/3.35in gun
 Secondary – 2 x 7.62mm/0.3in and
 1 x 12.7mm/0.5in machine-guns
Armour: Unspecified
Powerplant: Thought to be 12-cylinder diesel, 320.7kW/430hp
Performance: Speed – 60kph/37.3mph
 Range – 500km/310.7 miles

Type 62 Light Tank

The Type 62 Chinese Light Tank is based on the previous Type 59 and was introduced in 1962 as an indigenous scaled-down version of its predecessor with a much lower ground pressure to cope with the specific environments of rough and soft terrain. Weighing 21,000kg/20.7 tons and with a crew of four, the Type 62 was powered by a

320.7kW/430hp diesel engine providing a top speed of 60kph/37.3mph and a range of 500km/310.7 miles. In its Russian-style "mushroom head" turret it mounted an 85mm/3.35in rifled main gun, along with a coaxial 7.62mm/0.3in machine-gun, and another of 12.7mm/0.5in for anti-aircraft defence located by the loader's hatch. There was also

another 7.62mm/0.3in machine-gun in the bow operated by the driver. Approximately 800 are currently in Chinese service, and this AFV was widely exported to countries in Africa and Asia, especially Vietnam. The vehicle has been modified into ARV (Armoured Recovery Vehicle) and engineering variants, and there is also a tropicalized version.

Type 63 Light Amphibious Tank

The Type 63 is a light tank with amphibious capability and is of a similar size and weight to the Type 62. It also shares its turret and weapons systems, although its hull is based on the Type 77 APC. With a weight of over 18 tons, the Type 63 is powered by a

12150 LV12 diesel engine, giving a top speed of 64kph/39.8mph and a range of 370km/229.9 miles. Propulsion in the water is provided by hyrdro-jets located at the hull rear. It is estimated that some 1,200 are in service with the Chinese Army and Marine Corps, at least 500

of which have been upgraded to Type 63A standard, carrying a large three-man turret armed with a 105mm/4.13in rifled main gun. It is also in service with North Korea, Myanmar (Burma) and Vietnam.

RIGHT: **The Type 63 was the Chinese improvement on the Red Army PT-76 Light Amphibious Tank, which combined the T-54/T-55 turret on to the Type 77 APC chassis. It will most probably be replaced by the Type 99 Light Tank when it comes into full production.**

Type 63 Light Amphibious Tank

Entered service: 1963
Crew: 4
Weight: 18,400kg/18.1 tons
Dimensions: Length – 8.44m/27ft 8.5in
 Height (over turret hatch) – 2.52m/8ft 3.5in
 Width – 3.2m/10ft 6in
Armament: Main – 85mm/3.35in gun
 Secondary – 1 x 7.62mm/0.3in and
 1 x 12.7mm/0.5in machine-guns
Armour: Maximum – 14mm/0.55in
Powerplant: 12150LV 12-cylinder diesel, 298.3kW/400hp
Performance: Speed – 64kph/39.8mph
 Range – 370km/229.9 miles

Type 69 Main Battle Tank

The first firm sighting of a Type 69 was on a Beijing parade in 1982. It entered service earlier – perhaps even as early as 1969, hence its name. Although it looks much like its predecessor, the Type 59, it has had a whole raft of new fire-control, stabilization, NBC (Nuclear, Biological and

BELOW: **These Type 69s are in Iraqi desert livery, having been captured by Coalition forces in the first Gulf War. Note the large 12.7mm/0.5in heavy anti-aircraft machine-gun on the top of the turret of the nearest one.**

Chemical) protection, navigation and safety systems installed. At one time British Royal Ordnance produced a Type 59 armed with a 105mm/4.13in L7 series rifled gun for the export market. The Type 69-I MBT is now armed with a 100mm/3.94in smoothbore gun, while the Type 69-II MBT has a 105mm/4.13in rifled gun (possibly derived from the L7) and fitted with a thermal sleeve. There are also command, ARV (Armoured Recovery Vehicle), mine-clearing and twin 57mm/2.24in anti-aircraft variants.

TOP: **Two Chinese Type 69-IIs (sold to Pakistan) on parade with the Pakistan Army. Note that they have been upgraded by fitting the 105mm/4.13in gun.** ABOVE: **Captured by Coalition forces during the first Gulf War, this Type 69-II has lost its laser rangefinder, which is usually externally mounted over the main armament.**

Type 69 MBT	

Entered service: 1980 (or perhaps as early as 1969)
Crew: 4
Weight: 36,700kg/36.1 tons
Dimensions: Length – 6.24m/20ft 5.5in
 Height (over turret hatch) – 2.81m/9ft 2.5in
 Width – 3.3m/10ft 10in
Armament: Main – 100mm/3.94in gun
 Secondary – 2 x 7.62mm/0.3in and
 1 x 12.7mm/0.5in machine-guns
Armour: Maximum – 100mm/3.94in
Powerplant: 12010L-7BW V12 diesel,
 432.5kW/580hp
Performance: Speed – 50kph/31.1mph
 Range – 420km/261 miles

Type 74 Main Battle Tank

The Type 74 MBT was the next tank developed and produced by Japan to succeed the Type 61. Having tested two different prototypes – the primary difference between them being manual or automatic loading of the main gun – the manual version was chosen, with the vehicle being produced by Mitsubishi Heavy Industries and first appearing in 1975. Weighing 38,000kg/37.4 tons and fitted with a new vertically variable hydro-pneumatic suspension system, the Type 74 is powered by a Mitsubishi 10ZF22

WT 10-cylinder diesel engine, providing a top speed of 60kph/37.3mph and a range of 400km/248.5 miles. In the electrically powered turret – a sleeker looking version of the M47/48, but still with a rear bulge – the main armament is the British-designed 105mm/4.13in L7 type rifled tank gun, manufactured under licence in Japan. There is also one 7.62mm/0.3in coaxial machine-gun and one of 12.7mm/0.5in for Anti-Aircraft (AA) and close-quarter defence. Internally the vehicle is equipped with all the latest target and fire

ABOVE AND BELOW LEFT: **Designed by Mitsubishi in the early 1960s, the Type 74 was completed in 1969 when it was known as the STB 1. However, it was not until 1973 that the final production model was completed. Another two more years elapsed before the production run of some 560 were built and it replaced the Type 61.**

control, gun stabilization, NBC (Nuclear, Biological and Chemical) protection, communication, navigation, night-vision and safety systems. Variants include an ARV (Armoured Recovery Vehicle) and a twin 35mm/1.38in AA gun version. Approximately 560 were built, but all have now been phased out of front-line service.

Type 74 MBT	

Entered service: 1975
Crew: 4
Weight: 38,000kg/37.4 tons
Dimensions: Length – 9.42m/30ft 11in
    Height (over turret hatch) – 2.48m/8ft 1.5in
    Width – 3.18m/10ft 5in
Armament: Main – 105mm/4.13in L7 gun
    Secondary – 1 x 7.62mm/0.3in and
    1 x 12.7mm/0.5in machine-guns
Armour: Unspecified
Powerplant: Mitsubishi 10ZF22 WT 10-cylinder
    diesel, 536.9kW/720hp
Performance: Speed – 60kph/37.3mph
    Range – 400km/248.5 miles

LEFT: **The Type 80 became famous (or should it be infamous?) with the well-publicized scenes of crushing the students' revolt in Tiananmen Square. The Type 80 was a major advance in Chinese tank design, incorporating many new developments such as stabilization and a computerized fire-controlled system.** BELOW: **This Type 80 is showing off its ability to negotiate a sizeable vertical obstacle. To extend its operational range, it could be fitted with two large fuel drums at the rear (not fitted here) which could be jettisoned after use.** BOTTOM: **This immaculately painted Type 80-II was photographed in Beijing, probably during a military parade.**

Type 80 Main Battle Tank

Development of the Chinese Type 80 MBT began in the early 1980s, and full production was achieved towards the end of that decade. Although based on the Type 59/69 series, it has a newly designed chassis and running gear, with six road wheels and a torsion bar suspension system. Weighing 38,500kg/ 37.9 tons and with a crew of four, the Type 80 is powered by a VR36 V12 diesel engine, providing a top speed of 60kph/ 37.3mph and a range of 430km/267.2 miles. The turret has a "mushroom head" profile similar to the Type 69 but with a distinctive open grill stowage basket wrapped around the back and sides.

The main armament is an L7 type 105mm/4.13in rifled main gun fitted with a fume extractor and a thermal sleeve. There is also a coaxial 7.62mm/0.3in

machine-gun and a 12.7mm/0.5in anti-aircraft machine-gun mounted outside the loader's hatch. The Type 80 ports all the latest essential equipment, including a ballistics computer, a laser rangefinder integrated with stabilized sights, attack sensors and composite armour suites. To extend the operational range of the Type 80 MBT, two large drum fuel tanks (jettisonable) can be fitted at the rear.

Some 500 Type 80 Main Battle Tanks are in service with the Chinese army and a small number were exported to Myanmar (Burma).

Type 80 MBT

Entered service: 1988
Crew: 4
Weight: 38,500kg/37.9 tons
Dimensions: Length – 9.33m/30ft 7.5in
    Height (over turret hatch) – 2.29m/7ft 6in
    Width – 3.37m/11ft 0.5in
Armament: Main – 105mm/4.13in gun
    Secondary – 1 x 7.62mm/0.3in and
    1 x 12.7mm/0.5in machine-guns
Armour: Unspecified
Powerplant: VR36 V12 diesel, 544.4kW/730hp
Performance: Speed – 60kph/37.3mph
    Range – 430km/267.2 miles

Type 85-II Main Battle Tank

The Type 85-II Chinese MBT is an upgrade of the Type 80 with an improved chassis and a new, flatter welded turret, using the latest upgraded modular composite armour. Weighing just over 40 tons, it is powered by a V12 supercharged diesel engine, giving it a top speed of 62kph/39mph and a range of 450km/280 miles. Initially it mounted the same 105mm/4.13in main armament as its predecessor, but this has recently been upgraded to a larger, fully stabilized 125mm/4.92in smoothbore main gun served by an autoloader, thus reducing the crew to three. This weapon enables the Type 85 to fire accurately on the move – the first Chinese MBT to be able do so, which is a significant advantage.

ABOVE: **The Type 85-II initially had a 105mm/4.13in rifled gun, which has now been replaced by a 125mm/4.92in smoothbore gun with an automatic loader. In recent years China has exported more than 250 to Pakistan – known as the Type 85-IIAP, which is shown in this photograph.**

The most recent version, the Type 85-III is in service with the Chinese army and is built under licence in Pakistan, where its nomenclature is the Type 85-IIAP.

Variants

The Type 85-IIM, known in the People's Liberation Army as the Type 88C MBT, was first seen in 1999. It weighs 41,000kg/ 40.35 tons and is armoured with an automatic loader. It has the ISFCS 22 computerized fire-control system fitted. Some also appear to have been fitted with a laser-jamming device operated from inside the turret and mounted on the left side of the turret roof.

Type 85-II MBT

Entered service: 1995

Crew: 3

Weight: 41,000kg/40.35 tons

Dimensions: Length – 10.1m/33ft 1.5in
Height (over turret hatch) – 2.37m/7ft 9.5in
Width – 3.50m/11ft 6in

Armament: Main – 125mm/4.92in gun
Secondary – 1 x 7.62mm/0.3in and
1 x 12.7mm/0.5in machine-guns

Armour: Unspecified

Powerplant: Perkins V12 diesel, 894.8kW/1,200hp

Performance: Speed – 62kph/38.5mph
Range – 450km/279.6 miles

Type 88 K1 Main Battle Tank

Emerging in 1987 from a joint US–South Korean project begun in 1980, the Type 88 K1/K1A1 MBT is now entirely South Korean-built, with various parts manufactured under licence. It resembles the Abrams in appearance, with its flat faceted composite armoured turret. Weighing 51,100kg/50.3 tons and fitted with a hybrid suspension system combining hydro-pneumatic elements and torsion bar springs, the Type 88 K1 is powered by an MTU MB 871 Ka-501 turbocharged diesel engine, giving a top speed of 65kph/40.4mph and a range of 440km/273.4 miles.

Main armament in earlier models was the same as the M1, the 105mm/4.13in gun, along with three machine-guns, two of 7.62mm/0.3in and one of 12.7mm/0.5in. However, the latest version, the K1A1, mounts the M1A1's 120mm/4.72in smoothbore main gun. The vehicle also ports the latest target and fire control, gun stabilization, NBC (Nuclear,

Biological and Chemical) protection, communication, navigation, night-vision and safety systems.

There are also up-armour packages as well as ARV (Armoured Recovery Vehicle), mine-clearing vehicle and bridge-layer variants, all of which are currently being marketed to other countries, but to date without success.

TOP: **In early 1980 the Republic of South Korea chose the General Dynamics Company of the United States to design and build a new main battle tank for them. A few years later the Type 88 K1 appeared, which looks very like the Abrams M1 and mounts the same 105mm/4.13in gun.**
ABOVE: **Over 1,000 K1s have been built by Hyundai for the South Korean Army. Future developments may include a lighter model, that would include fitting ERA, to sell to other Far Eastern armies.**

Type 88 K1 MBT

Entered service: 1987
Crew: 4
Weight: 51,100kg/50.3 tons
Dimensions: Length – 7.48m/24ft 6.5in
  Height (over turret hatch) – 2.25m/7ft 4.5in
  Width – 3.59m/11ft 9.5in
Armament: Main – 105mm/4.13in gun
  Secondary – 2 x 7.62mm/0.3in and
  1 x 12.7mm/0.5in machine-guns
Armour: Unspecified
Powerplant: MTU MB 871 Ka-501 diesel,
  984.8kW/1,200hp
Performance: Speed – 65kph/40.4mph
  Range – 440km/273.4 miles

Type 90 Main Battle Tank

In 1976, development of the next indigenous Japanese tank was initiated as soon as the Type 74 had entered service and, in 1990, the Type 90 was produced by a consortium of Japanese companies headed by Mitsubushi Heavy Industries. Weighing 50,000kg/49.2 tons and fitted with a hybrid hydro-pneumatic and torsion bar suspension system, the Type 90 is powered by a Mitsubishi 10ZG 10-cylinder liquid-cooled diesel engine, giving it a speed of 70kph/43.5mph and a range of 400km/248.5 miles. The German Rheinmetall 120mm/4.72in smoothbore main gun – the same armament as Leopard 2 – is mounted in a wide, flat turret resembling that of the Abrams M1A1 and is armoured with a combination of the latest composite and laminate packages. This weapon was chosen after extensive testing in preference over the original Japanese design, and it is served by an autoloader, thereby reducing the crew to three.

Secondary weaponry includes the normal 7.62mm/0.3in coaxial and 12.7mm/0.5in machine-guns. The vehicle is also equipped with the latest digital fire-control,

ABOVE AND BELOW LEFT: **Mitsubishi was the prime contractor for this Japanese MBT that was first designed in 1976. Apart from its 120mm/4.72in smoothbore Rheinmetall gun, it was completely Japanese-designed and built. Later, two prototypes with Japanese 120mm/4.72in guns (firing Japanese ammunition) were also built. It is now in service with the Japanese Ground Self-Defence Force, and has never been offered on the export market.**

navigation, night-vision, communication and safety systems. The Type 90 is currently in Japanese service but has not been offered for export. There are the usual ARV (Armoured Recovery Vehicle), AVLB (Armoured Vehicle Launched Bridge) and mine-clearing variants.

Type 90 MBT

Entered service: 1991
Crew: 3
Weight: 50,000kg/49.2 tons
Dimensions: Length – 9.76m/32ft
    Height (over turret hatch) – 2.34m/7ft 8in
    Width – 3.43m/11ft 3in
Armament: Main – 120mm/4.72in gun
    Secondary – 1 x 7.62mm/0.3in and
    1 x 12.7mm/0.5in machine-guns
Armour: Unspecified
Powerplant: Mitsubishi 10ZG 10-cylinder diesel,
    1,118.6kW/1,500hp
Performance: Speed – 70kph/43.5mph
    Range – 400km/248.5 miles

Type 90–II (MBT 2000) Main Battle Tank

The NORINCO Type 90-II MBT, also now known as MBT 2000, first emerged in 1991 and was a development of the Type 85 design, with the first model never reaching production stage. Having undergone armour, engine and main gun upgrades, the new improved model, Type 90-II, weighed over 47 tons and was powered by a Perkins V12 diesel engine, providing a top speed of 62kph/38.5mph and a range of 450km/279.6 miles. Mounted in a flat turret tapering at the front and fitted with a kind of composite armour, the

125mm/4.92in smoothbore main gun is served by an automatic loader, allowing the tank to be crewed by three men – commander, gunner and driver. Secondary armament consists of two machine-guns – one of 7.62mm/0.3in and one of 12.7mm/0.5in.

Internally, the digital fire-control system includes a stabilized laser rangefinder sight, passive thermal imaging and crosswind, tilt and angular velocity sensors, allowing the Type 90-II to engage targets accurately while on the move in day or night conditions.

Currently in Chinese service, this AFV has been marketed for export under the name of MBT 2000 and, following a further agreement, Pakistan has been licensed to produce the Type 90-II, renaming it the Al-Khalid.

LEFT: **The Type 90 appeared in the early 1990s, and had considerable improvements in firepower, protection and mobility over previous Chinese MBTs. The main armament of this 48,000kg/ 47.2-ton three-man tank is a 125mm/4.92in smoothbore gun with an automatic loader and Image Stabilized Fire-Control System. Additional fuel drums can be mounted on the rear.**

Type 90-II (MBT 2000) MBT

Entered service: 1995
Crew: 3
Weight: 48,000kg/47.2 tons
Dimensions: Length – 10.1m/33ft 1.5in
 Height (over turret hatch) – 2.37m/7ft 9.5in
 Width – 3.50m/11ft 6in
Armament: Main – 125mm/4.92in gun
 Secondary – 1 x 7.62mm/0.3in and
 1 x 12.7mm/0.5in machine-guns
Armour: Unspecified
Powerplant: Perkins V12 diesel, generating
 894.8kW/1,200hp
Performance: Speed – 62kph/38.5mph
 Range – 450km/279.6 miles

Type 98 Main Battle Tank

A little-seen upgrade development of the Type 90-II is the Type 98 MBT, first glimpsed in 1999 at the 50th Anniversary of the Chinese People's Republic. It is an upgrade of the Type 90-II, with the same armament mounted on a modified turret with a new modular armour package. Improvements will no doubt include substantial enhancement of its fire-control, navigation, NBC

(Nuclear, Biological and Chemical) protection and safety systems. It is currently in production and has been deployed with the People's Liberation Army (PLA).

Development is continuing, and an improved Type 98 with a heavier combat weight (52,800kg/52 tons) has appeared. It retains the 125mm/4.92in smoothbore main gun and is said to be more reliable

and better protected, possibly using the "arrowhead"-type armour as on the latest Leopard 2.

Type 98 MBT

Entered service: 1998
Crew: 35
Weight: 50,793kg/50 tons
Dimensions: Length – 11m/36ft
 Height (over turret hatch) – approximately 2m/6ft 6in
 Width – 3.4m/11ft 2in
Armament: Main – 125mm/4.92in gun
 Secondary – 1 x 7.62mm/0.3in and
 1 x 12.7mm/0.5in machine-guns
Armour: Not known
Powerplant: 894.8kW/1,200hp diesel
Performance: Speed – 65kph/40.6mph
 Range – 450km/280 miles (600km/375 miles with
 external fuel tanks)

LEFT: **Yet another parade and another immaculate Chinese tank, this time a Type 98, one of their most modern tanks, clearly showing its 125mm/4.92in smoothbore gun.**

Vickers Mark 1 (Vijayanta) Main Battle Tank

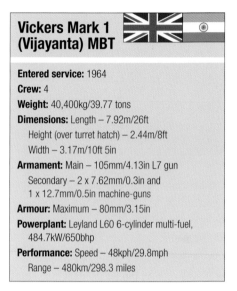

Vickers Mark 1 (Vijayanta) MBT	

Entered service: 1964
Crew: 4
Weight: 40,400kg/39.77 tons
Dimensions: Length – 7.92m/26ft
   Height (over turret hatch) – 2.44m/8ft
   Width – 3.17m/10ft 5in
Armament: Main – 105mm/4.13in L7 gun
   Secondary – 2 x 7.62mm/0.3in and
   1 x 12.7mm/0.5in machine-guns
Armour: Maximum – 80mm/3.15in
Powerplant: Leyland L60 6-cylinder multi-fuel,
   484.7kW/650bhp
Performance: Speed – 48kph/29.8mph
   Range – 480km/298.3 miles

The Vickers Mark 1 was based on the Chieftain MBT but produced in a lightly armoured configuration in 1964 for the Asian and Arab export market. This was a viable AFV, if not of NATO MBT quality, and was built using as many existing parts as possible. Weighing 38,600kg/38 tons, it was powered by a Leyland L60 Mk 4B 6-cylinder water-cooled multi-fuel engine which provided a top speed of 48kph/29.8mph and a range of 480km/298.3 miles. It was armed with the Royal Ordnance L7 105mm/4.13in main gun as well as two 7.62mm/0.3in and one 12.7mm/0.5in machine-guns. These were mounted in a turret that resembled the Centurion's in appearance, having an angular flat box shape with a rear stowage bustle, rather than the Chieftain's more ergonomic turret shape. The main customer of the Vickers Mark 1 was India, where a prototype had been sent in 1963. Accepted by India, it was renamed the Vijayanta (Victory), and local production was started in 1965 by an Vickers Indian subsidiary in Madras.

Local modifications were made over the years that followed, and these included a new engine, new fire-control, night-vision and navigation systems, and add-on suites of passive armour. In this way the life of the vehicle was extended until the Arjun came into service.

Some 2,200 Vijayantas were built before production ceased. Other countries who also bought the Vickers Mark 1 included Kuwait, who purchased 70 from 1970–72.

ABOVE: **The Kartik AVLB is based upon the lengthened chassis of the Vijayanta, which is also used for the Catapult SP artillery system.**

Vickers Mark 3 Main Battle Tank

An upgrade of the Mark 1 with changes to the hull, a new engine and a new turret, the Vickers Mark 3 MBT first appeared as an export model in 1977. Weighing 38,700kg/38.1 tons and fitted with a torsion bar suspension system, it was powered by a Detroit Diesel 12V-71T engine, giving it a top speed of 50kph/31.1mph and a range of 530km/329.3 miles. The vehicle's armament remained the same as its predecessor, the 105mm/4.13in L7A1 main gun and two 7.62mm/0.3in machine-guns (one coaxial), but mounted in a newly designed steel turret, with a reloading port on the left-hand side and a commander's cupola and hatch for the loader on the turret top. Fifty rounds of main gun ammunition were carried – 18 in the turret itself and a further 32 in the hull. Other changes included up-rated fire-control, night-vision, NBC (Nuclear, Biological and Chemical) protection, communication and safety systems, making the Mark 3 an infinitely more sophisticated weapon system than the Mark 1.

Another version developed for sale to Malaysia included an ERA (Explosive Reactive Armour) armour package and a GPS (Global Positioning System) Satellite Navigation (SatNav) system, as well as a range of further optional enhancement packages.

LEFT, ABOVE AND ABOVE RIGHT: **The next Vickers MBT was the Mark 3, of similar weight and size to the Mark 1, with a 105mm/4.13in gun, complete with laser rangefinder. The first Mark 3 production order was placed in 1977 by Kenya, followed by Nigeria. Sadly, others did not follow.**

Vickers Mark 3 MBT

Entered service: 1977
Crew: 4
Weight: 38,700kg/38.1 tons
Dimensions: Length – 7.56m/24ft 9.5in
  Height (over turret hatch) – 2.48m/8ft 1.5in
  Width – 3.17m/10ft 5in
Armament: Main – 105mm/4.13in L7A1 gun
  Secondary – 2 x 7.62mm/0.3in and
  1 x 12.7mm/0.5in machine-guns
Armour: Maximum – 80mm/3.15in
Powerplant: Detroit Diesel 12V-71T diesel,
  536.9kW/720bhp
Performance: Speed – 50kph/31.1mph
  Range – 530km/329.3 miles

Vickers VFM Mark 5 Light Tank

The VFM Mark 5 was first seen in 1986 at the British Army Equipment Exhibition (BAEE), and was another AFV developed by Vickers for the export market. The vehicle was developed in conjunction with an American company – FMC – using its Close Combat Vehicle (Light) or CCV(L) as the basis on which to mount a turret containing British armament. This produced a light tank with a considerable punch.

Weighing 19,750kg/19.4 tons with welded aluminium armour, the VFM was powered by a modular Detroit Diesel V6 turbocharged engine, delivering a top speed of 70kph/43.5mph and a range of 480km/298.3 miles. The power pack is housed in the distinctly raised rear hull and fitted with a ramp door to enable speedy access. The turret echoes the rising hull by also tapering at its rear, while mounting the L7 105mm/4.13in smoothbore main gun, along with two 7.62mm/0.3in machine-guns.

Designed to be air-portable in both the C130 Hercules and C141 Starlifter transport aircraft, it could also be dropped using the Low Altitude Parachute Extraction System (LAPES).

ABOVE LEFT, ABOVE AND BELOW LEFT: **The Vickers VFM 5 was a 19,750kg/19.4-ton light tank that was a joint venture between Vickers Defence Systems and the FMC Corporation of USA. The first prototype was on show at the 1986 BAEE, and a year later it had completed its firing and mobility trials. It was designed to be air-portable in both the C130 Hercules and the C141 Starlifter transport aircraft, and to be dropped by LAPES (Low Altitude Parachute Extraction System). It did not find a market, so never went into full production.**

Vickers VFM Mark 5 Light Tank	
Entered service: 1987	
Crew: 4	
Weight: 19,750kg/19.4 tons	
Dimensions: Length – 6.20m/20ft 4in	
Height (over turret hatch) – 2.62m/8ft 7in	
Width – 2.69m/8ft 10in	
Armament: Main – 105mm/4.13in L7 gun	
Secondary – 2 x 7.62mm/0.3in machine-guns	
Armour: Unspecified	
Powerplant: Detroit Diesel V6, 739.9kW/992hp	
Performance: Speed – 70kph/43.5mph	
Range – 480km/298.3 miles	

Vickers Mark 7 Valiant Main Battle Tank

Originally developed as a technology demonstrator at the same time as the VFM Mark 5, the Vickers Mark 7 Valiant represented another strand in the dynamic export market push of the mid-1980s undertaken by Vickers. This time the development partner was Germany and the resulting Vickers Mark 7 was even more versatile than its Mark 5 predecessor in being able to port a wide variety of European-manufactured equipment. Using British composite armour (known as Chobham after the town where it was developed) and a British turret, combined with a German chassis, engine and running gear (essentially the bottom of the Kraus-Maffei-built Leopard 2), the Valiant could mount a variety of main guns. The first option was the British rifled 120mm/4.72in L11A5, the second a French Giat

CN 120-26 120mm/4.72in, and the third a German Rheinmetall smoothbore 120mm/4.72in.

The vehicle is also fitted with the Marconi Centaur integrated gun and fire control as well as navigation, NBC (Nuclear, Biological and Chemical) protection and fire-suppression systems. The Mark 7 Valiant was overtaken by events (the first

ABOVE, LEFT AND BELOW LEFT: **Shortly after news of the development of the revolutionary Chobham armour in 1976, details were passed to Vickers, and the following year it was decided to produce a Chobham-armoured MBT weighing 54,640kg/53.4 tons, to be called the Vickers Mark 7 MBT (Valiant). Unfortunately Valiant was overtaken by events and never went further than the prototype stage. However, it did provide much useful experience in the production of a Chobham-armoured tank, which would eventually lead on to Challenger.**

Gulf War of the early 1990s) and never went into production, but it did provide much useful experience, which led to the development of the Vickers Challenger 2 MBT.

Vickers Mark 7 Valiant MBT	

Entered service: 1985
Crew: 4
Weight: 54,640kg/53.4 tons
Dimensions: Length – 7.72m/25ft 4in
  Height (over turret hatch) – 2.54m/8ft 4in
  Width – 3.42m/11ft 2.5in
Armament: Main – 120mm/4.72in L11A5 gun
  Secondary – 2 x 7.62mm/0.3in machine-guns
Armour: Unspecified
Powerplant: MTU MB873 V12 diesel, delivering
  1,118.6kW/1,500hp
Performance: Speed – 72kph/44.7mph
  Range – 550km/343.75 miles

Glossary

"A" vehicle An armoured vehicle, wheeled or tracked.

AEV Armoured Engineer Vehicle – AFV based upon an MBT chassis, crewed by engineers with the equipment to carry out engineering tasks.

AFV Armoured Fighting Vehicle – any armoured vehicle, whether tracked or wheeled, normally carrying an offensive weapon.

AP Armour-Piercing – ammunition that will penetrate armour plate rather than shatter or glance off on striking it.

APC Armoured Personnel Carrier – an AFV primarily designed to carry a number of fully equipped infantry soldiers.

APDS Armour-Piercing Discarding Sabot – a form of AP with a small, heavy core surrounded by a calibre-sized casing, which breaks up on leaving the gun muzzle. The core then flies on to the target with added velocity.

APFSDS Armour-Piercing Fin-Stabilized Discarding Sabot – the same as APDS but with a longer, finned core to give better penetration.

ARV Armoured Recovery Vehicle – an AFV based on a tank chassis, crewed by fitters with the equipment to carry out the repair and recovery of most AFVs.

Ausf *Ausführung* (German) – the word used to differentiate between various batches or models of the same type of AFV.

automatic gun A weapon that loads, fires, extracts, ejects and reloads continually while the firing mechanism is engaged and the feed mechanism supplies ammunition.

automatic loader A mechanism which, together with some form of magazine or dispenser, allows for automatic loading of a tank gun, thus dispensing with one crew member.

AVLB Armoured Vehicle Launched Bridge – an AFV based upon a tank chassis, normally crewed by engineers and carrying some type of vehicular bridge.

AVRE Armoured Vehicle Royal Engineers – British nomenclature for an AEV.

ball mount A spherical machine-gun mount permitting firing in various directions.

BARV Beach Armoured Recovery Vehicle – an ARV specially designed to recover "drowned" AFVs and keep exits from landing craft clear during assault landings.

"B" vehicle Any unarmoured vehicle normally wheeled. Also known as a "soft-skinned" vehicle.

bogie Units of a tank's suspension that help to distribute the sprung weight along the track.

BT *Bystrochodny Tankovy* (Russian) – Fast Tank.

calibre The diameter of the bore of a gun.

Carro Armato (Italian) – Tank.

Char (French) – Tank.

chassis That part of the tank that makes it mobile as opposed to the part for fighting.

coaxial The mounting of two weapons in the same mount.

cradle The non-recoiling part of the gun mount that allows elevation of the gun about the trunnions, houses the recoil system and guides it in recoil.

Cruiser Tank British term used to describe the series of lighter, faster, less well armoured tanks in between the lights and the mediums. Their role was to attack or counterattack with speed and panache, while the heavier infantry tanks supported the foot soldiers in the main assault. They would be absorbed into the medium range of tanks by the end of World War II. The term is now no longer used.

cupola A small protuberance above the main turret, equipped with vision devices and a protective lid, mainly for use by the tank commander.

CV *Carro Veloce* (Italian) – Fast Vehicle.

DU Depleted Uranium – a very heavy metal used for the cores of certain types of AP ammunition to give better penetration.

ERA Explosive Reactive Armour – explosive plates attached to the outside of a tank that explode outwards when struck, thus negating penetration.

fascine A large bundle of pieces of wood (or nowadays metal pipes) carried on an AFV to be dropped into a ditch or hole to enable the tank to cross.

fume extractor A device fitted to the barrel of a tank gun to enable the gases remaining behind after firing to be sucked out of the muzzle before the breech is opened, so that they do not enter the turret during reloading.

FV Fighting Vehicle, usually plus a number – British Defence Department nomenclature for British-built AFVs.

glacis plate The thick armour plate at the front of a tank, normally sloped at an angle so as to deflect enemy shot.

hatch An opening complete with cover and often vision devices, giving access in and out by crew members.

HE High-Explosive – the standard bursting explosive.

HEAT High-Explosive Anti-Tank – a type of projectile with a shaped charge that concentrates the explosion into a thin jet enabling it to penetrate armour plate.

Heavy Tank While the heavy tanks of World War I weighed only 28,449kg/28 tons, those of World War II were generally in the 50,802–60,963kg/50–60-ton bracket, or even heavier. Now they have been incorporated with the mediums under the general term MBT.

HESH High-Explosive Squash-Head – HE filled with plastic explosive that "squashes" on the armour plate before exploding, blowing a "scab" of metal off the inside surface rather than penetrating.

idler The undriven guide wheel carrying the tank track.

Infantry Tank British term. These heavily armoured, relatively slow and, initially, cumbersome tanks were designed primarily to support dismounted infantry attacks, so speed was of little importance. However, infantry tanks like the Churchill would soon show their versatility as the British moved towards the universal tank.

KwK *Kampfwagen Kanone* (German) – Tank Gun.

Light Tank In the past this term was used to describe small, fast, lightly armoured tanks in the 5,080–15,241kg/5–15-ton range, used mainly for reconnaissance, liaison and similar tasks. They were also ideal for training purposes because they were cheap and relatively easy to manufacture. In World War II their main reconnaissance role was taken over by armoured cars, but now they are coming more into vogue again with the need for strategic air mobility and the advent of lighter, more powerful weapon systems.

mantlet The moveable piece of armour plate that surrounds the hole into which the main armament is fitted into the turret. This hole has to be large enough to allow the gun to elevate and depress. It both protects and conceals this opening.

MBT Main Battle Tank – since World War II this term has been used to cover all types of modern medium and heavy tanks, from about 30,481kg/30 tons upwards to 60,963kg/60 tons and over. MBT is in essence the modern-day term for the British Universal Tank.

Medium Tank In the past this term was used to describe a tank of some 25,402–35,562kg/25–35 tons, reasonably well armoured and armed, with a good all-round performance. A perfect World War II example was the Russian T-34. Medium tanks have now been incorporated under the collective term of MBT.

muzzle brake An attachment screwed on to the end of the gun barrel, deflecting the gases laterally so as to reduce recoil.

NBC Nuclear, Biological and Chemical.

PAK *Panzer Abwehr Kanone* (German) – Anti-Tank Gun.

PzKpfw *Panzerkampfwagen* (German) – Tank.

rifling The spiral grooves in the bore of the gun that impart accuracy and stability to a projectile in flight.

roadwheel One of the wheels in contact with the track, which supports the tank.

semi-automatic gun A gun that requires the trigger to be pulled for each round fired.

separated ammunition Ammunition that requires separate loading of the projectile, propelling charge and primer.

skirting plates or side skirts Sheets of thin armour that hang in front of the upper run of the tracks and suspension. These cause HEAT projectiles to explode and thus dissipate their main force before reaching the hull.

SPAT Self-Propelled Anti-Tank – an anti-tank gun mounted on either wheels or tracks with an engine, so that it does not need a towing vehicle.

sponson A projection mounting a weapon, located upon a tank hull.

sprocket A toothed wheel which engages with the track to drive it, and is itself driven by the engine.

suspension The wheels, tracks, rollers, roadwheels, bogies etc, on which the tank runs.

TD Tank Destroyer – a self-propelled anti-tank gun on a similar chassis to a tank but normally with lighter armour and an open top.

track The part of a tank that is in contact with the ground and is guided by the idler, sprocket and top rollers.

thermal sleeve An insulated cover to keep the gun barrel at an even temperature and reduce differential expansion, which otherwise causes barrel bend and inaccuracy.

turret basket The floor attached to the rotating turret, so that the crew are rotated as the turret turns.

Universal Tank By 1945 British policy was moving towards the universal tank chassis, capable of mounting larger calibre guns and being continually improved. The Centurion is a perfect example, combining as it did the best qualities of the cruiser and infantry tanks, but with far superior firepower and performance.

vision slot/slit An opening in the hull or turret through which a crew member can get a limited view outside.

Acknowledgements

The author would like to thank the staff of the Tank Museum, Bovington, especially David Fletcher, Janice Tait and Roland Groom, for all their help.

The publisher would like to thank the following for the use of their pictures in the book (l=left, r=right, t=top, b=bottom, m=middle). Every effort has been made to acknowledge the pictures properly; however, we apologize if there are any unintentional omissions, which will be corrected in future editions.

© **Crown Copyright/MOD.** Reproduced with the permission of the Controller of Her Majesty's Stationery Office: 7tl; 7tr; 39b; 158b; 169t; 169m; 170b; 171m.

Deutsche Panzermuseum Munster: 46t.

Simon Dunstan: 30t; 30b; 31t (US Army); 31m (US Army); 31b (US Marine Corps); 155tr; 164t; 182t; 182b; 183br; 189tl; 189m; 191t; 191m; 197ml.

David Eshel: 10t; 34t; 34b; 35tl; 35tr; 35b; 153m; 160b; 181t; 203t; 203b; 204t; 204b; 205t; 205m; 205b; 210t; 214t; 214m; 214b; 221t; 221m; 221b.

Bob Fleming: 224b.

George Forty: 12b; 20t; 20b; 21t; 21br; 22–3t; 24t; 24b; 26b; 27tr; 27b; 28t; 29bl; 29br; 32; 33tr; 36l; 36r; 38; 39tl; 39tr; 39mr; 42b; 51br; 74m; 79t; 102tr; 102b; 134b; 135m; 142b; 146tr; 158m; 159b; 162m; 167t; 188t; 195t; 195b; 201b; 202tr; 207t; 207m;

207b; 208t; 208b; 213b; 215t; 248b.

Christopher F. Foss: 156t; 156b; 157t; 157b; 158t; 164b (Indian MoD); 165m; 165b; 167b; 176b; 184t; 184m; 184b; 185t; 197tr; 199t; 199b; 212t; 212b; 217b; 222b; 230m; 234t; 234b; 235t; 235b; 237b; 238b; 239b; 241m; 241b; 242; 243t; 243b; 245t; 246bl; 246br.

General Dynamics Land Systems Division: 6b; 154t; 155m.

Richard P. Hunnicutt: 103tl (US Army); 193b; 198t (US Army); 206m (US Army); 206b (US Army).

Imperial War Museum: 54tr (TR 939).

Jim Osborne: 106b; 108b.

RTR Publications Trust: 6t; 7b; 41tr; 41b; 42t; 43tr; 168b; 169b; 170t; 171t; 171b.

The Tank Museum, Bovington: 1; 3; 8–9; 10br; 11tl; 11tr; 11b; 12t; 13tl; 13tr; 13b; 14t; 14b; 15t; 15m; 15b; 16tl; 16tr; 16br; 17; 18t; 18b; 19tl; 19tr; 19b; 21bl; 22b; 23t; 23m; 23b; 24m; 25t; 25ml; 25mr; 25b; 26t; 27tl; 28b; 29t; 33tl; 33m; 33b; 37tl; 37tr; 37b; 40tl; 40–1t; 40b; 43tl; 43bl; 43br; 44–5; 46b; 47t; 47bl; 47br; 48t; 48b; 49t; 49b; 50t; 50b; 51t; 51bl; 52t; 52b; 53t; 53b; 54tl; 54b; 55t; 55b; 56; 57; 58t; 58b; 59t; 59b; 60t; 60b; 61t; 61b; 62t; 62b; 63t; 63bl; 63br; 64t; 64b; 65t; 65b; 66t; 67t; 67b; 68t; 68b; 69t; 69b; 70t; 70b; 71t; 71m; 71b; 72t; 73tl; 73tr; 73b; 74t; 74b; 75t; 75b; 76t; 76b; 77t; 77m; 77b; 78t; 78b; 80t; 80b;

Key to flags

Argentina
Australia
Austria
Brazil
Britain
Canada
China
Croatia
Czechoslovakia
France
Germany: World War I
Germany: World War II
Germany
Hungary
India
Israel
Italy: World Wars I and II
Italy
Japan
Poland
Romania
Russia
South Africa
South Korea
Spain
Sweden
Switzerland
Ukraine
USA
USSR

81t; 81b; 82t; 82b; 83t; 83b;
84t; 84b; 85tl; 85tr; 85b; 86t;
86b; 87t; 87m; 87b; 88t; 88b;
89t; 89m; 89b; 90t; 90b; 91t;
91b; 92t; 92b; 93t; 93b; 94t;
94m; 94b; 95t; 95b; 96t; 96b;
97t; 97m; 97b; 98t; 98b; 99t;
99m; 99b; 100t; 100b; 101t;
101m; 101b; 102tl; 103tr;
103b; 104t; 104b; 105t;
105ml; 105mr; 105b; 106t;
107t; 108t; 110t; 110b; 113t;
113m; 113b; 114t; 114b;
115t; 115b; 116b; 117t; 117b;
118t; 118b; 119t; 119m;
119b; 120t; 120b; 121t;
121ml; 121b; 122t; 122b;
123t; 123b; 124t; 124b; 125t;
125b; 126t; 126b; 127t;
127ml; 127mr; 127b; 128t;
128m; 128b; 129t; 129b;
130t; 130m; 130b; 131t;
131b; 132t; 132b; 133t; 133b;
134tl; 135t; 135b; 136tl; 136tr;
136b; 137t; 137b; 138t; 138b;
139t; 139b; 140t; 140b; 141t;
141b; 143t; 143bl; 143br;
144t; 144m; 144b; 145t;
145b; 146tl; 146b; 147t; 148t;
148b; 149; 150–1; 152t; 152b;
153t; 153b; 155tl; 159t; 159m;
160t; 161t; 161m; 161b; 162t;
163t; 166t; 166b; 168t; 172t;
172b; 173t; 173m; 173b;
174t; 174b; 175t; 175b; 176t;
177t; 177m; 177b; 178t;
178b; 179t; 179b; 180t;
180m; 180b; 181m; 181b;

186t; 188b; 189tr; 189b; 190t;
190b; 191b; 192t; 192b; 193t;
193m; 194t; 194b; 195m;
196t; 196b; 197tl; 200t; 200b;
201t; 201ml; 201mr; 202tl;
202b; 206t; 210b; 211tl;
211tr; 211b; 213t; 215b;
217m; 218t; 218b; 219t;
219m; 219b; 220t; 220b;
222t; 222m; 223t; 223m;
223b; 224t; 225tl; 225tr;
225m; 225b; 226t; 226bl;
226br; 228t; 228b; 229ml;
229mr; 229b; 230t; 230b;
231t; 231b; 232t; 232b; 233t;
233m; 233b; 236t; 236m;
236b; 237t; 237m; 238t; 239t;
239m; 240t; 240b; 241t; 244t;
244b; 245b; 246t; 247t; 247bl;
247br; 248tl; 248tr; 249t;
249m; 249b; 250; 251; 252;
253; 254; 255; 256;
endpapers.

TRH Pictures: 66b; 72b;
79b; 109t; 109b; 111t; 111b;
112t; 112b; 116t; 134tr; 142t;
143m; 147b; 162b; 163m;
163b; 165t; 183t; 183bl; 185b;
186b; 187tl; 187tr; 187m;
187b; 198b; 209t; 209m;
209b; 216t; 216b; 217t; 227t;
227m; 227b.

US Army: 2; 107b; 121mr;
154b; 155b; 197b; 229t.

US Marine Corps: 107m.

Index